Magna Carta and Due Process of Law: The Road to American Judicial Activism

Magna Carta and Due Process of Law: The Road to American Judicial Activism

Published by *Common Consent Press*

First Edition

Burrell, Thomas H., 1975-

ISBN 978-1-945104-00-8

Printed in the United States of America

Magna Carta and Due Process of Law: The Road to American Judicial Activism

By

Thomas H. Burrell

2016

Common Consent Press

PREFACE

I began this project with the intent to write an article. As the material filled the pages, it became apparent that the content extended beyond that allowed by an article. If the discussion appears to be compressed at points, I blame the original design. Perhaps a future edition will fully discuss points relegated to footnotes and parentheticals.

I am indebted to the works of many English historians, but especially noted are John Edward Austin Jolliffe, Bertie Wilkinson, George O. Sayles, Theodore F.T. Plucknett, James. F. Baldwin, and Walter Ullmann. And a special thanks to Kristin Scearce and Jessica Filippi for editing and Exodus Web Design and Graphics Studio for design. *The views expressed in the publication are the author's own views and do not represent the views of any state or federal agency.*

Thomas H. Burrell, 2016

Contents

I

Introduction

In 2015, nations across the world celebrated the Magna Carta's 800th anniversary. In 1215, a group of powerful barons secured a Great Charter of liberties from King John. The barons believed that John had ruled arbitrarily and violated the customs and laws of the realm. A long-brewing struggle between the barons and the king erupted. The result, under threat of civil war, was a forced promise of liberties from John to the barons.

The Magna Carta's influence did not end in 1215. As we will see below, the Magna Carta became a pillar of the English Constitution—the body of fundamental law emerging from successive political struggles that ultimately demoted the monarchy, established the High Court of Parliament, and secured the liberties of Englishmen.

The Magna Carta's anniversary spurs debate. From the English side, we are reminded of Parliament's evolution, the House of Commons, and famous English institutions such as taxation only with representation, impeachment, habeas corpus, and parliamentary sovereignty.[1] England celebrated the ascent of Parliament's representative government, which rose alongside the reduction of the monarchy.

In America, commentators trace the United States Constitution to the English Constitution and the Magna Carta. But the conversation in America turns away from participatory government to the American notion of "due process of law." Without much difficulty, American constitutionalism connects due process of law to Chapter 39 of the Magna Carta.[2] Chapter 39:

> No free men shall be arrested or imprisoned or disseised or outlawed or exiled or in any way victimised, neither will we attack him or send anyone to attack him, except by the lawful judgment of his peers or by the law of the land.[3]

The Fifth Amendment's Due Process Clause: "No Person shall . . . be deprived of life, liberty, or property, without due process of law."[4]

In America, due process of law means different things to different people. Most attribute a body of procedure to the

---

[1] *Infra* Chapter VIII.

[2] Several fourteenth-century statutes connect the Magna Carta to due-process-of-law language. *Infra* Chapter VI sec. E.

[3] MAGNA CARTA ch. 39 (1215) *in* 3 HARRY ROTHWELL, ENGLISH HISTORICAL DOCUMENTS 1189-1327, at 320 (D.C. Douglas ed. 1975) (hereinafter ENG. HIST. DOCS.).

[4] U.S. CONST. amend. V (1791); *see also* U.S. Const. amend. XIV § 1 (1868) ("No State shall . . . deprive any person of life, liberty, or property, without due process of law").

phrase.[5] For them, due process of law in the Fifth Amendment and Fourteenth Amendment entitles citizens to judicial customs and processes such as fair notice, a hearing, and trial by jury.

Others go much further and champion "substantive due process of law."[6] For advocates of substantive due process, the Constitution's use of due process of law extends to not only a body of judicial processes but also to generic concepts of reasonableness and social justice. Government actions or even enacted laws that violate a particular judge's notion of right and wrong, privacy, happiness, dignity, equality, or some other social principle also violate due process of law.[7] The problem with this subjective standard is self-evident.

As we will see below, the Magna Carta and due process of law in medieval English history established and protected participatory government.[8] The two cornerstones of the Magna Carta and the English Constitution are: (1) the concept of judgment and process before enforcement; and (2) common counsel or participation in extraordinary taxation and government. Medieval constitutionalism challenged the king's arbitrary rule and introduced the sovereignty of the Lords and Commons in Parliament. This book surveys the medieval era and highlights the rise of participatory government, which made its debut and obtained some success by Richard II's reign before receding some during the Tudors. Though the United States Constitution's genesis borrowed from English institutions and praised the "people" and representative government, the American judiciary's concept of due process of

---

[5] *Infra* Chapter X sec. A.

[6] *Id.*

[7] *Infra* Chapter X.

[8] *Infra* Chapters IV–VI.

law violates these principles and is not compatible with the origin and concept of due process of law in medieval English history.

II

Medieval Institutions and Political Theory

BEFORE WE DISCUSS the Magna Carta, we must introduce medieval political theory and the relationships between the king, pope, and God.

A. Saint Peter and the Vicar of Christ

Many medieval legal concepts and relationships take their origin from the Bible and canon law.[9] In Matthew 16:18-19, we learn of God's gift to Peter.

> Thou art Peter and upon this rock I will build my church . . . and I will give unto thee the keys of the kingdom of heaven; and whosoever thou shall bind on earth shall be bound in heaven; and whatsoever thou shall loose on earth shall be loosed in heaven.[10]

---

[9] WALTER ULLMANN, MEDIEVAL POLITICAL THOUGHT 21-23 (rev. ed. 1970) (hereinafter ULLMANN, MEDIEVAL POLITICAL THOUGHT).

[10] MATTHEW 16:18-19. *See also* ULLMANN, MEDIEVAL POLITICAL THOUGHT, *supra* note 9, at 22-23, 25 (discussing Petrinacy); I.S. Robinson, *Church and*

God rules through Saint Peter and the men who stand in the place of Peter. Under medieval Petrine principles, the power of Peter resided in the pope, whose office enjoyed a corporate status as Peter's power endowed the office rather than the body.[11]

The pope viewed the Christian population as an empire in its own right. The medieval pope had the absolute power of speaking and giving the law.[12] The Christian empire did not have a place for government by consent. The medieval pope was supreme within the Christian community and gave power to offices below. There was no questioning power above.[13] Medieval canon law epitomized the concept of superior and inferior: lower church authority was appealable to higher church authority and inferior law was "null and void."[14]

The pope also entertained appeals from the Christian population.[15] The pope told Henry I that appeals to Rome were

---

Papacy in THE CAMBRIDGE HISTORY OF MEDIEVAL POLITICAL THOUGHT C.350–C.1450, at 279–82 (J.H. Burns ed. 1988) (hereinafter CAMB. HIST. MED. POL. THOUGHT) (same); J.A. Watt, *Spiritual and Temporal Powers*, CAMB. HIST. MED. POL. THOUGHT, *supra*, at 376–77; BRIAN TIERNEY, THE CRISIS OF CHURCH AND STATE 1050–1300, at 8 (1964).

11 ULLMANN, MEDIEVAL POLITICAL THOUGHT, *supra* note 9, at 22–28.

12 *Id.* at 27.

13 WALTER ULLMANN, *The Papacy and the Faithful (VIII) in* JURISPRUDENCE IN THE MIDDLE AGES 23–27 (1980) (hereinafter ULLMANN, JURISPRUDENCE).

14 GWILYM DODD, JUSTICE AND GRACE, PRIVATE PETITIONING AND THE ENGLISH PARLIAMENT IN THE LATE MIDDLE AGES 36–38 (2007) (influence of papal appeals on Edward I's petitions in Parliament).

15 COLIN MORRIS, THE PAPAL MONARCHY: THE WESTERN CHURCH FROM 1050 TO 1250, at 211–15 (1989); I.S. Robinson, *Church and Papacy in* CAMB. HIST. MED. POL. THOUGHT, *supra* note 10, at 286.

available for great issues and for those who were oppressed.[16] And the pope's decision was final; there was no review of papal authority.[17] As the lord of the church, the pope did not necessarily exercise jurisdiction or judgment by feudal hierarchy but instead by "reason of sin" and "common utility."[18]

Within this paradigm, the medieval king's acts were subject to papal review.[19] The lay emperor or king was a Christian and thus subject to God's "reason" and Christian laws, for example, the pope's canon law and decretal.[20] A passage from Paul read: the prince "does not bear the sword without reason."[21] And the "reason" was God's divine plan for the prince.[22] Reason might be used synonymously with divine equity.[23] Reason guided both

---

16 MORRIS, *supra* note 15, at 211. The pope sat as an overseer of the king on matters of justice. *Id.* at 568-77; *see also* TIERNEY, CRISIS, *supra* note 10, at 98 (papal appeals).

17 ULLMANN, MEDIEVAL POLITICAL THOUGHT, *supra* note 9, at 29-30, 106.

18 J.E.A. JOLLIFFE, ANGEVIN KINGSHIP 314 (2d ed. 1963) (hereinafter JOLLIFFE, ANGEVIN KINGSHIP); ULLMANN, MEDIEVAL POLITICAL THOUGHT, *supra* note 9, at 103, 111-12.

19 I.S. Robinson, *Church and Papacy in* CAMB. HIST. MED. POL. THOUGHT, *supra* note 10, at 300-05 (papal supremacy over both material and spiritual realms); *see also* MORRIS, *supra* note 15, at 126-30.

20 ULLMANN, MEDIEVAL POLITICAL THOUGHT, *supra* note 9, at 39, 78-79; D.E. Luscombe, *Introduction: The Formation of Political Thought in the West in* CAMB. HIST. MED. POL. THOUGHT, *supra* note 10, at 167-69 (papal deposition of kings). St. Ambrose declared that the emperor was a member of the body of Christ, not above it. ULLMANN, MEDIEVAL POLITICAL THOUGHT, *supra* note 9, at 40; TIERNEY, CRISIS, *supra* note 10, at 9, 97-99, 117-19 (papal power and authority).

21 ROMANS 13:4.

22 ULLMANN, MEDIEVAL POLITICAL THOUGHT, *supra* note 9, at 40.

23 John Procope, *Greek and Roman Political Theory in* CAMB. HIST. MED. POL. THOUGHT, *supra* note 10, at 26 (reason as a form of *epieikeia* or equity).

the king and natural law. Reason was natural justice but complied with public utility as the necessity arose. Ernst H. Kantorowicz wrote:

> [The emperor] is free from all laws; he is above the ties of Positive Law, which Reason, complying with public Utility and changing Necessity, may alter at any time, and of which Reason is the mother as he is the father; but Reason is also above the Prince as she is above any king, and to her the emperor is bound: he is *legibus solutus*, but *ratione alligatus*" (unbound by laws but bound by reason).[24]

Albert F. Pollard wrote:

> The king was the minister of the church, and was subject to its law, not merely the divine law, but the canon law, the *lex positiva* imposed by the pope. This was universal law, and municipal legislation like acts of parliament, which conflicted with it, was *ipso facto* null and void.[25]

Under Petrine principles of binding and loosing, the pope was able to absolve subjects from fealty to wicked kings, who then might be excommunicated and deposed.[26] Excommunication resulted in the loss of participation in ecclesiastic ceremonies and

---

[24] ERNST H. KANTOROWICZ, THE KING'S TWO BODIES: A STUDY IN MEDIAEVAL POLITICAL THEOLOGY 105-07, 110 (1957); FRITZ KERN, KINGSHIP AND LAW IN THE MIDDLE AGES 71-72 (S.B. Chrimes Trans. 1939).

[25] A.F. POLLARD, THE EVOLUTION OF PARLIAMENT 222 (2d ed. 1926); *see also* ULLMANN, MEDIEVAL POLITICAL THOUGHT, *supra* note 9, at 78-80, 112-13; *supra* note 20 (church supremacy over kings and emperors).

[26] ULLMANN, MEDIEVAL POLITICAL THOUGHT, *supra* note 9, at 78-80, 112; KERN, *supra* note 24, at 101; Ludwik Ehrlich, *Proceedings against the Crown (1216-1377) in* 6 OXFORD STUDIES IN SOCIAL AND LEGAL HISTORY 46 (Paul Vinogradoff ed. 1921) (hereinafter Ehrlich, *Proceedings*).

services. It also provided a stigmatism and social scorn; the excommunicate was a "spiritual leper." Excommunicated officials in office might be ignored. Oaths to the excommunicated were released.[27] Before the fourteenth century, excommunication and deposition were papal matters.

In late medieval times, kings also considered themselves to be the vicar of God. For most of the medieval age, the theory of kingship was theological in origin.[28] Medieval political thought identified two theories of sovereignty: the temporal and spiritual swords.[29] The pope was the sword bearer over spiritual matters but theoretically left temporal matters alone.[30] The pope could not shed blood so he had to appoint a secular prince to handle the needs of the "material sword."[31]

---

[27] J.A. Watt, *Spiritual and Temporal Powers in* CAMB. HIST. MED. POL. THOUGHT, *supra* note 10, at 384-85 (effects of excommunication).

[28] TIERNEY, CRISIS, *supra* note 10, at 2. The Christian emperor was God's viceregent. And like the pope, the emperor's power was God's gift to the emperor. ULLMANN, MEDIEVAL POLITICAL THOUGHT, *supra* note 9, at 33-38; *id.* at 47-48 (Justinian's position of imperial authority); J.A. Watt, *Spiritual and Temporal Powers in* CAMB. HIST. MED. POL. THOUGHT, *supra* note 10, at 378-80 (emperors came before priests, so emperor's power comes from God); TIERNEY, CRISIS, *supra* note 10, at 100, 107-08, 122.

[29] LUKE 22:36-38. *See also* J.A. Watt, *Spiritual and Temporal Powers in* CAMB. HIST. MED. POL. THOUGHT, *supra* note 10, at 370-423; I.S. Robinson, *Church and Papacy, ibid.*, at 300-05; D.E. Luscombe & G.R. Evans, *The Twelfth-Century Renaissance, ibid*, at 317-20.

[30] SELECTED LETTERS OF POPE INNOCENT III CONCERNING ENGLAND (1198-1216), at x-xi (C.R. Cheney & W.H. Semple eds. 1953); JOLLIFFE, ANGEVIN KINGSHIP, *supra* note 18, at 314.

[31] TIERNEY, CRISIS, *supra* note 10, at 88; MORRIS, *supra* note 15, at 17.

But was canon law supreme over the "material sword"? TIERNEY, CRISIS, *supra* note 10, at 116-19, 122; *supra* note 19 (pope and church were supreme law); *infra* note 57 (the pope claimed to be the overseer of both the spiritual and temporal swords).

The king or emperor, once lawfully crowned and anointed, was king or emperor "*gratia Dei*" (by the grace of God) and under a sworn oath to God's justice.[32] As part of his sworn oath, the king was the fountain of justice and was responsible for the welfare of the realm—the "common utility" of the people. God's justice was administered through the king as his delegatee.[33] The king was the tutor of his kingdom, which was in the relationship of ward.[34] All rights flowed from the king and his assenting assembly of advisors.[35] Serving justice and equity might require creating new law or dispensing with the law for the necessity or the welfare of the realm.[36]

---

[32] P.D. King, *The Barbarian Kingdoms in* CAMB. HIST. MED. POL. THOUGHT, *supra* note 10, at 128-29, 141-44; *see also* ULLMANN, MEDIEVAL POLITICAL THOUGHT, *supra* note 9, at 33, 53-54, 86-87, 130. Fritz Kern discussed the *gratia-Dei* formula. KERN, *supra* note 24, at 36-37, 42-44, 51-61.

[33] 2 BRACTON ON THE LAWS AND CUSTOMS OF ENGLAND 22-23 (George E. Woodbine ed., Trans. Samuel. E. Thorne 1968).

[34] ULLMANN, MEDIEVAL POLITICAL THOUGHT, *supra* note 9, at 55-57.

[35] John Procope, *Greek and Roman Political Theory in* CAMB. HIST. MED. POL. THOUGHT, *supra* note 10, at 26, 34; P.D. King, *The Barbarian Kingdoms, ibid.*, at 143-44 (king preserved law for justice, welfare, or utility of people).

[36] John Procope, *Greek and Roman Political Theory*, *ibid.*, at 34, 46 (The Roman doctrines were "king unbound by the law," *rex legibus solutus*, and "what pleases the king has the force of law," *quod habet vigorem legis principi placuit*); D.M. Nicol, *Byzantine Political Thought*, *ibid.*, at 64-65; *see also* JOLLIFFE, ANGEVIN KINGSHIP, *supra* note 18, at 5-6, 344 (king ruled by will, *per voluntatem*).

For Romano-canonical theory on common utility and necessity, see GAINES POST, STUDIES IN MEDIEVAL LEGAL THOUGHT: PUBLIC LAW AND THE STATE, 1100-1322, at 18-21, 372-78 (1964) (hereinafter POST, STUDIES); G.L. HARRISS, KING, PARLIAMENT, AND PUBLIC FINANCE IN MEDIEVAL ENGLAND TO 1369, at 22-23, 39-41, 45-48 (1975) (hereinafter HARRISS, KING & PARLIAMENT) (king of the community and law of "necessity"); *see also supra* notes 20-24 (natural law's "reason" trumps positive law).

The author of the treatise known as Bracton, who was a famous thirteenth-century jurist, posited with some inconsistency that the king was under the law but not subject to the law.[37] The king ought to submit to the law of man, following Christ's example; however, the king was above legal process and enforcement—subject only to his own conscience and God's judgment. The king must have no peer, much less a superior, in doing justice. Though in doing justice, no one should be below him.

> The king has no equal within his realm. Subjects cannot be the equals of the ruler because he would thereby lose his rule, since equal can have no authority over equal. The king must not be under man but under God and under the law because the law makes the king. Let him therefore bestow upon the law what the law bestows upon him, namely rule and power, for there is no rex where will rules rather than lex. Since he is the vicar of God, he ought to be under the law, which appears clearly in the analogy of Jesus Christ, whose vicegerent on Earth he is. Though many ways were open to Jesus for his ineffable redemption of the human race, the true mercy of God chose this most powerful way to destroy the devil's work. Jesus would not use the power of force but the reason of justice. Thus, Jesus willed himself to be under the law that he might redeem those who live under it.

---

[37] There's ambiguity in Bracton's two theories of kingship. KANTOROWICZ, *supra* note 24, at 104-05 (describing antinomy in two maxims of kingship: the king bound by the law but above the law). On the tension between Bracton's theory of *sub lego* and *sub curia* but accountable only to God, see Gaines Post, *Bracton on Kingship* 42 TUL. L. REV. 519, 521-23, 527-28, 544-46 (1968); KANTOROWICZ, *supra*, at 147-48 (noting a complication of relying on Bracton's use of "law" interchangeably for both divine law and positive law); RALPH V. TURNER, THE KING AND HIS COURTS: THE ROLE OF JOHN AND HENRY III IN THE ADMINISTRATION OF JUSTICE, 1199-1240, at 236-37 (1968) (hereinafter TURNER, KING & COURTS) (noting doubts of authenticity of conflicting passages in Bracton's treatise; passages possibly added later by editors sympathetic to the baronial-reform party).

> For He did not wish to use force but judgment. . . . Let the king, therefore, do the same, lest his power remain unbridled. There ought to be no one in his kingdom who surpasses him in the doing of justice, but he ought to be the last, or almost so, to receive it, when he is plaintiff. If it is asked of him, since no writ runs against him there will only be opportunity for petition, that he correct and amend his act; if he does not, it is punishment enough for him that he await God's vengeance. No one may presume to question his acts much less contravene them.[38]

The point that the king was below justice but above the state's positive law was not controversial. The controversial aspect of Bracton's treatise was the statement that the barons and the community control the king. In discussing a royal writ, the author of the treatise noted that the king was bound by his conscience but also suggested that the king could be bound by the judgment of his court or the community of the kingdom.

> If it is the prince or king or another who has no superior except God, the remedy by assise will not lie against him; there will only be opportunity for a petition, that he correct and amend his act. If he fails so to do, let it suffice him for punishment that he await God the Avenger, who says, "Vengeance is mine and I will repay," unless one says that the *universitas regni* and his baronage may and ought to do this in the king's own court.[39]

In discussing the power of a judge to question royal charters, Bracton commented that private persons cannot question the

---

[38] 2 BRACTON, *supra* note 33, at 33; *see also id.* at 109-110, 166, 305-06. I've taken the liberty to put the text and additions into one voice.

[39] 3 *id.* at 43.

acts of kings or the meaning of royal charters. If there is doubt as to the charter's provisions, the king's counsel must be sought.[40] If there is an injury, the king ought to correct it, for he is under God and under "the law by which he is made king. [He is also under] his *curia*, namely, the earls and barons, because if he is without bridle, that is without law, they ought to put the bridle on him."[41]

Setting aside the inconsistencies, the rightful king, according to Bracton, lived under the law of God and law of nature.[42] The king was under natural law but above positive law.[43] Natural law might be defined as "reason" or God's law that animates all men. Natural rights cannot be alienated though they may be restricted or diminished by civil society.[44] Bracton wrote that natural law is the law that God taught all living things. Natural law is the first-order impulse that animates animals and men and is not in man's control.[45]

---

[40] 2 *id.* at 109-10.

[41] *Id.* at 110.

[42] *Id.* at 305-06 (using "law" for man's law and natural law interchangeably); JOLLIFFE, ANGEVIN KINGSHIP, *supra* note 18, at 16 (king's duty to seek grace for the realm; king not bound by the law, only by his own character); *infra* notes 263-265, 312, 372-376 (same).

[43] The king "under natural law" harmonizes with medieval theory. The law of God was the source of "right," "justice," and the "law." *Supra* notes 20-24. The king was not under any secular jurisdiction. Post, *Bracton on Kingship*, *supra* note 37, at 519-25.

[44] 2 BRACTON, *supra* note 33, at 26, 28.

[45] *Id.* at 26.

The law of nations is a subset of the law of nature.[46] The law of nations rules men and the second order of impulses. The law of nations is law used by all nations but falls short of natural law because natural law operates on all things—man and creature. The law of nations is common to men only, such as religion to God or obeying parents and country.[47] We receive liberty, however, from the law of nature. Natural rights, such as liberty, are immutable. Liberty cannot be taken away by the law of nations, only obscured by it.[48] Manumission, for example, does not accurately give liberty but only reveals liberty which exists as part of nature.

B. The Coronation Oath

The discussion of the king, pope, and God meets in the coronation oath. The oath was important in medieval society: coronations, charters, gilds, contracts, and judicial proofs were all formalized with oaths.[49] The oath's power resides in "con-

---

46 *Id.* at 27-28, 166-67.

47 *See* R.A. Markus, *The Latin Fathers in* CAMB. HIST. MED. POL. THOUGHT, *supra* note 10, at 111 (Augustine: God's providence creates two orders of law—natural law and law of man).

48 2 BRACTON, *supra* note 33, at 28.

49 ALAN HARDING, THE LAW COURTS OF MEDIEVAL ENGLAND 24-29 (1973) (oath and oath-helping as a form of judicial proof in Anglo-Saxon era); SUSAN REYNOLDS, KINGDOMS AND COMMUNITIES IN WESTERN EUROPE, 900-1300, at 33 (1984) (hereinafter REYNOLDS, KINGDOMS & COMMUNITIES); H.G. RICHARDSON & G.O. SAYLES, THE GOVERNANCE OF MEDIAEVAL ENGLAND FROM THE CONQUEST TO MAGNA CARTA 205-06 (1963) (hereinafter RICHARDSON & SAYLES, GOVERNANCE) (Normans preferred battle or duel for judicial proof; English preferred oath, compurgation, and ordeal).

The oath was an important part of Anglo-Saxon justice, as the king required oaths of peace from the nation to protect the king's peace. J.E.A. JOLLIFFE, THE CONSTITUTIONAL HISTORY OF MEDIEVAL ENGLAND: FROM THE ENGLISH SETTLEMENT TO 1485, at 8-10 (4th Ed. 1961) (hereinafter JOLLIFFE, CONST. HIST.) (oath-helping in Anglo-Saxon life); *id.* at 57-60 (oath, compurga-

science," a belief in divine justice and the afterlife. The oath was a call to God to torment the violator's soul who broke his oath.[50]

The king was sworn into office through a coronation ceremony.[51] The coronation ceremony and coronation oath became central to kings and emperors. The coronation, as far back as the tenth century, included the king's promise to do justice, to protect the church and the good laws and customs but to suppress evil laws and customs.[52] The oath's traditional form was three parts:

> It is the duty of a king newly ordained and inthroned to enjoin on the Christian people subject to him these three precepts; first, that the Church of God and all the Christian people preserve true peace at all times; secondly, that he forbid rapacity and all iniquities to all degrees; thirdly, that in all judgments he enjoin equity and mercy, that therefore the clement and merciful God may grant us His mercy.[53]

---

tion, and neighborhood status improved upon kindred justice); *id.* at 115-18 (oaths and peace-gilds); *see also* 2 DAVID C. DOUGLAS & GEORGE W. GREENAWAY, ENG. HIST. DOCS. (1042-1189), *supra* note 3, at 431 (all freemen swore an oath of fealty to Norman kings); *infra* notes 60-63 (oaths and charters).

50 William Hamilton Bryson, *Papal Releases from Royal Oaths*, 22 J. OF ECCLESIASTICAL HIST. 19, 19 (1971).

51 ULLMANN, MEDIEVAL POLITICAL THOUGHT, *supra* note 9, at 74-75, 85-87.

52 J.R. MADDICOTT, THE ORIGINS OF THE ENGLISH PARLIAMENT, 924-1327, at 98 (2010) (hereinafter MADDICOTT, ORIGINS); WALTER ULLMANN, *Law and the Medieval Historian (I) in* ULLMANN, JURISPRUDENCE, *supra* note 13, at 57.

53 1 WILLIAM STUBBS, THE CONSTITUTIONAL HISTORY OF ENGLAND IN ITS ORIGIN AND DEVELOPMENT 164-65 (6th ed. 1903). On the coronation oath, see H.G. Richardson, *The English Coronation Oath*, 24 SPECULUM, 44 (1949); B. Wilkinson, *The Coronation Oath of Edward II and the Statute of York*, 19 SPECULUM 445 (1944); Robert S. Hoyt, *The Coronation Oath of 1308: The*

The coronation provisions were equivalent to law codes.[54] The coronation promise to keep the laws and customs was considered, at least theoretically, a minimal restriction on the legislative power of the theocratic king ruling *gratia Dei*, by the grace of God.[55] The coronation bound the king to divine justice and papal oversight.[56] If kings ruled *gratia Dei*, the pope stood as a seat of justice or a court of appeal for the king's actions.[57] If the pope so determined, it was justified to excommunicate or depose an evil king for violating divine justice.[58]

Background of "Les Leys et Les Custumes," 11 TRADITIO 235 (1955); *infra* Chapter VI sec. A (Edward II's Coronation Oath).

54 WALTER ULLMANN, LAW AND POLITICS IN THE MIDDLE AGES: AN INTRODUCTION TO THE SOURCES OF MEDIEVAL POLITICAL IDEAS 208 (1975) (hereinafter ULLMANN, LAW & POLITICS); *cf.* J.P. Canning, *Law, Sovereignty and Corporation Theory in* CAMB. HIST. MED. POL. THOUGHT, *supra* note 10, at 462 (king's duty to protect the community's inalienable rights).

55 WALTER ULLMANN, *Law and the Medieval Historian (I) in* ULLMANN, JURISPRUDENCE, *supra* note 13, at 57-58; *see also supra* notes 19-24, 31 (church supremacy over secular realm).

56 I.S. Robinson, *Church and Papacy in* CAMB. HIST. MED. POL. THOUGHT, *supra* note 10, at 295-96; J.A. Watt, *Spiritual and Temporal* Powers, *ibid.*, at 405.

57 WALTER ULLMANN, *Law and the Medieval Historian (I) in* ULLMANN, JURISPRUDENCE, *supra* note 13, at 46, 58; J.A. Watt, *Spiritual and Temporal Powers in* CAMB. HIST. MED. POL. THOUGHT, *supra* note 10, at 378-79, 381-84, 388-89 (Petrinacy and papal authority over both swords; emperor under pope by coronation oath); *see also supra* notes 9-31 (Petrinacy and church supremacy).

58 WALTER ULLMANN, *Law and the Medieval Historian (I) in* ULLMANN, JURISPRUDENCE, *supra* note 13, at 44, 53; *see also supra* note 26 (papal deposition of king); *infra* Chapter IV (excommunication and near deposition of John).

The coronation oath was often memorialized and expanded into a coronation charter of liberties.[59] Royal charters were oaths in writing promising privileges and immunities to the grantee under penalty of God's judgment to keep the charter's promise.[60]

Because the oath was a call to God, the charter oath was voidable by the church or pope on the circumstances attached to the making of the contract.[61] The pope nullified charters and oaths conflicting with the absolute law and supremacy of the church.[62] Popes also set aside charters and royal acts when those charters and royal acts were obtained by duress or violated other contract principles.[63]

---

[59] *E.g.*, Henry I's Charter of Liberties, *infra* Chapter III sec. A; *see also* AUSTIN LANE POOLE, FROM DOMESDAY BOOK TO MAGNA CARTA 1087-1216, at 5-6 (2d ed. 1955); THEODORE F.T. PLUCKNETT, TASWELL-LANGMEAD'S ENGLISH CONSTITUTIONAL HISTORY: FROM THE TEUTONIC CONQUEST TO THE PRESENT TIME 66 (11th ed. 1960) (hereinafter PLUCKNETT, CONST. HIST.).

[60] Charters were quasi-ecclesiastic documents combining church and state, authored by the church in the name of the state. The charter bestowed privileges and immunities—a joint effort by church and state to give tribute to saints and to God. Thomas H. Burrell, *Privileges and Immunities and the Journey from the Articles of Confederation to the United States Constitution: Courts on National Citizenship and Antidiscrimination*, 35 WHITTIER L. REV. 199, 202-03 & nn. 16-20 (2014).

[61] The violation of an oath (perjury, false swearing) was within the jurisdiction of the ecclesiastical authorities. Bryson, *supra* note 50, at 19-20; CHENEY & SEMPLE, *supra* note 30, at x-xv.

[62] *Supra* Chapter II sec. A (church supremacy); *see also* Bryson, *supra* note 50, at 21. There were several baronial upheavals that resulted in papal intervention: the Magna Carta of 1215; the baronial-reform oath of 1258; and the era of the *Confirmatio Cartarum* of 1297. Bryson, *supra*, at 20-33; Janet Nelson, *Kingship and Empire in* CAMB. HIST. MED. POL. THOUGHT, *supra* note 10, at 247.

[63] *See, e.g.*, *infra* note 291 (Innocent III's release of Magna Carta on grounds of duress).

The king's oath to protect the rights of the crown was an obligation for the king to act for the welfare of the realm.[64] Popes set aside charters and royal acts because they conflicted with the king's obligation to protect the rights of the crown.[65] The king, too, could challenge baronial reforms on the basis of his coronation oath and the common utility of the realm.[66] The Romano-canonical maxim was "necessity knows no law."[67] The king's determination of "necessity," or the welfare of the realm, trumped positive laws, even the king's own positive law.

C. Feudalism

Divine justice was not the only force acting upon the English king. We have briefly discussed the theocratic theory of kingship. Feudalism provides a second theory. It flourished in the late medieval period. Feudalism was the relationship between man, lord, and land, and it served the king's duty to protect the peace.[68] At this time, there was very little national government for private concerns and men could not count on the government for protection. Though there were codes, there was not yet a na-

---

64 *Supra* notes 32-36 (king's duty to welfare and law of necessity); *cf.* KANTOROWICZ, *supra* note 24, at 95-96 (discussing the notion that the king's private person is under the law but his public person is above the law).

65 Ernst H. Kantorowicz, *Inalienability: A Note on Canonical Practice and the English Coronation Oath in the Thirteenth Century*, 29 SPECULUM 488 (1954); SIR MAURICE POWICKE, THE THIRTEENTH CENTURY 1216-1307, at 5-7 (1953) (hereinafter POWICKE, THIRTEENTH CENTURY).

66 Supremacy of necessity and common utility superseded private agreements, even the king's private charters. POST, STUDIES, *supra* note 36, at 17-21; Richardson, *supra* note 53, at 68-69; *supra* notes 20-24, 32-36.

67 POST, STUDIES, *supra* note 36, at 21; *supra* notes 20-24, 32-36.

68 JOLLIFFE, CONST. HIST., *supra* note 49, at 18-23 (origins of lordship).

tional law that punished individuals and provided general peace. The king's peace was reserved to his house and to the servants and dependents to whom he extended it.[69]

The Anglo-Saxon era was marked with violence. Feudalism served the state's need for justice. Feud and violence generated alliances as the poor or those pledging service commended themselves to lords for protection in exchange for service.[70] Kings and powerful men also had men in service as bodyguards and retainers.[71] Because lords had dominion over their vassals, feudalism was a check on feud and violence.[72]

Law and peace required surety and warranty. J.E.A. Jolliffe wrote that the law and administration of the late middle ages did not and could not operate on the individual. Law and justice operated on the individual through his kin or some other communal substitute serving as surety.[73] Justice was based on the feud and

---

69 *Id.* at 7-8, 44-46, 114-20. On a national level, the king had a role to pursue outlawry and keep order if one entity was too strong and the kin or community could not keep a basic level of safety, security, and justice. *Id.* at 44-46, 107-10; HARDING, *supra* note 49, at 13-24. National peace grew from the king's peace of special persons and special places. 1 FREDERICK POLLOCK & FREDERIC W. MAITLAND, THE HISTORY OF ENGLISH LAW BEFORE THE TIME OF EDWARD I, at 44-46 (2d ed. 1899) (describing the king's peace over house, highways, and special lands).

70 F.L. GANSHOF, FEUDALISM 3-9 (Philip Grierson, Trans. Rev. ed. 1964).

71 *Id.* at 3-9, 165.

72 JOLLIFFE, CONST. HIST., *supra* note 49, at 3-4, 14-17 (kinship as an institution of peace and justice; lordship in place of kinship); GANSHOF, *supra* note 70, at 23, 58-61 (lords provided protection from violence of civil war and invasion, but feudalism also presented problems for governance).

73 JOLLIFFE, CONST. HIST., *supra* note 49, at 2-4; *supra* notes 69-70.

private justice by the kindred. The kin of the injured avenged the wrong. Kin also provided warranty.[74]

Lordship arose from circumstances in which persons left their kin to join the service of another.[75] Lords and communities were responsible for justice, for reporting crimes and producing criminals, and telling the truth upon inquiry. Lord, neighborhood, and later territorial units such as the township and hundred replaced kin in the system of surety and warranty.[76] High lords were oath-worthy because of their status or wealth.[77] The landless and slaves were not oath-worthy.[78] The lord provided surety and protection for his tenants.[79]

The lord maintained the vassal. The lord's feudal protection and maintenance included food, clothing, and oftentimes,

---

[74] JOLLIFFE, CONST. HIST., *supra* note 49, at 2-18. Anglo-Saxon leaders sought to reduce violence, feud, and self-help. To address clan violence and self-help, wrongdoers had to compensate the other party. The wergild or blood-price was a system of damages designed to help the administration of peace. Damages were set by the class of the injured and by the injury received. If a high-class person had been slain, the slayers had to pay the relatives of the deceased a higher set of damages.

[75] *Id.* at 14-17; *supra* notes 69-74.

[76] JOLLIFFE, CONST. HIST., *supra* note 49, at 8-10, 14-19, 57-63, 115-21; *supra* note 49 (oath and neighborhood).

[77] GANSHOF, *supra* note 70, at 27-30 (fealty under continental feudalism was a sign of higher status; the privilege of swearing an oath was a sign of status, an honorable and oath-worthy man; lower class were not oath-worthy).

[78] JOLLIFFE, CONST. HIST., *supra* note 49, at 14, 19-23.

[79] PLUCKNETT, CONST. HIST., *supra* note 59, at 21 (tenth-century law that required every landless man have a lord for surety); *see also* BRYCE LYON, A CONSTITUTIONAL AND LEGAL HISTORY OF MEDIEVAL ENGLAND 80 (2d ed. 1980); *supra* notes 69-74.

land.[80] Land was critical during times of war to provide military service.[81] Land was status; powerful men had it. Land grants from powerful kings and lords elevated commendation and vassalage from a status akin to slavery to one of nobility—establishing a class of powerful tenants and tenants in chief providing military service.[82]

After the Norman Conquest, these relationships were absorbed by the feudal contract as Norman feudalism and homage worked its way into pre-existing institutions.[83] Property was an all-encompassing element of the Conquest as William the Conqueror assumed lordship of all the land.[84]

In return for maintenance and protection, the tenant rendered services[85] to the lord, attending his court and providing counsel (*consilium*) when summoned.[86] Feudal courts provided a vital service. Lords had some civil and criminal jurisdiction, and many matters were dealt with in the lord's court by local customs

---

80 GANSHOF, *supra* note 70, at 6-12, 36, 95-96 (lord's obligations included protection, defense, and warranty of vassals).

81 *Id.* at 16 (the tenant or vassal's possession of land aided military service); *id.* at 22-23 (subvassalage for contributions to military service).

82 *Id.* at 19, 23-24.

83 JOLLIFFE, CONST. HIST., *supra* note 49, at 139-40, 153-56.

84 DAVID C. DOUGLAS, WILLIAM THE CONQUEROR, THE NORMAN IMPACT UPON ENGLAND 271-76 (1964).

85 The average tenant had several obligations. Even for those holders of great immunities, there were the three common burdens of military service and bridge and wall work. Thomas H. Burrell, *A Story of Privileges and Immunities: From Medieval Concept to the Colonies and United States Constitution*, 34 CAMPBELL L. REV. 7, 11-12 & nn. (2011).

86 GANSHOF, *supra* note 70, at 92-93 (providing *consilium* was an obligation of feudalism and grew alongside the vassal's duty to attend court); JOLLIFFE, CONST. HIST., *supra* note 49, at 168-69.

and the suitors to the lord's court.[87] The judgment of tenants or equals is better known as *judicium parium* (judgment of peers), though the term "peer" was historically reserved for a high lord.[88] George Burton Adams described *judicium parium* as the judgment of equals or the barons but not itself definitive of a specific type of judicial proof. The judgment of the peers could include a number of judicial proofs including oaths, compurgation, ordeal, battle, and juries of witnesses.[89] Susan Reynolds described collective judgment as a president of a local tribunal directing an assembly in judgment by various proofs such as oaths, ordeals, or battle if there were a factual dispute.[90]

A principle accompanying *judicium parium* was that the *judicium* take place before enforcement. We can find the feudal rule of "judgment before enforcement" on the continent before the Norman Conquest. To end disputes between lords and vas-

---

[87] Feudal courts were prohibited from outlawry and could not conduct ordeals. DORIS M. Stenton, ENGLISH JUSTICE BETWEEN THE NORMAN CONQUEST AND THE GREAT CHARTER 1066-1215, at 57 (1963).

[88] JOLLIFFE, CONST. HIST., *supra* note 49, at 147-48, 151, 168-69. Small and petty matters were heard in the lord's court. The lord might hear minor violations of other laws including criminal matters. J.H. BAKER, AN INTRODUCTION TO ENGLISH LEGAL HISTORY 8-9 (4th ed. 2002); POOLE, *supra* note 59, at 57; HARDING, *supra* note 49, at 32-35; JOLLIFFE, ANGEVIN KINGSHIP, *supra* note 18, at 29, 52.

Suitors to the lord's court declared law and gave judgment. PLUCKNETT, CONST. HIST., *supra* note 59, at 44-45; FREDERIC W. MAITLAND, THE CONSTITUTIONAL HISTORY OF ENGLAND 48-50, 105-06, 169-70 (1908) (peers or equals of feudal courts); GANSHOF, *supra* note 70, at 92-93 (oath of fealty required that vassals declare the law in matters arising before the lord).

[89] GEORGE BURTON ADAMS, COUNCIL AND COURTS IN ANGLO-NORMAN ENGLAND 266 (1926); *see also* PLUCKNETT, CONST. HIST., *supra* note 59, at 23-24.

[90] REYNOLDS, KINGDOMS & COMMUNITIES, *supra* note 49, at 25-34. The president alone may direct judgment if the matter involved a charter or examination of witnesses.

sals, Emperor Conrad II pronounced in 1037 that certain tenants shall not lose their lands without certain or convicted fault except by the custom and constitution of our ancestors and judgment of his peers. Conrad II:

> No knight, whether of bishops, abbots, abbesses, marquises, counts, or anyone else, who held a benefice on royal or church land was to lose it [without certain and convicted guilt] unless formally and properly convicted of an offence according to the law of Conrad's predecessors and the judgment of the accused's peers.[91]

If the accused were caught red-handed committing the crime or with the weapon, he would be dealt with summarily: no proof was needed, no ability to answer, just execution.[92]

Lordship required an oath of allegiance. Homage and fealty were two types of feudal ties between man and lord. Fealty was less formal and required an oath that was sworn standing up.[93] Homage was a more formal tie and required kneeling and taking the lord's hand.[94] Homage was the complete dedication of oneself to the lord. Violation of homage was actionable at law; a violation of fealty was more of a moral offence.[95]

---

[91] SUSAN REYNOLDS, FIEFS AND VASSALS: THE MEDIEVAL EVIDENCE REINTERPRETED 200-03 (2001); BARNABY C. KEENEY, JUDGMENT BY PEERS 7-8 (1949).

[92] POOLE, *supra* note 59, at 404.

[93] RICHARDSON & SAYLES, GOVERNANCE, *supra* note 49, at 105-13 (discussing homage and fealty); *supra* note 77 (fealty and oath were a sign of oath-worthiness).

[94] JOLLIFFE, CONST. HIST., *supra* note 49, at 153; RICHARDSON & SAYLES, GOVERNANCE, *supra* note 49, at 107.

[95] JOLLIFFE, CONST. HIST., *supra* note 49, at 153, 162-63 n.2.

A particular subject might have more than one lord; the king was the ultimate lord or liege lord. The basic feudal formula after the Conquest was that all land was held of the king,[96] and thus all swore allegiance to the king.[97] Tenants in chief held land directly of the king. Tenants in chief also had tenants, who held indirectly of the king and owed allegiance to their lords as well as to the king.

Having reviewed the basic definition of feudalism, we can discuss the outcome if the lord or tenant broke his side of the feudal contract.[98] As noted above, the tenant was bound by several obligations. The lord could distrain or disseise the tenant if the tenant abandoned the lord in need or neglected another duty which the tenant owed to the lord.[99] In the twelfth century, the lord generally had to obtain a judgment before distraining the tenant's chattels or land.[100] Most matters involved land and services. If the lord deprived a tenant of his land unjustly—without judgment—the tenant would likely sue the lord if he had an avail-

---

[96] FREDERIC W. MAITLAND, DOMESDAY BOOK AND BEYOND 241, 300 (1897); *see also supra* note 84.

[97] PLUCKNETT, CONST. HIST., *supra* note 59, at 34.

[98] For definition and discussion of homage and homage as a bilateral contract, see JOLLIFFE, CONST. HIST., *supra* note 49, at 153-54.

[99] JOLLIFFE, ANGEVIN KINGSHIP, *supra* note 18, at 73-76; Joseph Biancalana, *For Want of Justice: Legal Reforms of Henry II*, 88 COLUM. L. REV. 433, 467 (1988). The king could outlaw after following specified procedure. Whether or not the Angevin king needed to pursue judgment before disseisin was a central point of the Magna Carta. *Infra* Chapter IV sec. B.

[100] JOLLIFFE, CONST. HIST., *supra* note 49, at 155; Biancalana, *supra* note 99, at 452. *See also supra* notes 85-88 (*consilium* and judgment of suitors).

able remedy in the county or king's court.[101] Jolliffe discussed the theory that the tenant could renounce his oath and defy the lord (*diffidatio* or diffidation).[102] Diffidation was the means of legally breaking the contract of homage and allegiance between man and lord. Jolliffe clarified that diffidation was acceptable not merely when the tenant was wronged but when he was wronged and denied justice after having pursued the proper legal remedies.[103] Feudal injustice did not center on the substantive outcome but instead on the absence of the adjudication as a whole.[104]

The national law of the middle ages did not cover many subjects, and justice resided in a variety of sources. But feudalism did protect rights in land. And for those tenants who failed to receive justice in private or local courts, the tenant might have an extraordinary action against the erring lord in the king's

---

101 PAUL BRAND, THE MAKING OF THE COMMON LAW 308–10 (1992); STENTON, *supra* note 87, at 57; Robert C. Palmer, *The Feudal Framework of English Law*, 79 MICH. L. REV. 1130, 1141–42 (1981).

102 JOLLIFFE, CONST. HIST., *supra* note 49, at 155; GANSHOF, *supra* note 70, at 98-99; Biancalana, *supra* note 99, at 461. For diffidation, see D.E. Luscombe, *Introduction: the Formation of Political Thought in the West in* CAMB. HIST. MED. POL. THOUGHT, *supra* note 10, at 160; *infra* note 133 (diffidation in Stephen's reign); *infra* notes 242-244 (diffidation in John's reign). *But see* RICHARDSON & SAYLES, GOVERNANCE, *supra* note 49, at 148–49 (finding that England had several different processes binding the king that substituted for pure feudal diffidation, which was more of a continental practice).

103 JOLLIFFE, CONST. HIST., *supra* note 49, at 156–60.

104 *Id.* at 157; Biancalana, *supra* note 99, at 439, 452–54.

court.[105] Within the feudal contract, the tenant was not permitted to do violence.[106] Self-help was not favored.

The leading barons were king's tenants and the rules of feudalism extended upwards. If the king's tenants in chief believed that the king had violated his duty, they could shed allegiance and rise in diffidation.[107]

Though justice flowed from the king, the king was not the only source of influence. The king was the head of the community but not the owner of it. As mentioned above, attending the lord's court was a component of feudalism.[108] The king's feudal council of tenants in chief served as suitors and advisors to his court providing *commune consilium* or common counsel. For

---

105 JOLLIFFE, CONST. HIST., *supra* note 49, at 156. If justice were denied to an individual a number of times by the normal methods, the king might intervene. But this role was extraordinary at first and then became more regular. *Id.* at 53, 107–08, 190–91. The twelfth-century king's position vis-à-vis subject was extra-judicial "to do right" when other justice failed. *Id.* at 45, 53; *infra* note 184 (development of assizes and judicial determinations from executive writs or orders "to do" justice). The royal court at this time did not provide a means for substantive appeal from a lower to higher court but rather served as a substitute court for defect of justice (no judgment provided) or false judgment. Biancalana, *supra* note 99, at 452–59. Ecclesiastic courts had the appeal to Rome, and the concept of appeal to higher authority eventually infiltrated secular courts. R.C. VAN CAENEGEM, ROYAL WRITS IN ENGLAND FROM THE CONQUEST TO GLANVILL: STUDIES IN THE EARLY HISTORY OF THE COMMON LAW 38, 40 (1959).

106 JOLLIFFE, CONST. HIST., *supra* note 49, at 156.

107 *Id.* at 155–59.

108 *Supra* note 86.

great matters, especially taxation and war, the king consulted with counselors, special assemblies, or great councils of barons.[109]

In pre-Conquest England, the king's Witan[110] and thegns regularly witnessed charters and attended special assemblies, festivals, and religious ceremonies.[111] Great crown-wearing assemblies provided an opportunity for the king to treat and parley with social and military advisors on national business.[112] Norman feudalism carried the function of the Witan past the Norman Conquest, and eventually to a formal body of royal councilors.

In the Norman-Angevin era, the king's court, the *curia regis*, was the supreme court where all branches of government met for the administration of the land.[113] The term "court" in

---

109 LYON, *supra* note 79, at 43 (Anglo-Saxon kings receiving informal counsel for custom and code); *infra* note 147 (common *consilium* on important matters).

110 The Anglo-Saxon "wita" were an aristocratic group of earls, bishops, king's thegns, abbots, and other influential subjects of the realm. "Wita" means "to know," witness. FELIX LIEBERMANN, THE NATIONAL ASSEMBLY IN THE ANGLO-SAXON PERIOD 6-7 (1913). The Witan were the wise men or the sapients of the kingdom: *boni* or *probi homines*. *Id.* at 8; *see also* LYON, *supra* note 79, at 44-51; JOLLIFFE, CONST. HIST., *supra* note 49, at 25-30. The king with the Witan could raise armies and levy extraordinary taxes. LYON, *supra*, at 48. The Witan were parties to grants of bookland and had appointment power of bishops and other officers. PLUCKNETT, CONST. HIST., *supra* note 59, at 19-20; LYON, *supra*, at 49-50.

111 MADDICOTT, ORIGINS, *supra* note 52, at 1-18, 31; LYON, *supra* note 79, at 43, 44-46 (Witan and national crown-wearing assemblies).

112 GEORGE O. SAYLES, THE KING'S PARLIAMENT OF ENGLAND 21-22 (1974) (hereinafter SAYLES, KING'S PARLIAMENT); *see also* JOLLIFFE, ANGEVIN KINGSHIP, *supra* note 18, at 166-67; MADDICOTT, ORIGINS, *supra* note 52, at 31, 49-52. These assemblies continued throughout the medieval period as Great Councils or Parliaments. *Infra* notes 147-156; SAYLES, KING'S PARLIAMENT, *supra*, at 27-34 (noting instances in which barons afforced courts of justices into Great Councils).

113 1 SIR WILLIAM HOLDSWORTH, A HISTORY OF ENGLISH LAW 32 (1966 reprint).

medieval times described a physical meeting place, served as a label referring to the meeting, or a name for the body of individuals attending the meeting. The court's function could be legislative and judicial without distinction.[114] The *curia regis* was the executive, financial, legislative, and judicial center of the Norman king.[115] The Norman *curia regis* did not have formal procedure.[116] The suitors or judges of the *curia regis* could invoke Norman, English, Roman, canon, or manorial customs to decide a case.

The Norman king was the fountain of justice, grace, and equity.[117] The king's court heard matters of equity or extraordinary appeals when local justice was denied.[118] Generally, justice was local; however, the king's royal jurisdiction was growing. During the twelfth century, reform movements put into motion forces that greatly expanded royal or national law.[119]

Walter Ullmann wrote that the history of medieval politics was a competition between the ascending and descending theories of government, between the feudal king responsible to his tenants in chief and the theocratic principle that kingship was a gift from

---

[114] THEODORE F.T. PLUCKNETT, A CONCISE HISTORY OF THE COMMON LAW 142-43 (5th ed. 1956) (hereinafter PLUCKNETT, CONCISE HISTORY).

[115] 1 HOLDSWORTH, *supra* note 113, at 32; PLUCKNETT, CONST. HIST., *supra* note 59, at 95-96.

[116] LYON, *supra* note 79, at 188-89.

[117] *Supra* Chapter II sec. A.

[118] *Supra* note 105.

[119] *Infra* Chapter III sec. B.

above.[120] Under the descending theory, God gave authority to the king. Governance was by the *voluntas princepis*, will of the king. Kings were privileged from above. In the ascending theory, kingship was part of the feudal hierarchy or developed by some aristocratic component of the people. Power resided in the king from a segment of the *voluntas populi*, will of the people—flowing upward based on some feature such as valor or bloodlines.[121]

Ullmann observed that medieval kingship was itself a paradox: placing sovereignty in the king and requiring an ultimate justice to God but also binding the king with feudal and *consilium* obligations.[122] The tension between the theocratic and feudal functions of the king characterized the latter part of the Middle Ages. The weak point of a theocratic king was his feudal responsibilities to receive common counsel from his court. Feudal *consilium* gave rise to conciliarism, community action, and participatory government—eventually eroding the power of the theocratic king ruling *gratia Dei* and substituting parliamentary sovereignty.

---

[120] ULLMANN, MEDIEVAL POLITICAL THOUGHT, *supra* note 9, at 12–13, 146–48.

[121] Germanic and Anglo-Saxon theories of kingship might be based on valor or blood supremacy. KERN, *supra* note 24, at 12–27; JOLLIFFE, CONST. HIST., *supra* note 49, at 30, 41–55.

[122] WALTER ULLMANN, *Law and the Medieval Historian (I) in* ULLMANN, JURISPRUDENCE, *supra* note 13, at 56–59.

III

Normans, Angevins, and the Magna Carta

A. The Norman Conquest and Henry I's Charter

WITH THIS ROUGH BACKGROUND of medieval political theory, we can briefly summarize the events leading up to the Magna Carta. William the Conqueror invaded England in 1066.[123] William, a Norman foreigner who claimed rightful inheritance, appeased the English with a promise to follow English laws.[124] He swore a coronation oath.[125] William's lasting accomplishment was the Domesday Survey and Book, an administrative inquest into the finances of the realm.[126] The inquest was a fact-finding device in which the king sought information based on the sworn verdicts or true statements of a

---

[123] DOUGLAS, *supra* note 84, at 181–210.

[124] PLUCKNETT, CONST. HIST., *supra* note 59, at 29.

[125] DOUGLAS, *supra* note 84, at 207; PLUCKNETT, CONST. HIST., *supra* note 59, at 66.

[126] V.H. GALBRAITH, THE MAKING OF DOMESDAY BOOK (1961).

group of worthy men with knowledge or able to obtain knowledge of the matter at issue.[127]

William's son and successor, William Rufus, was a poor king.[128] Following this lapse, William's other son, Henry I, who assumed kingship in 1100, was a strong monarch. Henry I swore out a set of promises in his coronation oath and charter.[129] Theodore F.T. Plucknett described Henry I's charter of liberties as an amplification of his coronation oath.[130] Henry's charter of liberties, among other things, promised to restore the laws of King Edward as amended by William and the counsel of his barons. Henry promised to abolish the evil customs of Rufus's reign and to refrain from assessing fines for offences at the king's mercy but instead to fine at a rate commensurate with the nature of the offense.[131]

The stronger administration of Henry I was lost with his nephew Stephen. During Stephen's reign, England fell into anarchy.[132] Barons in revolt defied the king and renounced their oath

---

[127] VAN CAENEGEM, *supra* note 105, at 40, 51-52; HARDING, *supra* note 49, at 36; JOLLIFFE, CONST. HIST., *supra* note 49, at 198-99.

[128] POOLE, *supra* note 59, at 98-99, 169-72.

[129] 2 DOUGLAS & GREENAWAY, ENG. HIST. DOCS., *supra* note 3, at 432-34. Henry's oath and coronation charter is not to be confused with the treatise under the name *Leges Henrici Primi*, though later generations often lump the two together. PLUCKNETT, CONST. HIST., *supra* note 59, at 50.

[130] PLUCKNETT, CONST. HIST., *supra* note 59, at *Id.* at 49-50.

[131] *Id.*

[132] THE ANARCHY OF KING STEPHEN'S REIGN (Edmund King ed. 1994).

of homage.[133] The baronial leaders became independent, usurped royal rights, and had to be restrained by force.

When young Henry, grandson of Henry I, became of age, he challenged Stephen and eventually invaded England.[134] Henry assumed the throne in 1154. Following the charters and oaths of Henry I and Stephen, Henry II also issued a coronation charter promising all the liberties of his grandfather, Henry I.[135]

B. *Consilium* and Henry II's Assizes

Henry II, though not without conflict, returned order to England following the anarchy of Stephen's reign. Henry II's reign transformed the source and scope of medieval legal authority. He greatly expanded the role of royal justice in local affairs through his development of royal assizes and writs.

In medieval times, authority and the law might come from a variety of sources. Positive law was the opposite of customary law.[136] Under Roman principles, positive law was given to the people by the ruler, *lex data* or *legisdatio*.[137] Norman rulers fol-

---

[133] ROBERT BARTLETT, ENGLAND UNDER THE NORMAN AND ANGEVIN KINGS 1075-1225, at 61 (2000); JOLLIFFE, CONST. HIST., *supra* note 49, at 159, 160.

[134] LYON, *supra* note 79, at 125-26.

[135] PLUCKNETT, CONST. HIST., *supra* note 59, at 56.

[136] Ullmann explained that customary law was the will of the people by toleration and usage; positive law was the ruler's law. Disuse and contrary custom challenged imperial authority. Because this was a dangerous principle, Constantine the Great made sure that positive law stood firm and that customary law could not derogate from the positive law. ULLMANN, LAW & POLITICS, *supra* note 54, at 62-63.

[137] Ullmann traced the etymology of "positive law" from "to place the law": "*ponere legem*; *lex posita*; *ius posit[iv]um*." ULLMANN, LAW & POLITICS, *supra* note 54, at 62; *see also* TIERNEY, CRISIS, *supra* note 10, at 103 (Jus-

lowed Roman imperial rulemaking.[138] It would be at least the middle of the thirteenth century before we see *lex lata* or *legislatio*, laws allowed by the people—in this case, the barons. The only universal law existed in the law of God or natural law.[139]

The king, the vicar of God, was the supreme law giver. The king had the right to decree the law through executive orders or adjudication. The king's writ was a royal order to do something.[140] The "original writ" originated an action at law. The plaintiff brought the matter to royal officials who, if the matter fit an available form of action, drafted a writ following a specified formula. The writ process was formal, and subsequent judicial procedure was writ-specific for summons, delays (essoins), and modes of proof.[141]

Royal legislation might take the form of oral orders, charters, and writs to the sheriff, or assizes.[142] Assize meant or was used interchangeably with "decision," "enactment," "provision," the sitting of a council, or establishment of a constitution.[143] The

---

tinian on law of nature, written law, statute law, and emperor's final authority on the force of law: "whatever the emperor settles by rescript, or decides in his judicial capacity, or ordains by edicts, is clearly a statute: and these are what are called constitutions.").

138 WALTER ULLMANN, *Roman Public Law and Medieval Monarchy: Norman Rulership in Sicily (V) in* ULLMANN, JURISPRUDENCE, *supra* note 13, at 165, 167, 173; REYNOLDS, KINGDOMS & COMMUNITIES, *supra* note 49, at 45-46.

139 KERN, *supra* note 24, at 71-72.

140 Biancalana, *supra* note 99, at 442-43.

141 VAN CAENEGEM, *supra* note 105, at 46-48, 111-12; BAKER, *supra* note 88, at 53-54.

142 2 HOLDSWORTH, *supra* note 113, at 178-80.

143 3 G.O. SAYLES, SELECT CASES IN THE COURT OF KING'S BENCH UNDER EDWARD I, at xi (1939) (hereinafter SAYLES, SELECT CASES); VAN CAENEGEM, *supra* note 105, at 82.

assize addressed conflicts and defects in custom.[144] Assizes were a precursor to statutes and represented royal legislation comparable to Roman imperial legislation.[145]

Royal legislative and judicial acts were framed and passed by the king with counsel.[146] On great matters, the king might summon others to afforce or add weight to existing opinion.[147] Popular attendance at the king's court served the function of disseminating orders and receiving oaths to assent to the law being developed or discussed.[148] By most accounts, any amendment to material law, especially tax matters, received the common counsel of the barons.[149] *Commune consilium* and the obligation to give

---

144 JOLLIFFE, CONST. HIST., *supra* note 49, at 239.

145 WALTER ULLMANN, *Roman Public Law and Medieval Monarchy: Norman Rulership in Sicily (V) in* ULLMANN, JURISPRUDENCE, *supra* note 13, at 167.

146 LYON, *supra* note 79, at 143-44; 1 HOLDSWORTH, *supra* note 113, at 39.

147 Great Councils were present throughout the period being examined. And while they might serve as an alternative to Parliament, their composition and function were not formal. SAYLES, KING'S PARLIAMENT, *supra* note 112, at 21-26, 129-33; BERTIE WILKINSON, THE CREATION OF MEDIEVAL PARLIAMENTS 44-46 (1972) (common counsel, and consent); *infra* notes 310-311, 330-333 (Council, Great Councils, and Parliaments).

148 H.G. Richardson, *The Origins of Parliament*, 11 TRANS. ROY. HIST. SOC. (4th Series) 137, 169 (1928). The full presence of the barons served the purpose of assisting royal policy by showing additional support for a matter of significance, especially when dealing with papal affairs, taxation, or foreign rivals. But at this early date, their presence was optional. LYON, *supra* note 79, at 142-51 (baronial *consilium* was a sounding board); JOLLIFFE, ANGEVIN KINGSHIP, *supra* note 18, at 168-69, 171.

149 SAYLES, KING'S PARLIAMENT, *supra* note 112, at 21, 24-25; *supra* notes 111-112 (kings "treating" with counselors). In the latter part of the twelfth century, councils were frequently called for extraordinary taxation. SAYLES, *supra*, at 31-32 (noting *consilium* for extraordinary taxes of the Saladin tithe and Richard I's ransom); MADDICOTT, ORIGINS, *supra* note 52, at 101-04. The thirteenth century can be described as the king con-

advice and share in judgment on important matters before the lord was a central duty of the tenant.[150]

It was a custom that the king consult with his barons, but "counsel" or "assent" was a loose requirement before thirteenth- and fourteenth-century reforms.[151] Baronial input was largely undefined.[152] Common counsel did not mean by vote or majority vote. It merely meant that action was tempered by some discussion and input was received or compromise was reached.[153] During this time, the king's power was virtually unrestrained and the counsel of the barons was a formality.[154] Jolliffe commented that the twelfth-century English king "held only of God and by the homages of his men[;] there was nothing but custom to govern the King and nothing but what influence or authority his own court could exert to enforce it; nothing but the counsel of his barons to prevent the suzerain's trust of power—[royal jurisdiction and dis-

---

ceding to baronial demands in exchange for taxation. *Infra* Chapter V; SAYLES, KING'S PARLIAMENT, *supra* note 112, at 25 (noting John's policy to indicate that action took place with the advice of counsel).

By the mid-thirteenth century, the barons would argue that even unwritten laws that have become law by the king and the common counsel cannot be changed significantly without the same common consent that made them law. 3 B. WILKINSON, CONSTITUTIONAL HISTORY OF MEDIEVAL ENGLAND 1216-1399 WITH SELECT DOCUMENTS 256-60 (3d imp. 1963) (hereinafter WILKINSON, CONST. HIST.). This may have been questionable at the end of the thirteenth century but mostly realized during the early to mid-fourteenth century. *Id.* at 333.

150 *Supra* notes 86-88, 108-109.

151 POOLE, *supra* note 59, at 10; LYON, *supra* note 79, at 143-46.

152 JOLLIFFE, CONST. HIST., *supra* note 49, at 238-39.

153 RALPH V. TURNER, MAGNA CARTA THROUGH THE AGES 74 (2003) (hereinafter TURNER, MAGNA CARTA).

154 J.F. Baldwin cited the controversy between Henry II and Becket as one of the first instances of advisors "debating" the king. JAMES FOSDICK BALDWIN, THE KING'S COUNCIL IN ENGLAND DURING THE MIDDLE AGES 10 (1913) (hereinafter BALDWIN, KING'S COUNCIL).

traint]—from becoming the ungoverned, irrevocable will of one man."[155]

C. The Assizes of Clarendon and Novel Disseisin

Henry II is remembered for his transformative legislation. Henry II gave us many assizes. We have the Assize of Clarendon and the petty assizes including the Assize of Novel Disseisin.[156] For purposes of this discussion, we focus on two assizes: the Assize of Clarendon and the Assize of Novel Disseisin.

Both assizes centered upon the royal inquest. We know that the royal inquest was used for financial and administrative purposes, for example, the Domesday Survey.[157] Supplementing the crown's administrative use, the inquest was also used for presenting those accused of crimes.[158] Henry II ordered that his courts use presentment juries to empanel jurors of the neighbor-

---

[155] JOLLIFFE, ANGEVIN KINGSHIP, *supra* note 18, at 5, 33-34.

[156] There were several other important assizes. Jolliffe described the age of assizes as a period of shared governance—possibly not a characteristic of Henry II's reign but might reflect how the assize was later viewed, for example, the assizes of John's reign. JOLLIFFE, CONST. HIST., *supra* note 49, at 239-41.

[157] *Supra* note 126.

[158] There were several juries in Anglo-Norman times. HARDING, *supra* note 49, at 55 (tracing presentment to the eleventh-century presentment of Englishry to avoid murder fines); Naomi D. Hurnard, *The Jury of Presentment and the Assize of Clarendon*, 56 ENG. HIST. REV. 374 (1941); *see also* A.L. BROWN, THE GOVERNANCE OF LATE MEDIEVAL ENGLAND, 1272-1461, at 102 (1989). There were juries of witnesses and compurgators: some chosen by parties, some elected from the neighborhood. JOLLIFFE, CONST. HIST., *supra* note 49, at 151, 198-99.

hood sworn to tell the truth of the crimes of great and powerful men who were able to evade justice.[159]

The principle of justice carried. In the Assize of Clarendon (1166), Henry formalized the process of the sworn presentment jury, what we know as the grand jury.[160] Royal itinerant judges[161] rode circuit (eyre) to receive sworn presentments covering a limited number of specified crimes.[162] In each county, twelve men from the hundred and four men from the township identified, under oath, those accused of specified crimes.[163] After the presenting jury accused him, the defendant was forced to de-

---

[159] 2 DOUGLAS & GREENAWAY, ENG. HIST. DOCS., *supra* note 3, at 766, 768 (Constitutions of Clarendon); POOLE, *supra* note 59, at 205; LYON, *supra* note 79, at 295. The Constitutions protected the accused from being sued or arraigned on insufficient evidence. POOLE, *supra* note 59, at 205 (arraigned only by lawful and responsible accusers).

[160] 2 DOUGLAS & GREENAWAY, ENG. HIST. DOCS., *supra* note 3, at 440–43; POOLE, *supra* note 59, at 398. The presenting jury and recognition in general were the predecessor of what we know as trial by jury.

[161] Itinerant justices were royal justices representing the *curia regis* in the local communal courts. The itinerant justices followed the practice of royal commissioners recording jurors' statements in the making of the Domesday Book. HARDING, *supra* note 49, at 38.

[162] BAKER, *supra* note 88, at 16 (eyres formalized after Assize of Northampton in 1176); POOLE, *supra* note 59, at 398–99. The eyre's jurisdiction was established by the "articles of eyre," which was a list of questions for the hundreds, towns, boroughs, and other units required to attend the eyre. ANTHONY MUSSON & W.M. ORMROD, THE EVOLUTION OF ENGLISH JUSTICE: LAW, POLITICS AND SOCIETY IN THE FOURTEENTH CENTURY 43 (1999) (hereinafter MUSSON & ORMROD, EVOLUTION OF ENG. JUSTICE).

[163] LYON, *supra* note 79, at 295; POOLE, *supra* note 59, at 398–99. The presenting jury used their own knowledge or the knowledge of others. 1 HOLDSWORTH, *supra* note 113, at 321–22; PLUCKNETT, CONST. HIST., *supra* note 59, at 107–10. The presenting jury flourished and was modified after the high number of complaints being brought before the justices. Individual complaints were made to the justices and verified in front of the presenting jury, a grand jury, swearing to a true bill or indictment. HARDING, *supra* note 49, at 89–90.

fend himself by a judicial proof, frequently compurgation or ordeal.[164] The petit jury (trial by jury, though not yet in modern form) was a natural outcome after the church abolished the ordeal as a means of judicial proof.[165] Thereafter, one jury would indict and another would convict.[166]

As discussed above, feudalism centered upon land, and lawful possession of land was a vital medieval concept.[167] The king sought to check self-help and feud.[168] Peace and justice required, at the least, a process of judgment before execution or enforcement.[169] One can trace the justice of the era by the law of distraint. Distraint and *judicium parium* went hand in hand as they were the means by which feudalism checked injustice.[170]

---

164 POOLE, *supra* note 59, at 401-02. Even if the accused were cleared by the ordeal, he would likely be outlawed. *Id.* at 402; *see also* LYON, *supra* note 79, at 296; JOLLIFFE, CONST. HIST., *supra* note 49, at 209.

165 The petit jury developed from the inquest and the need to ascertain the truth of a fact during litigation.

166 PLUCKNETT, CONCISE HISTORY, *supra* note 114, at 119-27 (describing development of jury trial in thirteenth century; noting that for convenience, judges on occasion found guilt by afforcing or adding jurors to presenting jury to find guilt from indictment).

167 For seisin to be valid, the gift, purchase, inheritance, or enfeoffment must have been accompanied by livery of seisin. VAN CAENEGEM, *supra* note 105, at 267. The definition of "seisin" was actual, visible, and noticeable use of the land. *Id.* at 306.

168 *Supra* notes 70-106.

169 *Supra* notes 88, 100-102.

170 JOLLIFFE, ANGEVIN KINGSHIP, *supra* note 18, at 24-29, 33-34, 52; *supra* notes 88-90.

The key to feudal justice was that the lord obtain judgment before distraint.[171]

Stephen's reign was full of chaos with frequent disseisin without judgment. In Stephen's reign, lords distrained and disseized their tenants unjustly without judgment (*sine judicio et injuste*).[172] Henry II had to address the state of affairs.[173] Henry II aimed to restore peace, and this meant restoring land ownership wrongfully taken.[174]

In 1166 or thereabouts, Henry II, with the goal of restoring order, issued an ordinance establishing the Assize of Novel Disseisin to address unlawful disseisin. The writ of novel disseisin provided a remedy for those disseized or dispossessed of their free tenement unjustly and without justice. The writ provided for a recognition jury to be empaneled in the presence of royal justices to decide the question of possession—not title, just possession.[175] The recognition jury, like the presentment jury, was based on the inquest of fact-witnesses.[176] The writ of novel disseisin grew from three trends: jury recognition, criminalization of wrongs, and royal executive intervention against unlawful dissei-

---

[171] Biancalana, *supra* note 99, at 439-40, 466-67.

[172] Distraint generally differed from disseisin as distraint was temporary confiscation in trust of chattels until trial. JOLLIFFE, ANGEVIN KINGSHIP, *supra* note 18, at 53. Distraint was also a means of enforcing judgment. *Id.* at 29-30, 52-53.

[173] VAN CAENEGEM, *supra* note 105, at 281.

[174] Biancalana, *supra* note 99, at 466.

[175] VAN CAENEGEM, *supra* note 105, at 261-67.

[176] *Id.* at 51-54; *supra* notes 126, 158-159.

sin.[177] A recognition, like the return from an inquest, was a response by a sworn body of jurors empaneled to give a true answer or verdict to an inquiry. The recognition served as an answer to a fact, a component of a judicial proof, or the judgment of the court itself.[178] When proceeding by the writ of novel disseisin, the sheriff or addressee summoned the defendant and the jurors and gave the time and place of the recognition.[179]

The assizes' method of proof and procedure greatly outweighed local procedures dependent upon older forms of proof.[180] Delays and excuses frustrating local courts were not permitted under novel disseisin.[181] Nonroyal courts were too slow in their procedure and inefficient.[182] Novel disseisin quickly and efficiently determined and restored possession. The question of the better "right" or title was left to different, more cumber-

---

177 VAN CAENEGEM, *supra* note 105, at 261, 292. The sworn jurors had personal knowledge or were able to obtain such knowledge. PLUCKNETT, CONST. HIST., *supra* note 59, at 104-05, 107-10.

178 VAN CAENEGEM, *supra* note 105, at 51.

179 *Id.* at 261, 298; *see also id.* at 271-82 (developing the judicial process of reseisin); BAKER, *supra* note 88, at 54-55. The Assize of Novel Disseisin originated through royal writs. BAKER, *supra* note 88, at 55. The writ directed the sheriff to summon twelve lawful men of the neighborhood to recognize before the king's justices whether B unjustly and without judgment recently disseized A of his free tenement. VAN CAENEGEM, *supra* note 105, at 261-62.

180 VAN CAENEGEM, *supra* note 105, at 290. Older forms of proof included proof by reputation oaths, or compurgation; trial by battle; as well as ordeal of water, fire, or another test. *Supra* notes 49, 88-90.

181 HARDING, *supra* note 49, at 61-62; VAN CAENEGEM, *supra* note 105, at 262 (recognition could take place without the defendant).

182 VAN CAENEGEM, *supra* note 105, at 268.

some procedure.[183] After seisin had been restored, the parties could pursue title.

Before the Assize of Novel Disseisin, kings dealt with unlawful disseisins on an equitable or extraordinary basis as the need arose. Norman executive writs were nonreturnable executive orders "to do" without a judicial inquiry evaluating the merits ("*juste*") of the action.[184] Henry's assizes added a judicial function to the executive writ. In the battle of jurisdiction between lord and king, lords claimed the defense that they had given justice to the tenant. From this, royal powers had to develop rules for what justice meant, including process and rules concerning distraint.[185]

Henry II reseized by assize and thus improved justice.[186] The writ of novel disseisin was a balance of royal and popular authority and was quite desired. Novel disseisin removed arbitrary enforcement, used the popular recognition form, and was quick and efficient as traveling justices gave speedy remedies.[187]

Henry II's assizes greatly enlarged the king's jurisdiction in local affairs. Royal reseisin was no longer characterized as equitable or extraordinary. The writ of novel disseisin took royal reseisin out of the extrajudicial equity category and made it judi-

---

[183] PLUCKNETT, CONCISE HISTORY, *supra* note 114, at 358-59.

[184] VAN CAENEGEM, *supra* note 105, at 239-43, 262, 274-77; STENTON, *supra* note 87, at 30-33; JOLLIFFE, ANGEVIN KINGSHIP, *supra* note 18, at 41-43, 45-46 (Norman reseisin by executive disseisin without judgment).

[185] VAN CAENEGEM, *supra* note 105, at 263, 272-80; Biancalana, *supra* note 99, at 484.

[186] JOLLIFFE, CONST. HIST., *supra* note 49, at 208.

[187] VAN CAENEGEM, *supra* note 105, at 290.

cial procedure and the law of the land.[188] No longer do we remember a time when the king's ban protected a few select crimes, special persons, and special places.[189] Henry II's writ system is credited with the birth of the common law. Henry II's justices carrying out the assizes replaced local judicial customs with a national judicial custom, which, during the twelfth century, was a collage of Norman and Frankish customs and Roman law. A national common law based on the writ system enveloped England's ancient judicial system.[190] John H. Baker noted that the common law became interchangeable with the law of the land and the law of the land with the common law.[191]

Henry II's legislation generated litigation, which reduced the power of the feudal magnates by drawing local litigation to his

---

[188] *Id.* at 300-02; PLUCKNETT, CONCISE HISTORY, *supra* note 114, at 355-57. As Jolliffe stated, the "Angevin writ of Novel Disseisin is the Norman disseizing writ tamed and rationalized." JOLLIFFE, ANGEVIN KINGSHIP, *supra* note 18, at 46. Henry II's famous legislation merely formalized his equitable command concerning executive justice into judicial procedure, though the king did not lose his ability to exercise executive power. *Id.* at 48; *see also id.* at 42-43.

[189] *Supra* note 69.

[190] R.H. Helmholz defined "*ius commune*" as the "amalgam of the Roman and canon laws that governed legal education in the European universities and influenced legal practice in Europe from the twelfth century forward." R.H. Helmholz, *Magna Carta and the Ius Commune*, 66 U. CHI. L. REV. 297, 300-01 (1999). When royal judges did not have a more authoritative principle to draw from, Roman and canon law fit the bill. *Id.* at 304-06.

[191] BAKER, *supra* note 88, at 56. Whether the law of the land was limited to the common law was a major point of contention in the seventeenth century as the Commons attempted to limit the king's prerogative. *Infra* notes 555, 686-694; *infra* Chapter X.

courts through his writ system.[192] The litigation eventually separated the king's *curia* into branches.[193] The common-law courts, centered upon formal process of assize and writ, broke away from the king's *curia*.[194]

While Henry II is remembered for his legislation and taming the sheriff, he himself was a strong monarch with a heavy hand. Though he legislated for greater rights for tenants against disseisin and injustice, he himself arrested and disseized by executive order without judgment. The king was not required to follow any legal process or have any trial before he took executive action.[195] He did not suffer the delays or procedural defects that other litigants had to suffer. The king might seize, disseize, outlaw, take hostages, or imprison men without judicial action or judgment of peers. When the king acted unilaterally, he was exer-

---

[192] The assizes removed jurisdiction from the feudal and local courts to the royal courts for specified crimes. 1 HOLDSWORTH, *supra* note 113, at 71; POOLE, *supra* note 59, at 386-87. This became an issue in the thirteenth century. While barons were content with some royal writs, they were aware of expanding national process and loss of jurisdiction. In the 1258 program, they ensured their participation in approving new writs. *Infra* Chapter V sec. B.

[193] PLUCKNETT, CONCISE HISTORY, *supra* note 114, at 146-50; BAKER, *supra* note 88, at 18-20.

[194] The *curia*'s ancient jurisdiction and equity remained with the king, but as time went by it conflicted with the common-law courts.

[195] JOLLIFFE, ANGEVIN KINGSHIP, *supra* note 18, at 5-6, 33-34, 39-40, 50-86, 328-29 (not only could the king disseize and arrest, but he also frustrated, delayed, or defeated the process of justice); BARTLETT, *supra* note 133, at 48-50; TURNER, KING & COURTS, *supra* note 37, at 56-101 (remarking on the king's authority to delay, close, or alter judicial proceedings in the royal courts). Certain executive acts of justice were implemented without judgment or customary limits because they did not attach to feudal rights for which judgment would precede enforcement and long-standing feudal custom would guide the punishment. JOLLIFFE, ANGEVIN KINGSHIP, *supra* note 18, at 105, 108.

cising his will by fiat (*voluntas princepis*).[196] In the twelfth century, there was little formal restraint on royal executive action. There was conscience and excommunication, which were papal matters. There was also feudal justice and diffidation, which were the equivalent of rebellion and civil war.[197] In theory, however, the king, as sword bearer, acted in the best interest of the community or the nation at large.[198] Both theocratic and feudal theories of kingship recognized that emperors and kings considered it a part of their royal duty to act for the public welfare.

D. Richard I: Regency and Community

Henry II's reign is credited with restoring order, but it also presented a great deal of strife. Henry was at war with his sons.[199] In the late 1180s, Henry's son Richard revolted against him.[200] But the conflict did not affect Richard's succession. At Henry's death in 1189, the throne went to Richard.

Richard I spent most of his time away from the realm on Crusades. Richard desired shared governance in his absence, which he placed with a commission or council of regents comprised of co-justiciars to rule along with Chancellor William Long-

---

[196] JOLLIFFE, ANGEVIN KINGSHIP, *supra* note 18, at 53, 55.

[197] *Id.* at 344; *see also supra* notes 98-104.

[198] JOLLIFFE, ANGEVIN KINGSHIP, *supra* note 18, at 43; *supra* Chapter II sec. A. The king's theocratic power and prerogative of necessity to act for the best interests or common utility of the realm served as a justification for the king's rule. *Supra* notes 32-36, 66-67 (common welfare, necessity).

[199] RALPH V. TURNER, KING JOHN 21 (1994) (hereinafter TURNER, KING JOHN).

[200] *Id.* at 34, 38.

champ and others.[201] During the twelfth century, the justiciar was the realm's chief official in the king's absence.[202] The chancellor was an official with many duties.

One of Richard's justiciars died and Longchamp received that office and ousted the other justiciar.[203] Longchamp combined his offices together, assuming all power to himself and evading Richard's intended council-regency.[204] Richard I learned of the discord and entrusted Archbishop Walter de Coutances with royal letters effectively placing him in the council-regency and ensuring that no business be done without him.[205] Richard ordered that his officers treat with other council members.[206]

Meanwhile, Richard's brother, Count John (later King John), and Longchamp fought each other. De Coutances mediated the conflict. John, Longchamp, and the barons agreed:

> It has been further agreed, that bishops, abbots, earls, barons, vavasours, and freeholders shall not, at the will of justices or deputies of our lord the king, be disseised of their land and chattels, but shall be dealt with by the judgment of the court of our lord king, according to the

---

[201] Bertie Wilkinson, *The Government of England during the Absence of Richard I on the Third Crusade*, 28 BULL. JOHN RYLANDS LIB. 485, 486-88 (1944); JOLLIFFE, CONST. HIST., *supra* note 49, at 228-29.

[202] HARDING, *supra* note 49, at 50 (Henry I created the office for his time away in Normandy).

[203] POOLE, *supra* note 59, at 351-52; Wilkinson, *supra* note 201, at 487-88.

[204] POOLE, *supra* note 59, at 354; JOLLIFFE, CONST. HIST., *supra* note 49, at 229-32.

[205] Wilkinson, *supra* note 201, at 495-508; POOLE, *supra* note 59, at 355.

[206] Wilkinson, *supra* note 201, at 504.

> lawful customs and assizes of the realm, or according to the command of our lord the king.[207]

After further disruptive events, John and the barons had had enough, and in 1191, they united against Longchamp. The barons accused Longchamp of assuming sovereignty proper for the king.[208] The community of barons, citizens, and justices deposed Longchamp, declaring that the realm's business ought to be managed by the community.[209]

The community included the "commune" of London citizens.[210] Londoners had been unofficially granted the right to form a commune, which was a community united under a common oath similar to the feudal oath but to the community rather than the lord.[211]

---

[207] 3 ROTHWELL, ENG. HIST. DOCS., *supra* note 3, at 67 (both Longchamp and John swore to the standard); *see also* J.C. HOLT, MAGNA CARTA 120-21 (2d ed. 1992) (hereinafter HOLT, MAGNA CARTA); TURNER, KING JOHN, *supra* note 199, at 43. As we saw above, the principle of judgment before action was a common rule of feudalism but did not apply to the king's executive action. *Supra* notes 88, 98-102. For the king, *judicium parium* in the king's court was a privilege to be sold. JOLLIFFE, ANGEVIN KINGSHIP, *supra* note 18, at 60, 70; *infra* note 218.

[208] LYON, *supra* note 79, at 236, 252-53.

[209] Wilkinson, *supra* note 201, *passim*. Longchamp was doing royal business and the realm's business through his own seal and not the royal seal that Richard had left for that purpose. *Id.* at 491-97.

[210] 3 ROTHWELL, ENG. HIST. DOCS., *supra* note 3, at 69; POOLE, *supra* note 59, at 69-71, 358.

[211] J.P. Canning, *Introduction: Politics, Institutions and Ideas in* CAMB. HIST. MED. POL. THOUGHT, *supra* note 10, at 353; LYON, *supra* note 79, at 276-77 (London's commune); MORRIS, *supra* note 15, at 41-42, 196-97; JOLLIFFE, ANGEVIN KINGSHIP, *supra* note 18, at 323-24. Richard later confirmed the grant of commune when he returned to England. LYON, *supra*, at 277. London's commune and organization contributed to borough develop-

Walter de Coutances, supported by Richard's orders, provided the necessary authority for Longchamp's deposition and likely subdued John's ambition. Thereafter, De Coutances was in charge and ruled by constitutional standards. Unless by royal command, he would not do anything but by the counsel of the community.[212]

Shortly after Longchamp's deposition, Richard I was captured on his return from the Crusades in 1192. He was released with a heavy ransom, which required an extraordinary tax.[213] Richard I died in 1199 by arrow. His death brought controversy over succession, which ultimately went to John through a series of negotiations.[214] Dispute over succession continued as Philip II of France had plans to supplant John with Arthur of Brittany, John's twelve-year-old nephew. John captured Arthur and was accused of killing him in captivity.[215]

---

ment. JAMES TAIT, THE MEDIEVAL ENGLISH BOROUGH: STUDIES ON ITS ORIGIN AND CONSTITUTIONAL HISTORY 291, 315-16, 347 (1936); *see also* Burrell, *Story of Privileges and Immunities*, *supra* note 85, at Part II.

[212] POOLE, *supra* note 59, at 355-56.

[213] *Id.* at 363-66.

[214] *Id.* at 378-79.

[215] *Id.* at 381-82.

IV

King John and the Magna Carta

LIKE HENRY II and Richard I before him, John, at face value, investigated his predecessors' wrongful acts.[216] John, by act of grace, allowed inquiries into Henry's and Richard's arbitrary disseisin without judgment.[217] John also conceded judicial liberties to foreign barons.

> They shall not through us or ours suffer loss or damage in any right or thing of which they are vested or seized, unless through the judgment of our court, for as long as they shall have

---

[216] After Henry II's death in 1189, his wife and Richard I attempted to restore some of the executive disseisins and remedy Henry II's executive arrests *per voluntatem* that had occurred during his reign. JOLLIFFE, ANGEVIN KINGSHIP, *supra* note 18, at 77, 308-09 (restore those who were imprisoned without "commune rettum" or common presentment); HOLT, MAGNA CARTA, *supra* note 207, at 119-20.

[217] TURNER, KING & COURTS, *supra* note 37, at 251-58, 266.

> served us faithfully and they shall have wished to stand in judgment in our court.[218]

But John was not considered a good king. John's reign was marked by arbitrary acts of will and excessive taxation ending in the Magna Carta. John was considered a tyrant, though academic inquiry often credits his many attempts at seeking the counsel of barons and attempting to remedy unjust disseisins.[219] Henry G. Richardson and George O. Sayles observed that the grievance of John's reign was not that John ignored his barons but that he did not sufficiently have their counsel on taxation.[220] John also increased the severity of distraint without judgment.[221] Landholders and barons were willing to submit to Henry II's financial burdens and arbitrary control because he provided good government and controlled the sheriffs. John required an even greater demand on the people but provided no good government.[222] John's demands for money resulted in a fight for more baronial power against arbitrary kingship.

John's leading folly was the loss of Normandy in 1202-1204.[223] In the conflict for the English crown following Richard's

---

[218] JOLLIFFE, ANGEVIN KINGSHIP, *supra* note 18, at 310. Jolliffe noted that English barons were excluded from John's grant. *Id.* at 311. Others could purchase the privilege. *See also supra* note 207.

[219] POOLE, *supra* note 59, at 425-29; RICHARDSON & SAYLES, GOVERNANCE, *supra* note 49, at 321-22.

[220] RICHARDSON & SAYLES, GOVERNANCE, *supra* note 49, at 145-46.

[221] JOLLIFFE, ANGEVIN KINGSHIP, *supra* note 18, at 131; JOLLIFFE, CONST. HIST., *supra* note 49, at 249-50.

[222] WILLIAM SHARP MCKECHNIE, MAGNA CARTA: A COMMENTARY ON THE GREAT CHARTER OF KING JOHN 50 (2d ed. 1914); 2 HOLDSWORTH, *supra* note 113, at 207-08.

[223] POOLE, *supra* note 59, at 384.

death, Philip II of France reclaimed Normandy.[224] What followed was an expensive war with France, which put John in need of taxes.

Following the loss of Normandy, John's next controversy began in 1205 with the death of Archbishop of Canterbury, Hubert Walter. By canon law, the monks of Christ Church were the electors of the Archbishop's replacement.[225] The king, however, often intervened. John and the monks fought over the nomination. Both parties appealed to Rome for clarification.

As discussed above, the medieval pope was the ruler of spiritual matters; kings were rulers of temporal matters.[226] By the thirteenth century, the English were accustomed to papal intervention. Pope Innocent III, 1198-1216, claimed to leave temporal jurisdiction to lay rulers. In fact, however, Innocent III was an aggressive pope who intervened in temporal affairs on multiple occasions.[227]

---

[224] D.E. Luscombe, *Introduction: the Formation of Political Thought in the West in* CAMB. HIST. MED. POL. THOUGHT, *supra* note 10, at 160; POOLE, *supra* note 59, at 384; *supra* note 215 (Arthur's death).

[225] POOLE, *supra* note 59, at 442-44.

[226] *See supra* notes 29-31 (Luke and two swords).

[227] CHENEY & SEMPLE, *supra* note 30, at x-xiii; JOLLIFFE, ANGEVIN KINGSHIP, *supra* note 18, at 313-18; MORRIS, *supra* note 15, at 430-32. Innocent III argued that he was the judge in all cases and possessed supreme jurisdiction, both civil and criminal. TIERNEY, CRISIS, *supra* note 10, at 129-30. Innocent was an integral part of John's affairs. JOLLIFFE, ANGEVIN KINGSHIP, *supra* note 18, at 318. The pope's favor in twelfth- and thirteenth-century England was a source of controversy in finances and politics. Having papal support or facing papal opposition was a factor in any dispute between the barons and the king. *See, e.g.*, *infra* Chapters IV, V sec. B (civil war and baronial uprising in 1215 and 1258).

Pope Innocent III suspended all proceedings to investigate the Archbishop's nomination. Innocent determined that the monks had the better right. The monks elected Stephen Langton, likely on Innocent's recommendation.[228] While Langton was consecrated in 1207, John refused to accept his appointment, and he remained on the continent for several years.[229] An angry John forced the monks into exile.

With John's refusal to accept Langton, tension between the pope and John was high. Innocent put England under an interdict in 1208, which prohibited ecclesiastic ceremonies for marriages and deaths, among others. John negotiated with papal messengers but no resolution was reached.[230] Innocent III excommunicated John in 1209, which threatened John's standing as king.[231]

John's problems extended beyond papal relations. John was busy fighting wars when he learned of a baronial insurrection.[232] He also received news that Philip intended to invade England and install his son Louis as king of England.[233] John, facing baronial rebellion and foreign invasion, needed support. In November of 1212, he submitted to papal demands and accepted Innocent's terms.[234] On May 15, 1213, John surrendered England

---

228 POOLE, *supra* note 59, at 444-45.

229 *Id.* at 445.

230 *Id.* at 446-47.

231 The excommunication did not result in formal deposition; however, Innocent III initiated or threatened deposition proceedings. MORRIS, *supra* note 15, at 429.

232 POOLE, *supra* note 59, at 455.

233 *Id.* at 456, 459.

234 HOLT, MAGNA CARTA, *supra* note 207, at 215-16.

to Innocent as a papal fiefdom, receiving it back after swearing homage and fealty to Innocent and providing payment of an annual sum.[235] John accepted Langton as Archbishop and agreed to readmit exiled clergy and to pay the church for losses.

John continued his fight with France,[236] but his barons refused to accompany him in service overseas because of his excommunication. Langton, who had the authority to restore John, arrived in England in early July 1213. Before restoring John, Langton insisted that John renew his coronation oath. Though a matter of obscurity, accounts state that John renewed his coronation oath and swore to observe the ancient laws of Henry I and Saint Edward or edited variations thereof.[237] The laws and charters of Henry I and Edward were a dead letter to Henry II and Stephen, but they came alive in new, fictitious form against King John.[238] After his oath, John was absolved of his excommunication.[239]

---

[235] 3 ROTHWELL, ENG. HIST. DOCS., *supra* note 3, at 307; POOLE, *supra* note 59, at 457. Poole explained that John's submission to Rome deprived Philip's invasion of the ecclesiastic authority that it would have otherwise enjoyed. POOLE, *supra* note 59, at 459.

[236] POOLE, *supra* note 59, at 461.

[237] HOLT, MAGNA CARTA, *supra* note 207, at 218-25 (noting the lack of evidence as to what John swore or what agreements were reached); POOLE, *supra* note 59, at 462.

[238] J.C. HOLT, MAGNA CARTA & MEDIEVAL GOVERNMENT 154-61 (1985) (hereinafter HOLT, MAGNA CARTA & MED. GOV.). James C. Holt observed that the doctoring of the *Leges Edwardi* and the use of *Leges Henrici Primi* leveraged the reputation of venerated kings. The same doctoring, and for similar reasons, took place in the seventeenth century by opponents of the Stuarts. The imaginary Magna Carta became a device invoked by Sir Edward Coke and associates for meaning never intended.

> To the fame gained by the Magna Carta in respect of its real and original meaning, must thus be added the fame gained by the imaginary Magna Carta, as evolved from

John lost a key battle in 1214 and his support faded. The barons sought papal support for enforcement of John's oath to good government.[240] By December 1214–January 1215, there was a coordinated effort for the king to keep his oath and honor the laws and charters of Saint Edward and Henry I.[241]

Eventually, the bridges that John had burned came back to take their toll. He faced a civil war and foreign invasion. Both sides appealed to Rome for intervention.[242] John sought to maximize his leverage with Innocent and took the cross in March 1215. This was a valued concession to the pope, who thereafter defended John. Innocent III threatened the barons with excommunication.

The controversy was coming to a head. England was in crisis; no one would pay any tax or obey John on any issue. Rec-

---

> the earlier Charter by the learning of Coke and his parliamentary associates. We have seen how, in the seventeenth century, it became a means of cloaking innovations in the guise of a return to the past, and how in an age averse from constitutional innovations, it enabled the opponents of the Divine Right of Kings to gain for their policy the approval of staid upholders of the venerated past.

William S. McKechnie, *Magna Carta Address in* MAGNA CARTA COMMEMORATION ESSAYS 19–20 (Henry Elliot Malden ed. 1917).

[239] HOLT, MAGNA CARTA, *supra* note 207, at 216; POOLE, *supra* note 59, at 461-62.

[240] HOLT, MAGNA CARTA, *supra* note 207, at 221–22.

[241] *Id.* at 222–23.

[242] *Id.* at 229–31.

onciliation efforts did not prevail and baronial diffidation proceeded on May 5, 1215.[243]

John sought to delay the barons by making efforts to arbitrate. The king was willing to grant most of the baronial demands.[244] On May 10, 1215, John, responding to Innocent's suggestion, proclaimed:

> Know that we have conceded to our barons who are against us that we shall not take or disseise them or their men, nor go against them [by force or arms], unless by the law of our land, or by the judgment of their peers in [our court], until consideration shall have been had by four whom we shall choose on our part and four whom they shall choose on their part, and the lord Pope who shall be oversman over them.[245]

But the barons refused the king's offer. This enraged John, and he retaliated. Civil war began.[246]

Meanwhile, the more sensible barons sought to take advantage of the king's concessions. They redrafted their articles of grievances and demands and put them into the form known as the Magna Carta, which the king agreed to on or about June 15, 1215, at Runnymede.[247] The Magna Carta's form was inspired by

---

243 POOLE, *supra* note 59, at 470-71; HOLT, MAGNA CARTA, *supra* note 207, at 235.

244 POOLE, *supra* note 59, at 472.

245 MCKECHNIE, *supra* note 222, at 34; HOLT, MAGNA CARTA, *supra* note 207, at 234-35.

246 HOLT, MAGNA CARTA, *supra* note 207, at 235.

247 3 ROTHWELL, ENG. HIST. DOCS., *supra* note 3, at 311-16; *see also* POOLE, *supra* note 59, at 473. The Barons had a draft of their grievances, com-

popular perceptions of the laws and coronation charters of Henry I and interpolations of *Leges Edwardi*.[248] The royal charter had long been a source of land grants and privileges and immunities to individuals, entities, and towns.[249] John had sold charters and confirmations of predecessors' charters for political gain. The Magna Carta was a charter for the realm.[250]

Several works have extensively analyzed the Magna Carta.[251] For purposes of this book, we highlight only a few key sections. In Chapter 12, the barons demanded common counsel for extraordinary aids and scutages (hereinafter referred to generically as taxation). In Chapter 39, the barons limited the king's arbitrary executive action. Finally, to enforce the Charter, the barons established a council of conservators in Chapter 61 to distrain the king for violations.

A. <u>Chapter 12</u>

---

monly referred to as the Articles of Barons. HOLT, MAGNA CARTA, *supra* note 207, at 239-40, 244-49.

[248] HOLT, MAGNA CARTA, *supra* note 207, at 93-95, 113, 115-16, 222-25. The barons focused on Henry I's charter and *Leges Henrici* because they were most beneficial to the reforms the barons wanted to achieve. 2 HOLDSWORTH, *supra* note 113, at 209-210; MADDICOTT, ORIGINS, *supra* note 52, at 100; PLUCKNETT, CONST. HIST., *supra* note 59, at 66, 69.

[249] HOLT, MAGNA CARTA & MED. GOV., *supra* note 238, at 161-66.

[250] *Id.* at 166.

[251] HOLT, MAGNA CARTA, *supra* note 207; HOLT, MAGNA CARTA & MED. GOV., *supra* note 238; TURNER, MAGNA CARTA, *supra* note 153; MCKECHNIE, *supra* note 222; JOLLIFFE, CONST. HIST., *supra* note 49; JOLLIFFE, ANGEVIN KINGSHIP, *supra* note 18; POOLE, *supra* note 59. For brief commentary on the Magna Carta's provisions, see PLUCKNETT, CONST. HIST., *supra* note 59, at 71-87. For more extensive but dated commentary, see MCKECHNIE, *supra* note 222. Thorough discussions are also found in David Carpenter's recent book, MAGNA CARTA (2015) as well as in ANTHONY ARLIDGE & IGOR JUDGE, MAGNA CARTA UNCOVERED (2014).

John's wars required continuous financing. Abusive taxation troubled the barons. The Magna Carta attempted to reduce the king's discretion over feudal obligations and taxation. The barons were concerned with extraordinary scutages and aids and required the king's promise that except for the three common feudal aids (marriage of daughter, knighting of son, and ransom) at reasonable rates, no scutage or aid would be assessed unless by the common counsel of the realm. Chapter 12:

> No scutage or aid shall be imposed in our kingdom unless by common counsel of our kingdom, except for ransoming our person, for making our eldest son a knight, and for once marrying our eldest daughter; and for these only a reasonable aid shall be levied.[252]

The scutage was an established feudal obligation that was historically free from specific baronial consent.[253] Feudal aids and reliefs also had customary amounts that were deemed just, legitimate, and reasonable.[254] John collected scutages and aids arbitrarily.[255] The barons resisted; they saw the kingdom as a large feudum whose obligations were fixed by custom and could not be changed arbitrarily, that is, without common counsel.[256]

---

[252] MAGNA CARTA, ch. 12 (1215) *in* 3 ROTHWELL, ENG. HIST. DOCS., *supra* note 3, at 316, 318.

[253] POOLE, *supra* note 59, at 16-17, 422.

[254] *Id.* at 20-21, 418-19; PLUCKNETT, CONST. HIST., *supra* note 59, at 36-38.

[255] TURNER, MAGNA CARTA, *supra* note 153, at 41-45; POOLE, *supra* note 59, at 422-24, 439-40.

[256] JOLLIFFE, CONST. HIST., *supra* note 49, at 242-46.

The Magna Carta's "common counsel" did not mean full participation by all classes.[257] Common counsel included the tenants in chief and lesser barons who were present.[258] The tenants in chief were the main body of individuals between the crown and the people. The mesne lords and other freemen derived their voice and rights from the tenants in chief.[259]

B. Chapter 39

As mentioned above, the Angevin king had a host of executive actions that he implemented without regard to judgment or the laws that applied to others.[260] Henry II's assizes were not intended to apply to the king.[261] The king might disseize, outlaw, or imprison men without judgment of peers or other legal process.[262] The king controlled justice and could suspend or dispense with any custom to the contrary.[263] Demands for the king to uphold the lawful laws and customs of the realm were not enforceable in the king's courts against the king himself if he did not concede the litigation or grievance.[264] There were few or no

---

[257] *Supra* notes 146-155.

[258] JOLLIFFE, CONST. HIST., *supra* note 49, at 257-58.

[259] *Id.* at 262.

[260] JOLLIFFE, ANGEVIN KINGSHIP, *supra* note 18, at 5-6, 33-34.

[261] *Id.* at 34, 36-37, 38.

[262] HOLT, MAGNA CARTA, *supra* note 207, at 81-84 (king's arbitrary disseisin, arrest, suspension of law and custom, hostage taking, and special fealty charters); *see also supra* notes 195-196. The rich could purchase the rights to a trial in the king's court by the judgment of its peers. JOLLIFFE, ANGEVIN KINGSHIP, *supra* note 18, at 60, 70; *supra* note 218.

[263] *Supra* notes 32-36, 66-67 (common welfare and necessity).

[264] HOLT, MAGNA CARTA, *supra* note 207, at 126-28; *see also infra* notes 372-376.

real constitutional limits on the king in the twelfth century.[265] There was diffidation, which was the equivalent of war.[266]

In the years before the Magna Carta, John fought with his barons and aggressively seized hostages.[267] Replacing customary fines, John arbitrarily, by will alone, fined or amerced his barons.[268] Injured tenants of the barons had protections but wronged barons themselves faced the king. The tenant in chief could not seek out a writ of right or the possessory assizes because the king's writ would not issue against himself.[269] In comparison to the laws that the barons had to abide by with their tenants, the king's actions against his tenants in chief were arbitrary. Addressing these grievances, the barons forced John to swear in Chapter 39 that:

> No free men shall be arrested or imprisoned or disseised or outlawed or exiled or in any way victimised, neither will we attack him or send

[265] POOLE, *supra* note 59, at 6-10.

[266] *Supra* notes 102, 133.

[267] RICHARDSON & SAYLES, GOVERNANCE, *supra* note 49, at 378-79 (commenting that taking hostages was common in the era).

[268] JOLLIFFE, CONST. HIST., *supra* note 49, at 224-25. Jolliffe discussed problems with Henry's reforms such as the arbitrary assessment of fines and arbitrary price for protective writs (replacing Anglo-Saxon wergild). *Id.* at 225-26; *supra* note 74 (Anglo-Saxon wergild compensation for justice); *see also* JOLLIFFE, ANGEVIN KINGSHIP, *supra* note 18, at 87-109 (discussing the king's special peace and benevolence along with his special anger and malevolence to fine, etc.). These matters were addressed in MAGNA CARTA, Chapters 20-22, 55. *Infra* note 273.

[269] H.G. RICHARDSON & G.O. SAYLES, SELECT CASES OF PROCEDURE WITHOUT WRIT UNDER HENRY III, at xxv (1941) (hereinafter RICHARDSON & SAYLES, PROCEDURE WITHOUT WRIT) (king was vicar of God and was not bound by writ system); TURNER, KING & COURTS, *supra* note 37, at 236-38, 251-63; HOLT, MAGNA CARTA, *supra* note 207, at 110, 128, 132, 163-64.

> anyone to attack him, except by the lawful judgment of his peers or by the law of the land.[270]

Chapter 39 broadly confronted executive abuses: the king shall not take, imprison, disseize, outlaw, exile, or destroy without judgment of his peers or by the law of the land.[271] John had manipulated the system by serving his own interests. The barons wanted judgment of peers to avoid the abuses of royal justice.[272] Penalties, amercements, and fines would be decided by neighbors, peers, or by a council.[273] Chapter 39 aimed to restrain the king's extraordinary executive action, leaving executive action permissible by law or by established custom.[274]

---

270 MAGNA CARTA, Chapter 39 (1215) *in* 3 ROTHWELL, ENG. HIST. DOCS., *supra* note 3, at 316, 320. The May 10 letters protected only the barons from arbitrary action. But the Magna Carta expanded the coverage to protect all free holders. For the Magna Carta extending to free men, see HOLT, MAGNA CARTA, *supra* note 207, at 276-77, 291.

271 JOLLIFFE, ANGEVIN KINGSHIP, *supra* note 18, at 333-35. *See also supra* notes 195-196, 262.

272 TURNER, KING & COURTS, *supra* note 37, at 243-44; HOLT, MAGNA CARTA, *supra* note 207, at 107-11.

273 MAGNA CARTA, Chapters 20, 21, 22, 55 *in* 3 ROTHWELL, ENG. HIST. DOCS., *supra* note 3, at 316, 319, 322 (peers and neighbors decide amercements and fine should fit the crime); *supra* note 268; *see also* HOLT, MAGNA CARTA, *supra* note 207, at 332-36, 363, 365.

274 JOLLIFFE, ANGEVIN KINGSHIP, *supra* note 18, at 330-35. The king likely retained legitimate power of prerogative arrest and disseisin (*per perceptum domini regis,* by the order of our lord king) when crisis or emergency called for executive arrests. F.M. Powicke, *Per Judicium Parium vel Per Legem Terrae, in* MAGNA CARTA COMM. ESSAYS, *supra* note 238, at 110-16; TURNER, KING & COURTS, *supra* note 37, at 56-57, 244, 250-51, 258-63 (executive disseisin less frequent after the Magna Carta than before in Henry II's and John's reign). Though most commentators would find that Chapter 39 meant to prevent executive arrests and disseisins, such a power in the king and national executive was consistent with medieval political theory. *See supra* notes 32-36, 66-67. The king likely dominat-

Chapter 39's language followed a common feudal principle of justice.[275] It was John's promise not to engage in arbitrary executive enforcement without process or judgment for matters in which judgment was the custom. Its inclusion was nothing extraordinary except that it was being invoked formally and more broadly against the king's arbitrary action.[276]

There is an abundance of literature discussing "judgment by peers" and "law of the land." Several scholars agree that "law of the land" was the broader phrase, which included written or positive law as well as ancient feudal custom worthy of the law of the land.[277] For example, law of the land included appeal and indictment, which could ultimately lead to different forms of judicial proof.[278] In other words, John's promise ensured that executive actions affecting life, limb, and property required process by the law of the land, which in some cases might include *judicium*

---

ed the determination of necessity but other factors such as open violence or a closed court could control the decision. *Cf.* T.F.T. PLUCKNETT, STUDIES IN ENGLISH LEGAL HISTORY, VI, at 550 (1983) (hereinafter PLUCKNETT, STUDIES).

[275] HOLT, MAGNA CARTA, *supra* note 207, at 327; WALTER ULLMANN, *Law and the Medieval Historian (I) in* ULLMANN, JURISPRUDENCE, *supra* note 13, at 60-61. Chapter 39 can be traced to the feudal laws of Conrad II before the Conquest. *Supra* note 91; *see also supra* note 207 (Community of 1191's concept of justice in the king's absence); *supra* note 218 (John's promise of feudal justice to foreign barons at the beginning of his reign).

[276] HOLT, MAGNA CARTA, *supra* note 207, at 76-77.

[277] Holt claimed that "law of the land" (*lex terrae*) in 1215 included both royal assize and local customs, both of which were to be consumed by statute in the fourteenth century. HOLT, MAGNA CARTA, *supra* note 207, at 327-32; JOLLIFFE, CONST. HIST., *supra* note 49, at 254 (describing Chapter 39 as judgment either by assize or *judicium*).

[278] HOLT, MAGNA CARTA, *supra* note 207, at 328; *supra* note 88 (*judicium parium*); *supra* Chapter III sec. B (assizes, presenting jury, judicial proofs).

parium. Ralph V. Turner wrote that Chapter 39 protected the free man from

> extralegal or illegal treatment by the king and his agents, enjoining him to proceed against them only by the writs and assizes of the common law courts or by combat, the ordeal, or compurgation, ancient processes of the shire and honor courts. In short, the king was to be bound by the law. . . .[279]

C. Chapter 61

It was one thing to secure the king's promise but the barons naturally wanted some means of enforcing the promise. Chapter 61 provided a Council of Twenty-Five barons to keep the peace and remedy all matters of unjust disseisin and unjust fines and amercements.[280]

> Since, moreover, for God and the betterment of our kingdom and for the better allaying of the discord that has arisen between us and our barons we have granted all these things aforesaid, wishing them to enjoy the use of them unimpaired and unshaken for ever, we give and grant them under-written security, namely, that the barons shall choose any twenty-five barons of the kingdom they wish, who must with all their might observe, hold and cause to be observed, the peace and liberties which we have granted and confirmed to them by this present charter of ours.[281]

---

[279] TURNER, KING JOHN, *supra* note 199, at 243; KEENEY, *supra* note 91, at 60-68.

[280] HOLT, MAGNA CARTA, *supra* note 207, at 343, 347.

[281] MAGNA CARTA, Chapter 61, *in* 3 ROTHWELL, ENG. HIST. DOCS., *supra* note 3, at 316, 323-24.

If John or his officers violated his oath and promise, four of the barons will petition the king, or the Chief Justiciar if the king were away. If the king refused to redress the grievance, the four barons would summon the Twenty-Five and they

> with the community of the whole land shall distrain and distress [the King] in every way they can, namely, by seizing castles, lands, possessions, and in such other ways as they can, saving [the King's] person and the persons of [the] queen and [their] children, until, in their opinion, amends have been made; and when amends have been made, they shall obey [the King] as they did before.[282]

Chapter 61's Council of Twenty-Five was to be elected and serve as conservators of the Charter. Chapter 61's Council might be described as a type of court to sit in judgment of the king or alternatively as the written extension and formalization of feudal diffidation and rebellion.[283]

Many scholars connect the Magna Carta to the political controversies of Richard I's reign. The community of 1191 opposed Richard I's officers operating unilaterally in his absence and without the common counsel of the community.[284] But the

---

[282] *Id.*

[283] JOLLIFFE, CONST. HIST., *supra* note 49, at 258-60. Holt described the Council of Twenty-Five as a court and not a council. HOLT, MAGNA CARTA, *supra* note 207, at 343. According to Holt, distraint by the court of twenty-five would not be diffidation but legal procedure. *Id.* at 347-48. Plucknett disagreed. PLUCKNETT, CONST. HIST., *supra* note 59, at 86-87 (commenting on the difficulty of describing the Council of Twenty-Five but that it was not a court because there was no position for the injured party); *see also* POOLE, *supra* note 59, at 476 n.3 (comparing the procedure to rebellion).

[284] *Supra* Chapter III sec. D; *supra* notes 195-196.

community's demands would not have applied to the king's executive justice and prerogative. In the agreement of 1191, Richard's barons, De Coutances, Longchamp, and John agreed that

> bishops, abbots, earls, barons, vavasours, and freeholders shall not, at the will of justices or deputies of our lord the king, be disseised of their lands and chattels, but shall be dealt with by judgment of the court of our lord king, according to the lawful customs and assizes of the realm, *or according to the command of our lord the king.*[285]

Up until this point, the will of the king was sufficient grounds for law and judgment; the king deprived barons of liberty and property arbitrarily.[286] And this is what the barons attempted to resolve in 1215. By the end of John's reign, baronial opposition evolved from challenging royal officers in the king's absence to challenging the sitting king himself. The Magna Carta was the king's promise for judgment before royal enforcement and common counsel for extraordinary taxation.[287]

Reviewing these three chapters and the Magna Carta's other provisions, the consensus is that the Magna Carta did not necessarily create new law but made the king promise in writing to refrain from arbitrary actions which the barons perceived to be against existing principle. Richardson and Sayles observed that the Magna Carta was revolutionary in its provisions applicable to the king but mostly a reaffirmation or restatement of law in its

---

285 3 ROTHWELL, ENG. HIST. DOCS., *supra* note 3, at 67 (emphasis added); *supra* note 207.

286 *Supra* Chapter III sec. C (Henry II's assizes).

287 TURNER, KING & COURTS, *supra* note 37, at 236-39, 244-51, 258-66 (describing justice against the king by petition after the Magna Carta).

other chapters.[288] Jolliffe suggested that if John had lived, the Magna Carta might be a document limited to his reign without any of the notoriety it achieved in the medieval period.[289]

---

288 RICHARDSON & SAYLES, GOVERNANCE, *supra* note 49, at 383; *see also* HOLT, MAGNA CARTA, *supra* note 207, at 112-13.

289 JOLLIFFE, CONST. HIST., *supra* note 49, at 259.

V

The Thirteenth Century after Runnymede

WHILE JOHN AGREED to the Magna Carta in June 1215, he soon sought a papal release from his oath and a nullification of the Charter.[290] In the summer of 1215, Innocent III excommunicated the barons, quashed the Charter, and absolved John from his oath on the premise that the barons had procured the Charter by duress and against the king's dignity.[291]

And thus the realm was back in a state of civil war. Invoking Chapter 61 was an option, but the barons were not united.[292]

---

[290] Many commentators state that John had no intention of following the Charter. Poole hypothesized that John attempted to abide by the Charter but that the barons were openly hostile and unfaithful to the agreement. POOLE, *supra* note 59, at 477-79.

[291] 3 ROTHWELL, ENG. HIST. DOCS., *supra* note 3, at 324-26; *see also* HOLT, MAGNA CARTA, *supra* note 207, at 370-75; POOLE, *supra* note 59, at 479.

[292] RICHARDSON & SAYLES, GOVERNANCE, *supra* note 49, at 390; POOLE, *supra* note 59, at 477-79. *See generally* HOLT, MAGNA CARTA, *supra* note 207, at 347-77 (detailing the period following the charter).

They agreed to swear homage to Philip II of France, and they nominated Prince Louis, his son, as their king.[293] In 1216, Louis, prepared for Conquest, landed in England.[294] But John died in October 1216, and the civil war and threat of foreign rule eventually subsided.[295]

A. Henry III and "Evil" Councilors

Henry III, John's son, became king. But Henry was only nine, a minor, so the regency would be with the king's counselors.[296]

With John's death, the major motives for baronial reform vanished. There was no longer an arbitrary king violating customs and ruling *per voluntatem.* The barons quickly reissued John's Charter in November 1216, but fundamental components of the original Charter were omitted as "doubtful."[297] The barons explained the omissions:

> [B]ecause there were certain articles contained in the former charter which seemed important yet doubtful, namely on the assessing of scutage and aids [among others], the above-mentioned prelates and magnates have agreed to these being deferred until we have fuller counsel, when we will, most fully in these as well as other mat-

[293] RICHARDSON & SAYLES, GOVERNANCE, *supra* note 49, at 390.

[294] POOLE, *supra* note 59, at 483-84.

[295] HOLT, MAGNA CARTA, *supra* note 207, at 376.

[296] F.M. POWICKE, KING HENRY III AND THE LORD EDWARD: THE COMMUNITY OF THE REALM IN THE THIRTEENTH CENTURY 38 (1966 reprint) (hereinafter POWICKE, HENRY III & EDWARD).

[297] HOLT, MAGNA CARTA, *supra* note 207, at 381-83. For the text of the 1216 reissue, see 3 ROTHWELL, ENG. HIST. DOCS., *supra* note 3, at 327-32.

> ters that have to be amended, do what is for the common good and the peace and estate of ourselves and our kingdom.[298]

The barons felt that they were able to influence extraordinary taxes, so requiring formal "common counsel" was not needed. Also missing was the provision authorizing distraint if the king violated the Charter (Chapter 61). These provisions were presumed unnecessary as there was no longer an arbitrary king but instead the regency of others more receptive to the barons. With the omissions, the Magna Carta's promise changed. Nonetheless, Henry III's minority passed without significant controversy concerning the Charters. Rebel and royal barons reached a consensus and both participated in the policy-making of the king.[299] The barons likely had a significant share in governance and the spirit of the Magna Carta was followed.

In 1223, the pope suggested that Henry III was of age, which became fact for all cases by 1227.[300] Despite the absence of the "common counsel" provision in the Magna Carta's reissue, extraordinary taxes were raised with the counsel of barons.[301] In exchange for a 1225 tax on all movables, Henry III reissued a modified Magna Carta with his own authority.[302] The 1225 version,

---

[298] 3 ROTHWELL, ENG. HIST. DOCS., *supra* note 3, at 331 (#42) (minor formatting added).

[299] D.A. CARPENTER, THE MINORITY OF HENRY III, at 54 (1990) (hereinafter CARPENTER, MINORITY) (noting that royal actions followed principle of "common counsel" during Henry III's minority); TURNER, MAGNA CARTA, *supra* note 153, at 85.

[300] 4 SAYLES, SELECT CASES, *supra* note 143, at xxix. Henry was deemed of age for some matters at 1223 and declared himself fully of age in 1227. POWICKE, HENRY III & EDWARD, *supra* note 296, at 43–44.

[301] HOLT, MAGNA CARTA, *supra* note 207, at 393–403.

[302] MADDICOTT, ORIGINS, *supra* note 52, at 119.

omitting several chapters, became the official version.[303] The 1225 reissue was accompanied by an ecclesiastic threat of excommunication for those who violated its provisions.[304] With the 1225 reissue and Henry III's sworn promise, the Charter was carried into Henry III's reign.

Henry III's majority caused problems with the barons. He began his majority continuing the policy of safeguarding royal assets.[305] The royal resumption and redistribution of castles, which had begun in Henry's minority, generated controversy among foreign and English barons, spilling into the 1230s.[306] Henry reclaimed rights that were without explicit charter authority through *quo warranto* (by what right) proceedings.[307] He annulled and cancelled several charters, having determined that such charters were wrongfully granted in his minority and thus

---

303 3 ROTHWELL, ENG. HIST. DOCS., *supra* note 3, at 341-47; TURNER, MAGNA CARTA, *supra* note 153, at 86-87.

304 TURNER, MAGNA CARTA, *supra* note 153, at 87; *see also infra* notes 315, 438 (instances of seeking excommunication for violations); FAITH THOMPSON, MAGNA CARTA: ITS ROLE IN THE MAKING OF THE ENGLISH CONSTITUTION 1300-1629, at 125 (1948) (discussing excommunication for violations of the Magna Carta).

305 1 WILKINSON, CONST. HIST., *supra* note 149, at 15-19, 86-88.

306 CARPENTER, MINORITY, *supra* note 299, at 189-90, 398 (In 1219, Pope Honorius III urged the counselor-regents to resume royal lands and castles to alleviate royal poverty); *id.* at 187-342 (recounting the successes and failures of the resumption process during Henry's minority); JOLLIFFE, CONST. HIST., *supra* note 49, at 266-70; TURNER, MAGNA CARTA, *supra* note 153, at 85-86, 90 (describing conflict between native and foreign barons).

307 POWICKE, THIRTEENTH CENTURY, *supra* note 65, at 38-39 (hereinafter POWICKE, THIRTEENTH CENTURY); POWICKE, HENRY III & EDWARD, *supra* note 296, at 323-29 (the crown reserved liberties and rights notwithstanding [*non obstante*] a claim or practice to the contrary; royal determination of common good trumped vested interests and the common law).

not binding. Lords who claimed such franchises had to repurchase them, and the justiciar arbitrarily assigned the amount of the repurchase.[308]

Henry was at odds with the barons throughout his reign. His reclaim of royal power identified a tension between those seeking shared governance and those who felt that the Charter was extorted by force during a time of weakness. The barons believed that Henry III, through "evil counselors," was restoring "evil customs" and depriving men of their property without the law of the land.[309]

The counsel that Henry received was a source and focus of reform. During Henry III's reign, his *consilium* received more definition. While Henry was a minor, the king's justiciar or council-regency functioned in the place of the king, much like the council-regency when the king was absent.[310] With the loss of Normandy, Henry III remained in England, and the undefined body of counselors providing advice along with those who would have ruled in the king's absence became a *concilium baronum*, a type of permanent advisory council to the king.[311] Depending on the era, the advisory Council might consist of offices such as the justiciar, chancellor, treasurer, among others.

---

[308] 1 WILKINSON, CONST. HIST., *supra* note 149, at 96-97.

[309] POWICKE, HENRY III & EDWARD, *supra* note 296, at 31. Jolliffe recounted that the king revived John's policies: the special charters of fealty and taking of hostages as pledges. JOLLIFFE, CONST. HIST., *supra* note 49, at 273; JOLLIFFE, ANGEVIN KINGSHIP, *supra* note 18, at 131-36.

[310] *Supra* Chapter III sec. D (council-regency in Richard I's reign).

[311] SAYLES, KING'S PARLIAMENT, *supra* note 112, at 27-30 (loss of Normandy resulted in Henry III remaining in England; officers and justices transitioned from regents in the king's absence to the king's continuous advisors); *see also* TURNER, KING JOHN, *supra* note 199, at 77-79, 202-03.

The next thirty years can be described as a struggle to increase baronial involvement in the king's council. Henry III favored foreign influence, but the barons despised his reliance on foreign "evil" councilors. Conflict became critical in the 1230s. Henry dismissed Justiciar Hubert de Burgh in 1232 at the urging of counsel. But these events soon spiraled into discord. Henry's action, among other arbitrary acts, generated a backlash that threatened the peace. In 1234, Henry yielded and permitted his outlawry of Hubert de Burgh to be judged by the customs of the realm. The outlawry was criticized and reversed because it did not follow procedure.[312] The barons were not satisfied with merely restoring de Burgh; they wanted to address the source. Henry conceded to the protests and dismissed several of his foreign councilors.[313]

Following the difficulties of the first half of the decade, the barons of 1236-1240 engaged in reform. Great Councils met to address affairs and legislate. In 1237, the barons required confirmation of the Charters before agreeing to taxation.[314]

---

[312] TURNER, KING & COURTS, *supra* note 37, at 177, 249 (petitions of those outlawed without procedure, which Henry allowed to go forward for adjudication according to custom); *id.* at 251 (emphasizing that the king allowed the petitions against his rights to proceed to judgment and that had the king not done so, rebellion would be the remaining option); SAYLES, KING'S PARLIAMENT, *supra* note 112, at 37; POWICKE, HENRY III & EDWARD, *supra* note 296, at 139-40.

[313] POWICKE, HENRY III & EDWARD, *supra* note 296, at 79-81, 123, 135-36; POWICKE, THIRTEENTH CENTURY, *supra* note 65, at 50-61; 1 WILKINSON, CONST. HIST., *supra* note 149, at 100-16.

[314] SAYLES, KING'S PARLIAMENT, *supra* note 112, at 40-41; *see also* B. WILKINSON, STUDIES IN THE CONSTITUTIONAL HISTORY OF THE THIRTEENTH AND FOURTEENTH CENTURIES 160-62 (2d ed. 1952) (hereinafter WILKINSON, STUDIES) (finding baronial demands of the 1230s a precedent for the reforms of 1258).

As we see throughout the first half of the thirteenth century, most of the battles took place when the king needed taxes. Henry III's request for money met with demands. When the king wanted taxes, the barons asked for a confirmation of the Charter, which Henry III granted.[315] Rejecting the Charter's principles would invite too much conflict.[316]

The king's confirmation might be more aptly viewed as a confirmation of the relationship in addition to the Charter's formal text. The Magna Carta was confirmed many times but its subject matter was improved upon and modified several times. A handful of provisions were repealed.[317] With the confirmations, the spirit of the Magna Carta lived on. The Magna Carta took its place as a bargaining chip, an ideal and aspiration in the struggle between barons and the king.

B. The Baronial Period of Reform, 1258-1265

Baronial discontent with foreign advisors and Henry III's policies continued throughout his reign, ultimately resulting in

---

315 *Supra* note 302 (1225 confirmation in exchange for taxation). The confirmation of 1237 was accompanied by the threat of excommunication. POWICKE, HENRY III & EDWARD, *supra* note 296, at 154.

316 1 WILKINSON, CONST. HIST., *supra* note 149, at 109.

317 THOMPSON, *supra* note 304, at 9-32; HOLT, MAGNA CARTA, *supra* note 207, at 9-11 (citing statutes extending the Magna Carta's principles beyond the original text); POWICKE, THIRTEENTH CENTURY, *supra* note 65, at 216-18 (enforcement of violations but also statutes updating, interpreting, and applying the Magna Carta); *infra* notes 384-397, 449-456 (same). The 1215 version was modified in later reissues. *Supra* notes 297-298. In the 1297 confirmation, provisions were added. The barons revisited the content in the *Articuli super Cartas*. *Infra* notes 410-415. The Ordinances of 1311 also improved upon baronial reform. *Infra* Chapter VI sec. B.

civil war during the baronial-reform movement of 1258-1265.[318] By 1258, Henry III and his son Edward were left with little financial room to negotiate and yielded to baronial demands.[319]

The baronial reform of 1258 was the fruition of an earlier vision, the Paper Constitution of 1244—a revolutionary draft of baronial ideals that was never implemented.[320] The Paper Constitution's aim, following the tumult of the 1230s, was to have four "conservators of liberty," elected by all and unable to be removed except by common counsel, join the king's Council, hear complaints or *querelae* of injustice, and treat with the king concerning the realm's business.[321] The four would have the power to call a Great Council at their discretion. The Paper Constitution also sought to reestablish offices as they were in Henry's minority, namely the justiciar. Justices and officers were to be elected. Documents were not to be sealed by the king without the chancellor, and if the king did so, they were null and void.[322] The king's finances were to be spent conservatively.[323]

---

318 *See generally* R.F. TREHARNE, THE BARONIAL PLAN OF REFORM, 1258-1263 (rev. ed. 1971).

319 *Id.* at 64-66.

320 3 ROTHWELL, ENG. HIST. DOCS., *supra* note 3, at 359-60; *see also* 1 WILKINSON, CONST. HIST., *supra* note 149, at 28, 30-32, 117-30; JOLLIFFE, CONST. HIST., *supra* note 49, at 292-94. There is some dispute that the Paper Constitution was drafted in the year 1238.

321 1 WILKINSON, CONST. HIST., *supra* note 149, at 123-24; MADDICOTT, ORIGINS, *supra* note 52, at 180, 236-37; Andrew H. Hershey, *Justice and Bureaucracy: The English Royal Writ and '1258,'* 113 ENG. HIST. REV. 829, 840 (1998).

322 POWICKE, HENRY III & EDWARD, *supra* note 296, at 291-92.

323 HARRISS, KING & PARLIAMENT, *supra* note 36, at 70-71.

The first act of reform in 1258 was Henry's unprecedented agreement to surrender governance to a committee of barons. The Committee of Twenty-Four was intended to be a permanent adaptation of Magna Carta's Chapter 61.[324] Twelve of the twenty-four were chosen by the king and twelve were chosen by the barons. The king promised to bind himself to the Committee's decisions.

The Committee's first order of work followed in the Provisions of Oxford.[325] The Provisions demanded that good government be with a permanent advisory council to the king. The king's Council of Fifteen was to be elected by four who were chosen from among the Committee of Twenty-Four.[326] Working with several barons and ministers, the Council of Fifteen became the essential component of governance.[327] As we saw above, the king's counselors had frequently come under attack in the first half of the thirteenth century.[328] To remedy the problem, the Provisions of Oxford defined the Council as a tool controlling the kingship, thereby giving it a formal role in government.[329]

---

324 TREHARNE, *supra* note 318, at 67; MADDICOTT, ORIGINS, *supra* note 52, at 233-36; BALDWIN, KING'S COUNCIL, *supra* note 154, at 30 (citing the Provisions' standing committee as an improvement upon Chapter 61's emergency council).

325 3 ROTHWELL, ENG. HIST. DOCS., *supra* note 3, at 361-67.

326 TREHARNE, *supra* note 318, at 74, 83.

327 *Id.* at 86; SAYLES, KING'S PARLIAMENT, *supra* note 112, at 51-54.

328 *Supra* Chapter V sec. A.

329 TREHARNE, *supra* note 318, at 30. The barons were resurrecting governance under the council-regency. Removing governance from the king would be a reoccurring baronial reform. *See also supra* notes 310-311; *supra* notes 320-323 (Paper Constitution's plan to return to governance of Henry III's minority); *supra* Chapter III sec. D (Richard I and the council-

As part of the Provisions of Oxford, Parliament was to meet three times a year, and the Council of Fifteen would be a required component.[330] The term "parliament" (Latin, "*colloquium*") had been used throughout the thirteenth century to describe assemblies and Great Councils treating, parleying, and discussing important business, judicial decisions, or extraordinary taxation.[331] T.F. Tout described Parliaments as afforced Great Councils and a Great Council as an afforced court of the king's household. The primary duty of each of these bodies was to give the king advice, and in this function they overlapped.[332] The Provisions of Oxford formalized the parliamentary process by combining the Council of Fifteen with a body of barons representing the Great Council's powers and functions.[333] The Council in Parliament would handle judicial business and other important matters.

Up until this time and throughout the thirteenth century, England's governance had been with the king or the king and bar-

regency); *infra* Chapter VI secs. A-C, F; *infra* note 599 (fourteenth-century efforts to place governance in council).

330 SAYLES, KING'S PARLIAMENT, *supra* note 112, at 53-55.

331 *Id.* at 32-33, 38-41; *supra* notes 108-112, 146-155; JOLLIFFE, CONST. HIST., *supra* note 49, at 336-43 (discussing thirteenth-century Parliaments). The distinction between the late medieval Parliament and Great Council is vexing. *See generally* H.G. RICHARDSON & G.O. SAYLES, *Parliaments and Great Councils in Medieval England*, (XXVI) *in* THE ENGLISH PARLIAMENT IN THE MIDDLE AGES (1981) (hereinafter RICHARDSON & SAYLES, ENGLISH PARLIAMENT). Sayles distinguished Great Councils and parleys outside of Parliament from those inside of Parliament by the barons' ability in Parliament to approach and petition the king and receive an answer. SAYLES, KING'S PARLIAMENT, *supra* note 112, at 130-32.

332 2 T.F. TOUT, CHAPTERS IN THE ADMINISTRATIVE HISTORY OF MEDIAEVAL ENGLAND 146-48 (1920) (hereinafter TOUT, CHAPTERS).

333 TREHARNE, *supra* note 318, at 86-87; *see also* SAYLES, KING'S PARLIAMENT, *supra* note 112, at 54-56 (afforced councils known as Parliaments were considered superior to other assemblies and councils).

ons. Other free men were not a focus or were deemed represented by others. During the thirteenth century, knights of the shire and burgesses of the borough were optional invitees to court at the king's discretion but more likely to be found when taxation was at issue, especially by the end of the thirteenth century.[334] During the baronial-reform movement, knights and burgesses were sent on behalf of their community to parleys and Great Councils.[335] When the barons were struggling with the king, it was advantageous to have the support of knights and burgesses, but their counsel was not a required element to government action.

The baronial-infused Council of Fifteen had power to nominate and supervise chief officials such as the justiciar, chancellor, and treasurer.[336] Rather than being in office for life or good behavior, the revived office of the justiciar was in office for one year

---

334 D.A. CARPENTER, THE REIGN OF HENRY III, at 390-408 (1996) (discussing the presence and role of knights and burgesses in the thirteenth century); SAYLES, KING'S PARLIAMENT, *supra* note 112, at 86-92 (knights and burgesses optional members of assemblies). Knights were community representatives for many functions, and their election to parleys was a natural one. BARTLETT, *supra* note 133, at 158-59. Jolliffe discussed the role of knights of the shire in judicial business as a precedent for knights and burgesses of the "Commons." JOLLIFFE, CONST. HIST., *supra* note 49, at 305-07, 344, 349-52 (optional presence of knights and burgesses during reigns of Henry III-Edward II).

335 SAYLES, KING'S PARLIAMENT, *supra* note 112, at 61-64 (knights and burgesses summoned to Parliament during the baronial-reform movement but their presence was not required); PLUCKNETT, CONST. HIST., *supra* note 59, at 133-36 (Simon de Montfort's contribution to what later became the House of Commons); TREHARNE, *supra* note 318, at 55, 348-54 (connecting the knights on hand to record complaints with the buzones or community representatives of the hundred and shire). On this topic, see generally J.C. Holt, *The Prehistory of Parliament in* THE ENGLISH PARLIAMENT IN THE MIDDLE AGES 1-28 (R.G. Davies & J.H. Denton eds. 1981) (hereinafter DAVIES & DENTON, ENG. PARL. IN THE MIDDLE AGES).

336 TREHARNE, *supra* note 318, at 73, 89, 344-45.

and his actions would be reviewed at year's end.[337] Given the problems with the realm's administration, the justiciar was empowered to hear complaints of maladministration from all corners as well as violations of law and of the Magna Carta.[338] Complaints (*querelae*, bills, or petitions) were bills in which the plaintiff simply asked that justice be done.[339] *Querelae* were less formal than procedure by writ and were free.[340] It was the duty of the knights at county court sessions to record and bring forward every complaint in the administration of justice: trespasses, payments to royal officials, increases, exemptions, royal grants of lands, sales, escheats, and violations of the Magna Carta or royal rights.[341] Abuses by baronial bailiffs and the sheriffs were also collected and presented. The business of hearing complaints took place at special eyres, which were inquiries for hearing complaints.[342]

---

337 *Id.* at 90-93.

338 SAYLES, KING'S PARLIAMENT, *supra* note 112, at 51-52, 56-57, 77.

339 3 ROTHWELL, ENG. HIST. DOCS., *supra* note 3, at 361-62; *see also* POWICKE, THIRTEENTH CENTURY, *supra* note 65, at 351-53; TREHARNE, *supra* note 318, at 111, 147, 151-53 (noting that the *querela* process was the expansion of a procedure available before 1258 and that during the reform period the *querela* was being used in place of the writ for some transgressions); RICHARDSON & SAYLES, PROCEDURE WITHOUT WRIT, *supra* note 269, at xxv; S.F.C. MILSOM, HISTORICAL FOUNDATIONS OF THE COMMON LAW 82 (2d ed. 1981).

340 Hershey, *supra* note 321, at 831-32, 844-45.

341 POWICKE, THIRTEENTH CENTURY, *supra* note 65, at 143-44; 351-54; TREHARNE, *supra* note 318, at 99, 109-110, 137-39, 187-88, 199-200, 349-50 (noting that the inquest resembled previous ones, such as Henry II's Inquest of Sheriffs); RICHARDSON & SAYLES, PROCEDURE WITHOUT WRIT, *supra* note 269, at xxvi-viii, xxxiii-xxxvi (same); *see also infra* notes 362-364 (connecting the reform period's *querela* process with the petitions and returns of the late thirteenth century's *quo warranto* era).

342 TREHARNE, *supra* note 318, at 91-92, 356; HARDING, *supra* note 49, at 87.

The chancellor, like the justiciar, was in office for one year and was not to receive gifts or emoluments for office.[343] The chancellor, a high ecclesiastic and one of the highest members of the king's Council, was important because royal government came from his office.[344] Application to common-law courts went through the chancellor, as the chancery issued original writs.[345]

The barons complained that royal control of the writ process provided Henry with an opportunity to discriminate against others by arbitrarily denying justice to disfavored applicants.[346] The barons were also upset that the chancery clerks were issuing new writs and thus expanding national jurisdiction without consent.[347]

In the reform program, the barons provided that the chancellor was not allowed to authorize unapproved writs.[348] If a writ was routine "*de cursus*" (of course), then the clerks were permitted to issue a writ as common law, but if the remedy or relief were new or extraordinary or if the writ was framed "*per perceptum domini regis*" (by the order of the lord king), the issue should go

---

343 TREHARNE, *supra* note 318, at 93.

344 1 HOLDSWORTH, *supra* note 113, at 395-97.

345 *Id.* at 396, 398; *see also supra* notes 140-141 (discussing original writs).

346 Hershey, *supra* note 321, at 839-40, 842 (the barons charged Henry with violating the letter and spirt of Magna Carta's Chapter 40, which prohibited the king from denying, delaying, and selling justice arbitrarily).

347 *See also supra* Chapter III sec. C (Henry II's assizes expanding royal or national jurisdiction); BAKER, *supra* note 88, at 56 (identifying defendant's grievance in 1256 that a new, unheard of writ be quashed).

348 TREHARNE, *supra* note 318, at 93.

to the king and the Council of Fifteen for approval.[349] The barons felt that issuing new writs was equivalent to issuing new legislation.[350] Attacking arbitrary rule, baronial reforms sought to establish that the law, that is the common law, should not be changed by the king alone. Every writ must conform to the existing common law, unless approved by the king and Council of Fifteen.[351]

In the period of baronial reform, the king agreed to release sovereignty over his counselors and to accept coordinate government. The baronial-reform movement contained several legal and governmental reforms extracting power from the king in favor of a baronial committee or a council controlled by a community of barons. The barons of 1258 cited confirmation of the Magna Carta, but the reach of the barons was much deeper. Following the Paper Constitution's vision, the community of barons wanted a direct share in governance.[352] The Council of Fifteen was similar to the council-regency of 1191. But that council was established by the king or with the king's blessing. This council was forced upon the sitting king, of age, present in England.

Governance under the new plan was highly controversial. While Henry III agreed to the reforms, he frustrated their success by refusing to hold a required Parliament.[353] The barons also contributed to the unraveling of reform by failing to take respon-

---

[349] *Id.*; 3 WILKINSON, CONST. HIST., *supra* note 149, at 123-24; *cf.* TURNER, KING & COURTS, *supra* note 37, at 56-57.

[350] 1 HOLDSWORTH, *supra* note 113, at 398.

[351] WILKINSON, STUDIES, *supra* note 314, at 218-20.

[352] TREHARNE, *supra* note 318, at 67.

[353] SAYLES, KING'S PARLIAMENT, *supra* note 112, at 60-62.

sibility for the grievances against baronial bailiffs.[354] The king accused the barons of treating him and the dignity of the crown like a ward or minor.[355] In 1261, the king sought and received a papal release of his oath to the reform movement. The pope also ordered excommunication of any who enforced the provisions against the dignity of the crown.[356] The papal bull gave Henry the support that he needed to regain royal rights, only to lose it shortly thereafter.[357] The realm was in civil war. In 1265, the king defeated the baronial-reform movement, and governance was returned to the king.[358]

Above, we stated that the Magna Carta served as a symbol of a relationship, a tug-of-war between the barons and the king.[359] The gains of the baronial reform of 1258—appointment, accountability, conciliar governance—for a time added a building block to the Magna Carta. But even in their failure, the Provisions lived on as the new standard that the barons sought to obtain and secure.

---

[354] The "community of bachelors" was a group of knights from various corners who celebrated reform for the common good but complained that the king had done all that was asked of him but that the barons had done nothing. 1 WILKINSON, CONST. HIST., *supra* note 149, at 171; MADDICOTT, ORIGINS, *supra* note 52, at 246; TREHARNE, *supra* note 318, at 160-64.

[355] TREHARNE, *supra* note 318, at 344.

[356] *Id.* at 260 (papal bull of 1261); *see id.* at 250, 261, 275, 338; POWICKE, THIRTEENTH CENTURY, *supra* note 65, at 163, 165.

[357] POWICKE, THIRTEENTH CENTURY, *supra* note 65, at 167-68; *see also id.* at 183 (The papal bull influenced King Louis's arbitration decision against the barons in 1264).

[358] 1 WILKINSON, CONST. HIST., *supra* note 149, at 161-63.

[359] *Supra* note 317 and accompanying text (Magna Carta as a symbol of the relationship between king and barons).

When the barons regained their footing, the ideals of the baronial-reform plan of 1258 resurfaced.[360]

C. Edward I and the Council in Parliament

Edward I, Henry's son, was out of the country at the time of Henry's death but managed affairs abroad until his return in 1274.[361] Edward sought to reclaim royal rights and lands that had been usurped during the civil war.[362] In his inquest of 1274, every baronial liberty and franchise must have explicit charter authority or else fall back to the king in *quo warranto* proceedings.[363] Edward's inquiry into franchises blossomed into investigations of other abuses, and the whole process generated many petitions.[364] If individuals could not make their complaints to the king's representatives in the local districts, they could petition the Council in Parliament directly.[365]

---

[360] The Ordainers picked up where the baronial reform of 1258 ended. *Infra* Chapter VI secs. A–B.

[361] DONALD W. SUTHERLAND, QUO WARRANTO PROCEEDINGS IN THE REIGN OF EDWARD I 1278-1294, at 16–17 (1963).

[362] *Id.* at 17; HELEN CAM, THE HUNDRED AND THE HUNDRED ROLLS: AN OUTLINE OF LOCAL GOVERNMENT IN MEDIEVAL ENGLAND (1930) (hereinafter CAM, HUNDRED ROLLS).

[363] SUTHERLAND, *supra* note 361, at 17–18. For Henry III's *quo warranto* proceedings, see *supra* notes 306–308.

[364] SUTHERLAND, *supra* note 361, at 18–19, 24–25, 28–29 (describing the jurors' returns to the commissioners' inquiries as unofficial indictments and commenting on Edward's legislative and judicial responses to the returns); POWICKE, THIRTEENTH CENTURY, *supra* note 65, at 351–58; *cf. supra* notes 338–342 (*querelae* of the baronial-reform period).

[365] SAYLES, KING'S PARLIAMENT, *supra* note 112, at 78–79.

We saw above that the royal writ to initiate an action at law was obtained in the chancery.[366] The writ system, stemming from Henry II's reforms, was expensive, formal, and required technical pleading.[367] With the reforms of 1258, the register of writs was closed to unauthorized addition. The petition, however, was always available for subjects to petition the king for grace, as the king had a theocratic responsibility to justice.[368] The petition was informal and free.[369] They were in narrative form and asked for relief or justice on general, moral, or religious grounds.[370] Similar to the *querelae* of 1258, Edward I encouraged the practice of petitions into abuses, and the petition became a common practice in the late thirteenth and fourteenth centuries.[371]

The petition also served a second purpose: to seek a remedy against the king. Royal courts favored and were dependent on the king, who had privileges that other litigants did not have. Royal writ process did not run against the king the same way that

---

366 *Supra* notes 140-141, 345.

367 SAYLES, KING'S PARLIAMENT, *supra* note 112, at 76-77; Hershey, *supra* note 321, at 831-32, 837-38.

368 DODD, *supra* note 14, at 25-26, 283-84; *see also* Serena Connolly, *Petitioning in the Ancient World in* MEDIEVAL PETITIONS, GRACE AND GRIEVANCE 52 (W. Mark Ormrod, Gwilym Dodd, & Anthony Musson eds. 2009) (hereinafter Medieval Petitions) (use of petitions in Roman law).

369 DODD, *supra* note 14, at 29-30; *supra* note 340. The term "petition" was used until the fifteenth century when the term used was "public bills." SAYLES, KING'S PARLIAMENT, *supra* note 112, at 79 n.21.

370 BALDWIN, KING'S COUNCIL, *supra* note 154, at 282-83. Sayles noted that a plaint or *querela* often served as the source of the common-law writ which initiated the formal action. RICHARDSON & SAYLES, PROCEDURE WITHOUT WRIT, *supra* note 269, at xxii-xiii (chancery clerks examined petitions and plaints to determine the proper writ).

371 *Supra* note 364; *infra* Chapters VI, VII.

it did against a common individual.[372] Individuals petitioned the king's grace for debt owed by the king or some property matter involving the king.[373] Where a writ would be brought against a private person, a petition would be sought against the king. Sayles emphasized that while the king could refuse a petition—that's what a petition is—he respected the common law and often worked within its confines.[374] Courts were reluctant to change or alter the common law, even when it was deficient.[375] To ask for grace in a petition was to ask the king to waive royal prerogative and allow the common-law procedure to operate against the king's interest.[376]

If the king refused to remedy a wrong, there was not a clear role for enforcement against him in medieval times.[377] The king swore at his coronation oath to abolish bad laws and to pro-

---

[372] 3 SAYLES, SELECT CASES, *supra* note 143, at xliii-xlvi; *supra* note 269.

[373] Paul Brand, *Understanding Early Petitions: An Analysis of the Content of Petitions to Parliament in the Reign of Edward I in* MEDIEVAL PETITIONS, *supra* note 368, at 107-113.

[374] *Supra* notes 42, 263-265, 312.

[375] *Supra* note 149.

[376] 5 SAYLES, SELECT CASES, *supra* note 143, at lxxxiii-xxxviii (king allowing, as a matter of grace, petitions of right to be determined by common-law methods). Sayles criticized the Stuart concept of "petition of right" as either not applicable to medieval times or limited to a few instances of wrongs to individuals and not a device for constitutional challenges to the king or the theory of kingship. SAYLES, KING'S PARLIAMENT, *supra* note 112, at 59 (noting the fluidity of the law and its interpretation when the king's interest was at stake); *infra* Chapter VIII (Stuart England). On the petition of right, see William S. Holdsworth, *The History of Remedies against the Crown I, II*, 38 LAW Q. REV. 141, 280 (1922).

[377] *Supra* notes 37-41 (Bracton's antinomy); *see also* Ehrlich, *Proceedings*, *supra* note 26, at 45-47, 59.

tect good customs.[378] But this was a matter for his conscience or perhaps papal excommunication.[379]

In Edward I's reign and thereafter, petitions were addressed to the king, the Council, chancellor, Parliament or some combination thereof.[380] The judicial work of answering petitions constituted a large part of the Council's business. The work became too much, and petitions that could be handled by existing common-law processes or specific departments were referred out.[381] Appointed committees of receivers and hearers disposed of routine petitions.[382] And if a matter had not been decided by this point, it would go to the king for a decision.[383] The king was seen as the ultimate decision-maker for difficult cases.

---

[378] *Supra* Chapter II sec. B.

[379] *Supra* Chapter II sec. A.

[380] DODD, *supra* note 14, at 83-86; 1 HOLDSWORTH, *supra* note 113, at 401-02. Petitions were addressed to the king and King in Council and presented at a session of parliament. Later, when Parliament became a body, petitions were addressed to Parliament. FREDERIC WILLIAM MAITLAND, *Introduction to the Memoranda de Parliamento in* RECORDS OF THE PARLIAMENT HOLDEN AT WESTMINSTER [28 FEBRUARY 1305], at lxvi-lxvii (1893).

[381] DODD, *supra* note 14, at 80-81, 118-19; *see also* Gwilym Dodd, *Parliamentary Petitions? The Origins and Provenance of the 'Ancient Petitions' (SC8) in the National Archives in* MEDIEVAL PETITIONS, *supra* note 368, at 12.

[382] In 1280, it was decided that petitions be grouped and sent out to appropriate departments and courts. Those that could not be handled by courts and departments remained with King in Council. SAYLES, KING'S PARLIAMENT, *supra* note 112, at 79-82; *id.* (in 1305, receivers did the bundling and assignment but hearers or auditors disposed of routine matters); DODD, *supra* note 14, at 50-60, 103-08.

[383] Dodd, *Parliamentary Petitions in* MEDIEVAL PETITIONS, *supra* note 368, at 38.

Edward I's reign was the age of statutes.[384] Edward's statutes were based on judgments addressing petitions and jurors' returns to his inquests.[385] Changes to the law or the common law in Edward's reign took the form of statutes, constitutions, and provisions rather than writs and assizes.[386] The Edwardian statute was the king's declaration of law in written form.[387]

Toward the end of the middle ages, there was a significant difference between "statute" and royal "ordinance."[388] During Edward I's reign, however, it is difficult to define "legislation" or "statute" as we know those terms.[389] Plucknett wrote:

> The only safe course is to say, quite simply, that those things are statutes which contemporaries themselves describe by that word. In other words, the description of 'statute' is acquired by repute. We must regard as contemporaries, moreover, those who were best qualified to

384 T.F.T. PLUCKNETT, LEGISLATION OF EDWARD I (1949) (hereinafter PLUCKNETT, LEGISLATION).

385 SUTHERLAND, *supra* note 361, at 18-19; POWICKE, THIRTEENTH CENTURY, *supra* note 65, at 350-57, 376-78; *supra* note 364.

386 JOLLIFFE, CONST. HIST., *supra* note 49, at 334-35; SAYLES, KING'S PARLIAMENT, *supra* note 112, at 85-86 (king and council updated the law; statute and judicial actions overlapped in medieval period); 3 SAYLES, SELECT CASES, *supra* note 143, at xxxvi-vii (noting that statute law during the medieval era did not always abrogate the common law but was also merely a restatement of law). Many of the Magna Carta's provisions were modified and passed as statutes. *Supra* note 317 (modifying Magna Carta's promises); *infra* notes 448-454 (contrasting Edwardian statutes from Parliament's statutes); *infra* note 538.

387 3 SAYLES, SELECT CASES, *supra* note 143, at xi-xiv.

388 *Infra* Chapters VI sec. D, VII (common petition and High Court of Parliament).

389 PLUCKNETT, LEGISLATION, *supra* note 384, at 10-20.

> know—above all, the courts, for it was their duty to know. It is not necessary to believe that every scrap in private compilations which is there called a 'statute' is truly one.[390]

Edward I and his small advising Council were enough for statute and the judicial business before the king, though the Council could be afforced by barons and others.[391] The medieval king, except in times of rebellion such as that of 1258, was law giver. Edward I did not distinguish between statute and ordinance. His will was behind both the statute and the prerogative; they were read together. Edward I's reign was not the reign to differentiate or define variations of Council and Parliament or their respective function or composition. This differentiation became more pronounced during the fourteenth century.[392]

As a law giver, Edward I's reign was too early for constitutional controversies in the source of law. It was the king's duty to amend the laws for the good of the whole—to preserve good laws

---

[390] *Id.* at 11; RICHARDSON & SAYLES, *Early Statutes*, (XXV), *in* ENGLISH PARLIAMENT, *supra* note 331, at 32-47.

[391] JOLLIFFE, CONST. HIST., *supra* note 49, at 339, 350, 352 (Edwardian Council in Parliament included the sworn officers of state afforced with justices or barons or both depending on the matter before it); *id.* at 346 (King in Council in Parliament was the "essential authority" of statute); *id.* at 339, 352-54 (magnates not necessary for Edwardian statute or for all of Parliament's business; barons not required for statute until fourteenth century). Following the Magna Carta, however, the assent of barons was generally required for extraordinary taxation. *Id.* at 341, 352-63 (magnates called to assent to taxation or very serious matters but no real composition or requirement for the assenting body).

[392] J.F. Baldwin, *The King's Council in* 1 THE ENGLISH GOVERNMENT AT WORK, 1327-1336, at 145-46 (James F. Willard & William A. Morris ed. 1940) (hereinafter ENG. GOV. AT WORK); JOLLIFFE, CONST. HIST., *supra* note 49, at 344.

and abolish bad ones.[393] This was the essence of the king's divine royal prerogative and theocratic responsibility.[394] Necessity knows no law. The king swore in his coronation oath that he would preserve and protect ancient and good laws and abolish bad customs—that is, provide justice.[395] For the king, this meant that he was above the law and custom and could declare it void when it conflicted with common welfare.[396] Edward I considered statutes, along with all positive law, subject to the crown's duty to reason and common utility.[397] His actions to the contrary of common law were likely for public welfare or equity and thus not controversial.

---

393 *Supra* Chapter II sec. B.

394 *Supra* notes 32-36, 66-67, 263 (common utility, necessity).

395 *Supra* Chapter I sec. B.

396 PLUCKNETT, LEGISLATION, *supra* note 384, at 3-6; SAYLES, KING'S PARLIAMENT, *supra* note 112, at 86, 116-17 (king altered law outside of Parliament if it conflicted with his opinion on public welfare); 3 SAYLES, SELECT CASES, *supra* note 143, at xxxviii-xliii, xliv (noting that Edward I ignored and repealed statutes on his own accord but often worked within the common law); JOLLIFFE, CONST. HIST., *supra* note 49, at 335-37; JAMES CONWAY DAVIES, THE BARONIAL OPPOSITION TO EDWARD II: ITS CHARACTER AND POLICY, A STUDY IN ADMINISTRATIVE HISTORY 1-16, 27, 48 (1918) (royal prerogative in medieval times); *cf.* POWICKE, THIRTEENTH CENTURY, *supra* note 65, at 329-30; *id.* at 324 (noting political fallout if the king decided a matter without the barons for which the barons ought to have been consulted).

397 RICHARDSON & SAYLES, *Early Statutes*, (XXV), *in* ENGLISH PARLIAMENT, *supra* note 331, at 25-30; THOMPSON, *supra* note 304, at 17, 20, 34-35 (noting use of *non obstante* clause [notwithstanding] to disregard prior laws; royal prerogative trumped statutory text; royal judges did not give statutes literal force), *citing* 3 T.F. TOUT, THE HISTORY OF ENGLAND: FROM THE ACCESSION OF HENRY III TO THE DEATH OF EDWARD III (1216-1377), at 152 (1905) ("[A]ll medieval laws were rather enunciations of an ideal than measures which practical statesmen aimed at carrying out in detail."); TURNER, KING & COURTS, *supra* note 37, at 110-24 (king intervened to dispense with custom for justice and utility); *supra* notes 307, 386, 394-396 (Edward I's control over statute-making process); *infra* note 538.

Edward I was viewed as a strong and good ruler who worked with the barons.[398] A controversial reign was often followed by a conciliatory reign: the bitter reforms of the prior era ratcheted up to the accepted or semi-accepted policy of the successor. Henry III was a minor and the council-regency was receptive to baronial concerns.[399] Edward I likely avoided controversy because he followed the spirit of the baronial plan of reform.[400] The Council, as a nucleus of officers, had a strong and organized presence in Edward's reign. Edward I supported his executive acts acknowledging the Council's participation as advisor.[401] Many petitions cited abuse by royal ministers and officers. Edward addressed ministerial corruption of local officials by appointing committees of the Council in Parliament (*auditores querelarum*) to investigate petitions.[402] Edward's committee in Parliament was an important precedent for fourteenth-century reform efforts.[403]

But Edward I also had his fight with the barons. The last decade of his reign was controversial, akin to that of John and the Magna Carta. Edward demanded service and money for war, which he justified in terms of the common good of the realm.[404] The realm was not happy with his collection process, as he often

---

398 1 WILKINSON, CONST. HIST., *supra* note 149, at 47–48, 59.

399 *Supra* Chapter V sec. A.

400 MADDICOTT, ORIGINS, *supra* note 52, at 282–83; *supra* note 398.

401 WILKINSON, STUDIES, *supra* note 314, at 121–23.

402 BRAND, MAKING COMMON LAW, *supra* note 101, at 102-12; HARDING, *supra* note 49, at 87; *cf.* RICHARDSON & SAYLES, *The Origins of Parliament* (I), *in* ENGLISH PARLIAMENT, *supra* note 331, at 163–64; *see also supra* note 382.

403 *Infra* Chapter VI.

404 POWICKE, THIRTEENTH CENTURY, *supra* note 65, at 528 (connecting the war and need for money with the law of necessity).

levied taxes without the full spirit of common counsel.[405] Like his father, Edward I was pressured to confirm the Charters in the famous *Confirmatio Cartarum* of 1297.[406] In return for the confirmation, Edward received much-needed taxes.

"Common profit" and "common utility" had historically been a kingly responsibility but also served as a beachhead for baronial reform. The king argued that taxes were necessary for the profit of the realm. The barons also latched on to "*pro communi utilitate*" and "necessity" in the controversy leading up to the *Confirmatio*.[407] G.L. Harriss observed that while the king was the decision-maker, the *Confirmatio* balanced the king's "unilateral declaration of necessity" with baronial common assent.[408] The 1297 confirmation, adding several articles to the 1225 text, provided that certain taxes should be granted by the "common assent" for the "common profit" of the realm—suggesting concern

---

[405] JOLLIFFE, CONST. HIST., *supra* note 49, at 355-56, 359.

[406] 3 ROTHWELL, ENG. HIST. DOCS., *supra* note 3, at 485-86; 1 WILKINSON, CONST. HIST., *supra* note 149, at 62-65, 187-232; MICHAEL PRESTWICH, PLANTAGENET ENGLAND 1225-1360, at 165-68 (2005).

[407] HARRISS, KING & PARLIAMENT, *supra* note 36, at 40-41, 45-48; *see also* C.L. KINGSFORD, THE SONG OF LEWES (lines 890-920) 52-53 (1890).

[408] HARRISS, KING & PARLIAMENT, *supra* note 36, at 67-70; *supra* notes 32-36, 66-67, 263-265, 393-397 (common utility and necessity). "Common utility" is often discussed in connection with popular Romano-canonical principles such as "*quod omnes tangit ab omnibus approbetur*" (what touches all shall be approved all), which made a presence in late thirteenth-century secular documents. 3 WILKINSON, CONST. HIST., *supra* note 149, at 311 (maxim "*quod omnes tangit*" appeared in the summons to Parliament of 1295). Powicke observed that although Romano-canonical principles were present and influenced English affairs, they should not be viewed as the parent or root of English parliamentary principles. POWICKE, THIRTEENTH CENTURY, *supra* note 65, at 538-39 & nn. *See generally* POST, STUDIES, *supra* note 36, at 163-220.

for abusive spending and a baronial desire to attach strings to the purse.[409]

The episode of 1297 repeated a few years later when Edward I confirmed the *Articuli super Cartas* in exchange for further finances.[410] His promise in the *Articuli* acknowledged that the Charters had been violated despite the king's previous promises. The *Articuli* also noted that the common law provided little remedy against such violations. The king's use of the Privy Seal was chief among the judicial complaints. The Privy Seal was at this time the king's instrument and followed a less formal procedure than that of the Great Seal.[411] Specifically, the barons grieved that writs of the Privy Seal were being used to remove cases from the common-law courts.[412] In addition to judicial complaints, barons complained of the broader problem of the king's household and its grip over executive machinery, a problem that would resurface in the next reign.[413] The *Articuli* provided a commission of lawful men, similar to the *querela* process of 1258, to hear and punish violations of the Charters.[414] But Edward sought to derail these

---

409 3 ROTHWELL, ENG. HIST. DOCS., *supra* note 3, at 486.

410 *Id.* at 496; *see* HARRISS, KING & PARLIAMENT, *supra* note 36, at 99–106; PRESTWICH, *supra* note 406, at 172–75.

411 BALDWIN, KING'S COUNCIL, *supra* note 154, at 255–57, 260 (noting original intention of Privy Seal and discussing its transformation into other uses primarily due to the advantages of secrecy and freedom from restraint and procedure).

412 2 TOUT, CHAPTERS, *supra* note 332, at 153–55, 227; *see also infra* note 458 (similar complaints in the Ordinances); *infra* notes 545–548 (similar complaints in mid-fourteenth century).

413 2 TOUT, CHAPTERS, *supra* note 332, at 152–55 (failures of the financial system in the 1290s caused Edward I to rely more on his household service than traditional offices of state).

414 3 ROTHWELL, ENG. HIST. DOCS., *supra* note 3, at 496–97.

reform efforts. Like John and Henry III before him, Edward in 1305 sought and received a papal release from his promises.[415]

---

[415] 1 WILKINSON, CONST. HIST., *supra* note 149, at 230-32; MADDICOTT, ORIGINS, *supra* note 52, at 327-28; *supra* notes 61-67, 356 (papal releases).

VI

The Fourteenth Century and the Rise of Participatory Government

A. Edward II's Coronation Oath and Baronial Reform

EDWARD II'S REIGN COMMENCED in 1307 following Edward I's death. Edward II's reign was considered a disaster for various reasons, including the claim that he failed to fix England's financial woes. His officers were deemed tyrants ("evil councilors") oppressing the people in the name of the king's prerogative.[416] Chief among the initial complaints was Edward's elevation of favorite Piers Gaveston to Earl of Cornwall. The barons loathed Gaveston's greed, arrogance, and influence over royal patronage.[417] Gaveston had been exiled before and was permitted to return a second time. He was the focus of several

---

[416] DAVIES, *supra* note 396, at 359 (king and "evil counsel" wasted money set aside for certain purpose).

[417] HARRISS, KING & PARLIAMENT, *supra* note 36, at 161–85 (Edward II's reign was a competition between royal patronage and the common profit of the realm); PRESTWICH, *supra* note 406, at 178–79.

reforms. But the barons were ultimately successful in getting rid of Gaveston. He was murdered in 1312 by an informal tribunal.[418]

From the start, the barons wanted this reign to be different from those prior. In early 1308, Edward II swore to a fourth provision in addition to the common three-part coronation oath. Edward's 1308 Coronation Oath promised:

> 1. To grant and preserve and by your oath confirm to the people of England the laws and customs granted to them by former kings of England, your righteous and godly predecessors, and particularly the laws, customs and liberties granted to the clergy and the people by the glorious king St Edward, your predecessor
>
> 2. [Y]ou for God and holy church and for the clergy and for the people keep peace and accord in God, to the best of your ability
>
> 3. [Y]ou in all your judgments have impartial and proper justice and discretion done in compassion and truth to the best of your ability
>
> 4. [Y]ou agree to maintain and preserve the laws and rightful customs which the community of your realm shall have chosen and [you will] defend and enforce them to the honor of God to the best of your ability.[419]

Though not without debate, commentators argue that the fourth clause made the king promise not only to law and custom of pre-

---

[418] *See generally* J.S. Hamilton, Piers Gaveston, Earl of Cornwall 1307-1312, at 98-99 (1988).

[419] 3 ROTHWELL, ENG. HIST. DOCS., *supra* note 3, at 525.

decessors but also to laws elected by the commonalty or the barons.[420]

The fourth clause was a step forward from the Magna Carta and the baronial-reform efforts of 1258. As we saw throughout the thirteenth century, the king often repudiated promises.[421] Edward I, three years earlier, had disavowed his oaths by obtaining a papal release.[422] The coronation oath's fourth clause may have been an attempt to remedy that problem.[423] During baronial-reform movements, the king was not the sole law giver; the law came from below. The 1308 coronation oath envisioned law from below as a regular process rather than an achievement of rebellion or council-regency. The king would be bridled not only by natural law but also by the commonalty. The king's most sacred coronation promise, indeed his very authority, extended to the law chosen by the commonalty. Edward II's governance would be fused with baronial reform, in theory.

The barons wanted desperately to get rid of Gaveston, but as a royal minister he was protected from an action at law. In general terms, process did not apply to the king or his officers unless the king gave permission.[424] A faction of barons issued a Declaration in the spring of 1308 urging the king to fulfill his cor-

---

[420] 2 WILKINSON, CONST. HIST., *supra* note 149, at 91-99 (discussing scholarship on the fourth clause's meaning). *See generally* B. Wilkinson, *The Coronation Oath of Edward II and the Statute of York*, 19 SPECULUM 445 (1944).

[421] *Supra* notes 61-67, 356, 415 (papal releases).

[422] *Supra* note 415.

[423] 2 WILKINSON, CONST. HIST., *supra* note 149, at 92-93.

[424] Ehrlich, *Proceedings*, *supra* note 26, at 28-29; *supra* notes 42, 263-265, 269, 312, 372-377.

onation oath and banish Gaveston.[425] Without other civil means, the barons proclaimed that they were permitted to self-help, violence, and coercion if the king did not keep his oath. The barons:

> Homage and the oath of allegiance are more in respect of the crown than in respect of the king's person and are more clearly related to the crown than to the king's person; and this is evident because, before the right of the crown has descended to the person, no allegiance is due to him. And, therefore, if it should befall that the king is not guided by reason, then, in order that the dignity of the crown may be preserved the lieges are bound by the oath made to the crown to reinstate the king in the dignity of the crown or else they would not have kept their oath. The next question is how the king should be reinstated, whether by an action at law or by constraint [violence or coercion]. It is not, however, possible by recourse to the law to obtain redress, because there would be no other judge than royal judges, in which case, if the king's will was not accordant with right reason, the only result would be that error would be maintained and confirmed. Hence, in order that the oath may be saved, when the king will not right a wrong and remove that which is hurtful to the people at large and prejudicial to the crown, and is so adjudged by the people, it behoves that the evil must be removed by constraint, for the king is bound by his oath to govern his people, and his lieges are bound to govern with him and in support of him.[426]

---

[425] Richardson, *supra* note 53, at 67.

[426] 3 ROTHWELL, ENG. HIST. DOCS., *supra* note 3, at 525. The remainder of the Declaration refers to Gaveston without attribution. The 1308 Declaration was similar to Chapter 61 as it contemplated coercion or violence if the king failed to abide by his promises. 2 WILKINSON, CONST. HIST., *supra*

The treasonous effort of the Declaration promoted the separate capacities of the crown and the king's person.[427] The opposition barons were mostly looking past the king himself to his ministers, namely Gaveston. But Gaveston and other ministers were protected by the king and the concept of monarchy, which led to a competition over the monarch's powers. The barons supporting this radical Declaration pledged their loyalty, homage, and allegiance to the crown rather than to the king's person.[428] Separating the king from his title was a clever stratagem to turn his divine authority and prerogative against him. For if the king or his ministers violated the office of the crown, community loyalty was to the latter. The discretion the king identified for himself or his ministers became a source for the barons to claim for the community. The barons were either withholding money from the king or challenging other royal actions and thus had to make a better showing of common utility and necessity than the king's showing.[429] In the name of coronation oath, the barons seemed to be evaluating divine "reason"[430] and threatening coercive action if the king or his ministers fell below their definition of that standard.[431] The king had always treated his determinations of com-

---

note 149, at 12, 102; *see also* HARRISS, KING & PARLIAMENT, *supra* note 36, at 160-63.

[427] DAVIES, *supra* note 396, at 22-27 (separation of capacities); HARRISS, KING & PARLIAMENT, *supra* note 36, at 163-64.

[428] 2 WILKINSON, CONST. HIST., *supra* note 149, at 12, 100.

[429] HARRISS, KING & PARLIAMENT, *supra* note 36, at 108-09, 160-62; JOLLIFFE, CONST. HIST., *supra* note 49, at 361-62 (barons and king disputing whose interest better served the "rights of the crown").

[430] *Supra* notes 20-24 ("reason" in natural law).

[431] DAVIES, *supra* note 396, at 42-43.

mon utility and necessity as above positive law, even his own positive law.[432] Could these principles be controlled by the barons?

B. The Ordinances and the Competition for "Right and Reason"

The coronation oath and baronial Declaration provided a foundation for reform efforts. The financial problems that had emerged in Edward I's reign continued to plague Edward II.[433] To address financial difficulties, oppressive taxation, and injustice, the barons wanted a role in the common welfare of the realm, which was historically a kingly responsibility but now sought as a popular right. The king conceded and issued a charter on March 15, 1310, giving the barons the right to elect Ordainers who would protect the profit of God and the profit of the people according to right and reason.[434] The king approved the Ordainers' appointment in order to help with his ministers and the administration of the realm. The Ordainers blamed the king's evil ministers and advisors, like Gaveston, who had led Edward astray rather than attacking the king directly.[435] Ordainers were to guide the king,

---

[432] *Supra* Chapter II sec. A; *supra* notes 64-67, 195-198, 393-397, 408.

[433] J.R. MADDICOTT, THOMAS OF LANCASTER, 1307-1322, at 106-09 (1970) (hereinafter MADDICOTT, LANCASTER).

[434] 2 WILKINSON, CONST. HIST., *supra* note 149, at 124-25; HARRISS, KING & PARLIAMENT, *supra* note 36, at 160-65; *see also supra* notes 32-36, 64-67, 409, 410, 417 ("common utility" a kingly matter but later a baronial matter).

[435] DAVIES, *supra* note 396, at 27-40 (summarizing the baronial efforts against the king's ministers); *id.* at 369-71 (Ordainers removed the king's evil councilors); HARRISS, KING & PARLIAMENT, *supra* note 36, at 165-68 (describing grievances against royal patronage and Gaveston's influence upon the king).

resume royal profits and lands from unwise alienation, and restore justice and order.[436]

For the Ordainers to succeed, they needed to change their reform agenda from earlier baronial efforts. History had repeatedly demonstrated that the king's promises were not kept. We saw above how the Magna Carta's Chapter 61 was a type of rebellion or enforcement in the form of judgment and distraint.[437] Chapter 61 never materialized as it tried to civilize distraint against the king. Other enforcement methods also failed. Excommunication was threatened for violations of the Charters, thereby raising its character to "fundamental law." But this was not a viable secular option.[438] If a matter arose in litigation and there were a gap between baron and king, the royal judge would be bound by royal interests.[439] Despite the Magna Carta's assurances and numerous confirmations, the law provided little safety against the king. By 1258, reform efforts had evolved as the barons sought control of the king's Council to supervise royal government. But in 1258, change within the king's Council alone was insufficient. The 1258 program fell apart when the king regained power. The barons went back to seeking promises and confirmations. The barons in 1308 needed more. They had to find some enforcement role against the king and his ministers.

---

[436] HARRISS, KING & PARLIAMENT, *supra* note 36, at 161-85; SAYLES, KING'S PARLIAMENT, *supra* note 112, at 96-97.

[437] *Supra* Chapter IV sec. C.

[438] THOMPSON, *supra* note 304, at 125-26 (discussing the ineffectiveness of excommunication for violations of the Great Charter); ADAMS, *supra* note 89, at 325 (citing use of excommunication for Charter violations as an effort to make it "fundamental law"). *See also supra* notes 304, 315 (Magna Carta's confirmation with threat of excommunication for violations).

[439] 3 WILKINSON, CONST. HIST., *supra* note 149, at 155.

The barons found that answer in the Ordinances, Parliament, and reforming the king's household.[440] The first set of Ordinances was agreed upon in 1310, followed by the full set in 1311. The Ordinances follow the *Confirmatio, Articuli super Cartas,* and the Articles of Stamford 1309, which was mostly a reaffirmation of the *Articuli.*[441] The Ordinances sought to revitalize Parliament as a baronial center for reform and justice for individuals, a superior court to lower courts, and a place in which the king received counsel on national matters.[442] They required annual or semi-annual meetings of Parliament.[443]

The Council in Parliament had been a court for several different matters, but especially a court to hear petitions.[444] Building upon baronial and Edwardian reforms, the Ordinances provided for a committee of barons to hear petitions concerning violations of the Ordinances or the Charters by the king's ministers

---

440 2 WILKINSON, CONST. HIST., *supra* note 149, at 14-15 (contrasting the parliamentarian nature of baronial opposition to Edward II from the conciliarism of 1258); 2 TOUT, CHAPTERS, *supra* note 332, at 194-95 (Ordainers sought to reform the household as well as the realm).

441 Michael Prestwich, *The Ordinances of 1311 and the Politics of the Early Fourteenth Century in* POLITICS AND CRISIS IN FOURTEENTH-CENTURY ENGLAND 1-18 (John Taylor & Wendy Childs eds. 1990); MADDICOTT, LANCASTER, *supra* note 433, at 97-105; *supra* note 410.

442 3 ROTHWELL, ENG. HIST. DOCS., *supra* note 3, at 527; SAYLES, KING'S PARLIAMENT, *supra* note 112, at 97-99 (observing that Parliament's function remained as it had been; however, control would be with the Ordainers and not the king's ministers).

443 3 ROTHWELL, ENG. HIST. DOCS., *supra* note 3, at 536 (#29).

444 By this time, the Council in Parliament was a court of appeals from the King's Bench as well as a supreme court for deciding difficult matters. MUSSON & ORMROD, EVOLUTION OF ENG. JUSTICE, *supra* note 162, at 26.

and to punish accordingly (#40).[445] With accountability in the hands of a parliamentary committee, the Ordainers were reaching for an independent share of government, which would accomplish the needed enforcement power.[446] Parliamentary accountability of ministerial abuse was a step forward from the demand for promises and confirmation—for accountability assumed baronial standards and enforced them.

Supplementing Parliament's accountability powers, the Ordainers were to safeguard the profit of the realm and determine violations of "right and reason," which seemed to be public concerns along with the common law.[447] The king's statutes maintained against "right and reason," the Charters, or the Ordinances were to be held void.[448] Prior to the division between statute and ordinance and fourteenth-century reforms, the meaning and significance of statute was obscure.[449] Edward I's statutes were

---

[445] 3 ROTHWELL, ENG. HIST. DOCS., *supra* note 3, at 539. The thirteenth century was full of grievances against councilors. *Supra* Chapter V sec. A. Reform in 1258 had elected officers and governance by Council. Edward I inquired into the actions of ministers through a committee of Parliament. *Supra* notes 402-403. Later, Parliament was a center of accountability for impeachment of officers and others. *Infra* Chapter VI secs. F-G (Stratford, Richard II, impeachment, and judgment of peers in Parliament).

[446] DAVIES, *supra* note 396, at 368, 372.

[447] 3 ROTHWELL, ENG. HIST. DOCS., *supra* note 3, at 527 (preface), 528 (#6), 536 (#31, #32); *supra* Chapter VI sec. A. The king had long sworn to uphold good laws and customs. Canon law recognized that these duties were inalienable. For example, the king swore to protect royal lands and promote the fisc. *See generally* Kantorowicz, *supra* note 65; HARRISS, KING & PARLIAMENT, *supra* note 36. In the latter part of the thirteenth century and with the Ordinances, the barons were assuming a role in safeguarding that royal responsibility.

[448] 3 ROTHWELL, ENG. HIST. DOCS., *supra* note 3, at 528 (#6), 536 (#31).

[449] *Supra* Chapter V sec. C; *infra* notes 517-522.

mostly judicial acts of the King in Council.[450] The Ordainers provided that statutes were not to contravene the Charters or the Ordinances (#6, #31).[451] In this sense, the Ordainers likely equated "statute" with other royal acts when they claimed that statutes contrary to the Charters were void.[452] Despite this claim, this was not a reality of fourteenth-century jurisprudence.[453] Plucknett observed that there was an inconsistency between saying that enactments contrary to the Magna Carta were void but all the while having enactments modifying and repealing the Magna Carta's subject matter.[454] After the Ordainers' and other fourteenth-century reforms, Lords and Commons would consider a statute or reform provision approved of by the common counsel of Parliament the law of the land, on par with the Magna Carta.[455] For example, the Ordainers gave themselves authority to review and clarify the Magna Carta's provisions. If any point of the Charter

---

450 *Supra* Chapter V sec. C.

451 *See also* 42 Edw. III ch. 1 (1368) (late fourteenth-century statute providing: "That the Great Charter and the Charter of the Forest be holden and kept in all Points; and if any Statute be made to the contrary, that shall be holden for none"); THOMPSON, *supra* note 304, at 16-17.

452 *Cf.* Ordinance #32 (Ordainers proclaimed that the Common Law and the law of the land was supreme over the king's letters and the Privy Seal).

453 HELEN M. CAM, MAGNA CARTA, EVENT OR DOCUMENT? 17 (1965) (noting absence of evidence for premise that violations of Magna Carta resulted in voided statutes).

454 THEODORE F.T. PLUCKNETT, STATUTES AND THEIR INTERPRETATIONS IN THE FIRST HALF OF THE FOURTEENTH CENTURY 27 (1922); *see also* THOMPSON, *supra* note 304, at 14-19; *supra* note 317 (barons, Lords, and Commons improving, modifying, and repealing the subject matter of the Magna Carta and other laws).

455 *Infra* Chapter VI sec. D (Commons' petitions and the increased importance of the statute from Parliament's perspective).

were "obscure or doubtful, let it be made clear by the said Ordainers and others" in Parliament (#6, #38).[456]

The Ordainers also demanded common assent to several matters such as war (#9), removal of evil councilors (#13), and appointment of the king's ministers of both state and household (#14).[457] Whereas the Privy Seal was a symbol of kingly government by prerogative, the Ordainers declared that writs of the Privy Seal were not to frustrate the common law.[458] Weary of the king's abuse of finances, the Ordainers attempted to reign in the king's expenditures for personal use; national finances should be used for the common profit of the realm.

With all these changes, the Ordainers endeavored that Parliament no longer be just a session of the Council but instead a baronial body for reform and accountability. The Ordainers were living out the coronation oath, and Edward had sworn to abide by their election. The Ordinances provided an additional brick to the

---

456 3 ROTHWELL, ENG. HIST. DOCS., *supra* note 3, at 528 (#6), 538 (#38); *see also* THOMPSON, *supra* note 304, at 15, 16.

457 3 ROTHWELL, ENG. HIST. DOCS., *supra* note 3, at 529–30; *see also supra* note 435 (Ordainers' goal of removing evil counsel); *cf. supra* note 336 (Provisions of Oxford and Council of Fifteen's appointment power).

458 3 ROTHWELL, ENG. HIST. DOCS., *supra* note 3, at 536 (#32, neither law of the land nor common right ought to be delayed or disturbed by letters under Privy Seal; if anything shall be done against right or the law of the land by the Privy Seal, it shall be null); *see also* 2 TOUT, CHAPTERS, *supra* note 332, at 222, 284–310 (Ordainers and barons able to remove the king's Privy Seal away from royal control); DAVIES, *supra* note 396, at 133–77 (Privy Seal and royal orders were being used by the king and executive in a variety of ways contrary to Great Seal and normal administrative processes; Privy Seal was seen as an instrument of the king's personal will); *cf.* Article 6 of *Articuli super Cartas, supra* notes 410–412 (attempt to address Edward I's use of Privy Seal).

foundation of liberty initiated by the Charters.[459] Bertie Wilkinson commented that the Ordainers, beyond providing mere "*consilium*," wanted a partnership with the king in Parliament.[460] With the Ordinances, we see "common counsel" moving beyond a feudal rule of assent and advice, beyond a negative, toward parliamentary participation in several key and national areas for good government, accountability, and common profit and welfare.[461]

C. The Ordainers, Rebellion, and the Statute of York

The Ordainers' ambitious reform goals faced a host of royal obstacles. Gaveston's murder in 1312 converted powerful opponents to the king's side.[462] More importantly, baronial opposition was subdued by executive machinery.[463] Deflecting reform, Edward II was able to maintain control of affairs through the traditional components of a monarch: the king's household, royal officers, and his control of the Council. The Ordainers desired to revitalize Parliament as a center for reform. But that revitalization required extensive personnel management. Reducing the royal hold of the executive and household was a necessary part of baronial reform.[464] J.C. Davies commented that the Ordainers

---

[459] MADDICOTT, ORIGINS, *supra* note 52, at 346.

[460] 2 WILKINSON, CONST. HIST., *supra* note 149, at 14-15.

[461] JOLLIFFE, CONST. HIST., *supra* note 49, at 365-67, 369; *supra* Chapter VI sec. B.

[462] DAVIES, *supra* note 396, at 322-23; *supra* note 417.

[463] DAVIES, *supra* note 396, at 248, 281-87, 298, 304, 307-08, 322-27, 335, 341-42.

[464] *Id.* at 310-11, 343, 349-56.

sought appointment power over all, or nearly all, of the king's household and council.[465]

Accordingly, the era of the Ordainers marked a transition in the composition of Parliament, from being primarily composed of professional ministers and justices to one of knights, burgesses, and barons.[466] Jolliffe observed that by the end of Edward I's reign, the Council was the primary component of Parliament with barons as "spectators and auditors whose agreement might be sought at the king's discretion. . . ."[467] In Edward II's Parliaments, Ordainers and other nonprofessionals joined or infiltrated the Council, and the baronial element was seen as a superior force over the professionals.[468] "By the end of [Edward II's] reign[,] the magnates had established themselves as the king's primary Council in Parliament, absorbing the sworn [professional] Council into their larger body, and resuming [the professional Council's] primi-

---

[465] *Id.* at 371-72, 430. The Ordainer Council was to infiltrate the household to further the effectiveness of baronial coercion and restraint. *Id.* at 412-13, 420-21, 451-52, 464-68.

[466] SAYLES, KING'S PARLIAMENT, *supra* note 112, at 99-101 (Small Council of professionals afforced with Great Council for significant or difficult matters; Parliament no longer merely "Council in Parliament"; "peers" or lords held prominent role in Parliament's judgments). Knights and burgesses frequently attended Parliament after 1312. BROWN, *supra* note 158, at 185-206.

[467] JOLLIFFE, CONST. HIST., *supra* note 49, at 363.

[468] By this time, there was an inner council of advisors personal to the king. DAVIES, *supra* note 396, at 248-50. The larger council had the potential to be less personal to the king and subject to baronial influence. *Id.* at 282-83, 301-02 (commenting that the presence of opposition barons in Parliament and Great Councils made royal control more difficult); *see also id.* at 290-97 (noting difficulty of defining and separating Great Council from Parliament); *id.* at 304-05, 396-97 (weighty matters assigned from Council to Great Council with barons for final decision); *id.* at 352-53, 368 (baronial control over council); JOLLIFFE, CONST. HIST., *supra* note 49, at 365-67, 369 (barons took over Edwardian concept of Council in Parliament and required petitions and major actions go through it).

tive function as the enacting authority of legislation."[469] The Commons, in turn, gravitated toward the position that the barons held in Edward I's reign: present but not yet required.[470]

Edward II initially assented to the Ordinances but challenged them soon thereafter.[471] The Ordinances went far beyond what the king had envisioned and were too much for royalists. He recognized that the Ordinances supplanted his prerogative and conflicted with his coronation oath.

The king and royalists, however, lost support in 1314 due to a failed military campaign and were forced to yield to baronial opposition and compliance with the Ordinances.[472] Capitalizing on growing baronial influence, in 1316 Thomas of Lancaster, a leading Ordainer, became head of the king's Council. The Ordinances were confirmed. Lancaster required that the king address grievances concerning those matters that were not done for the "common profit" of the realm. Further, Lancaster required that evil councilors be dismissed.[473] All important matters were to go through Lancaster and the baronial Council.[474]

---

[469] JOLLIFFE, CONST. HIST., *supra* note 49, at 363.

[470] *Id.* at 363, 370.

[471] DAVIES, *supra* note 396, at 392-93, 486-90; Richardson, *supra* note 53, at 68-70 (the Ordinances conflicted with the king's coronation oath, right and reason, and king's duty).

[472] DAVIES, *supra* note 396, at 394-407.

[473] *Id.* at 412-24.

[474] *Id.* at 421-22.

But there was division among royalists, moderates, and opposition barons.[475] The years 1321-1322 saw a divided baronial uprising followed by a reversal of baronial success.[476] The end of Edward II's reign resembled the beginning. Father and son, both Hugh Despenser, counselors of the king like Gaveston, were a target for a renewed attack on Edward's administration.[477] The Despensers had unraveled the opposition's successes in reforming the king's household.[478] Symbolic of the Ordainers' transformation of Parliament, the barons or peers of Parliament exiled the Despensers and forced the king to agree.[479]

Shortly thereafter, Edward II and the Despensers were able to regain control and savagely took revenge against baronial rebels.[480] Lancaster and others were executed without common-law legal process, without arraignment or an opportunity to answer.[481]

---

[475] By the end of 1318, compromises reaffirmed the Ordinances and placed a standing council in control. 2 TOUT, CHAPTERS, *supra* note 332, at 205-06, 246-48. But these compromises failed to secure peace among the factions and conflict resumed. *Infra* notes 477-478. For the period 1311-1321, see MADDICOTT, LANCASTER, *supra* note 433; J.R.S. PHILLIPS, AYMER DE VALENCE, EARL OF PEMBROKE 1307-1324 (1972).

[476] N. FRYDE, THE TYRANNY AND FALL OF EDWARD II, 1322-1326 (1979).

[477] DAVIES, *supra* note 396, at 469-84.

[478] *Id.*

[479] 2 WILKINSON, CONST. HIST., *supra* note 149, at 18-19, 153-55 (Peers' judgment exiling Despensers); SAYLES, KING'S PARLIAMENT, *supra* note 112, at 100-101. The Despensers were exiled *in abstentia* without proper legal process, and the judgment was reversed the next year. THOMPSON, *supra* note 304, at 74-75.

[480] PRESTWICH, *supra* note 406, at 201-02.

[481] 2 WILKINSON, CONST. HIST., *supra* note 149, at 174. The king recorded Lancaster's notorious acts of treason and rebellion, which were common-

Edward's reclaim of royal authority was marked by the Statute of York, 1322, which formally rescinded parts of the Ordinances because they were in derogation of the rights of the crown.[482] Royalists rejected the idea that the barons controlled the "ideal" crown or "right and reason" over the king. Future baronial reforms placing governance in committees through nonroyal procedure (such as the Ordinances and the 1258 Committee and Council) were prohibited.[483] Governance was returned to the king.

But the king did not reject all of the previous decade's reform efforts, only those in derogation of his regalian rights. The Statute of York confirmed law by the "assent of the prelates, earls and barons, and the commonalty [community] of the realm, as has been accustomed formerly."[484] Scholarship debates the role of knights and burgesses, "the Commons," in 1322. "Commonalty" might mean Lords and Commons but it could also mean Lords

---

ly known among the barons. PLUCKNETT, STUDIES, VI, *supra* note 274, at 546-47; *see also* T.F.T. Plucknett, *The Origin of Impeachment*, 24 TRANS. OF ROYAL HIST. SOCIETY (4th Series) 47-71 (1942). Up until this era, the king's personal record was sufficient proof for judgment. PLUCKNETT, STUDIES, VI, *supra*, at 547. *See infra* note 591 (justices of peace and coroners could also record crimes committed in their presence). But the concept of sufficient process was changing in this era. Henry of Lancaster, Thomas's brother, petitioned in 1327 that his brother's conviction was without arraignment and answer and the king's ability to record guilt was limited to war times. PLUCKNETT, STUDIES, VI, *supra*, at 549-50. Henry claimed that any subject in time of peace ought to be arraigned, have the opportunity to answer, and be convicted by process of law. Nobles and barons agreed and reversed the judgment in 1327.

482 3 ROTHWELL, ENG. HIST. DOCS., *supra* note 3, at 543-44; *see also* Richardson, *supra* note 53, at 69-70.

483 2 WILKINSON, CONST. HIST., *supra* note 149, at 135, 155-56.

484 3 ROTHWELL, ENG. HIST. DOCS., *supra* note 3, at 543-44.

alone.[485] Sayles counseled against reading too much parliamentary procedure into the Statute of York as the days of king, Lords, and Commons would come later.[486] Soon, however, knights and burgesses would replace the barons as the "community," though the Lords as Peers remained the dominant component of Parliament (except for the king) throughout the medieval age.[487] After Edward II's reign, the king and Council alone were no longer enough for a statute as it had been in Edward I's day. The barons and the community were a permanent fixture of Parliament.[488]

Wilkinson posited that the royal reclaim of 1322 rejected baronial reform so thoroughly that it damned the stream of reform such that another crisis or overflow was inevitable. "The more the monarchy was made unchangeable, the more men's minds were likely to turn to the possibility of changing the ruler."[489] The barons fell back to the coronation oath and the 1308 Declaration. Separating the crown from the king's person, the barons concluded that Edward II was not fulfilling the crown's obligations. In 1326, Queen Isabella and Roger Mortimer, Earl of March, led a rebellion against Edward II.[490] Having tasted accountability in Parliament, the lords tried to depose him in the

---

485 2 WILKINSON, CONST. HIST., *supra* note 149, at 144-46; GAILLARD T. LAPSLEY, CROWN, COMMUNITY AND PARLIAMENT IN THE LATER MIDDLE AGES: STUDIES IN ENGLISH CONSTITUTIONAL HISTORY 153-62 (1951).

486 SAYLES, KING'S PARLIAMENT, *supra* note 112, at 101-106 (Lords and not Commons were the essence of "community" in the thirteenth century and early fourteenth century).

487 *Infra* Chapter VI sec. D.

488 *Supra* note 484; *see also* Morris, *Introduction in* 1 ENG. GOV. AT WORK, *supra* note 392, at 13-29.

489 2 WILKINSON, CONST. HIST., *supra* note 149, at 21.

490 3 TOUT, CHAPTERS, *supra* note 332, at 1.

form of a judgment in Parliament, but the court of Parliament was still with the king.[491] For the king was an essential component and still, at this time, initiated law for his Parliament.[492] He could not be deposed in Parliament unless he condemned himself.[493] Jolliffe observed that the attempted deposition resembled formal diffidation as barons renounced homage in Parliament. Parliament, though a branch of the king's tree, acted independently of the king, a precedent for its impeachment power in the latter part of the century.[494] Edward II, facing deposition, abdicated his throne in 1327 in favor of his son.[495]

Edward III was a minor in 1327, and a council-regency influenced by the Lancasters was in charge.[496] Isabella and Mortimer were able to prevent the council from rule, which contributed to division between the Lancasters and Mortimer.[497] In the disorder, Mortimer's grip failed, and in 1330 Edward III ousted him. Mortimer stood accused by the king's record for various misdemeanors and for assuming royal power. As a symbol of Parliament's growth as a center for accountability during Edward II's

---

[491] 2 WILKINSON, CONST. HIST., *supra* note 149, at 160-62.

[492] *Id.* at 160.

[493] *Id.* at 161.

[494] JOLLIFFE, CONST. HIST., *supra* note 49, at 371-72. But the Lords and Commons attempted to use a quasi-judicial procedure and gave some structure to Parliament's judgment. 2 WILKINSON, CONST. HIST., *supra* note 149, at 162.

[495] Claire Valente, *The Deposition and Abdication of Edward II*, 113 ENG. HIST. REV. 852 (1998). Edward was later executed.

[496] 3 TOUT, CHAPTERS, *supra* note 332, at 10.

[497] *Id.* at 14-15.

reign, Edward III yielded Mortimer's fate to Parliament's judgment of peers.[498]

Like Edward I's succession following Henry III, Edward III was receptive to the previous reign's reforms.[499] Encouraged by the Ordainers' energy, the end of Edward II's and the beginning of Edward III's reign was marked with populist ideals. The *vox populi* (voice of the people) gave legitimacy to the law.[500] In 1330, Edward III promised to govern the realm's business according to conscience, right, and reason, and by the common counsel of the Lords.

> And we wish all men to know that in future we will govern our people according to right and reason, as is fitting our royal dignity; and that the matters which touch us and the estate of our realm are to be disposed of by the common counsel of the magnates of our realm, and not in any other manner.[501]

---

[498] The events of 1327 influenced young Edward III's process against the younger Mortimer in 1330. The king provided notorious facts to the Lords but allowed the Lords in Parliament to convict by *judicium parium*, which was essentially automatic as the king's facts were not subject to defense and proof. PLUCKNETT, STUDIES, VI, *supra* note 274, at 550-51. In 1354, an heir successfully challenged the peers' conviction of Mortimer. Mortimer was brought to trial based on notorious facts and the king's record but without indictment and answer. *Id.* at 552; *see also* Alan Rogers, *Parliamentary Appeals of Treason in the Reign of Richard II*, 8 AM. J. OF LEGAL HIST. 95, 112 (1964).

[499] 2 WILKINSON, CONST. HIST., *supra* note 149, at 168-69 (Edward III's succession); *see also supra* notes 296-299 (Henry III's succession); *supra* notes 398-403 (Edward I's succession).

[500] Valente, *supra* note 495, at 865-66 (noting the perception of "authority of the people" in the deposition of Edward II and coronation of Edward III: "*vox populi, vox Dei,*" voice of the people, voice of God; "*populi dat iura voluntas,*" will of the people gives [authority to the] laws).

[501] 2 WILKINSON, CONST. HIST., *supra* note 149, at 173-74.

D. The Commons' Petition

As we saw with the Ordainers and Ordinances, the change that took place during the first half of the fourteenth century was an expansion of the meaning and membership of a session of Parliament. The barons, knights, and burgesses, and the functions of assenting to taxes and important matters converged on the petition and judicial sessions of the Council in Parliament.[502] Throughout Edward I's reign, "Parliament" was an expanded session of the King in Council addressing petitions.[503] During the era of the Ordainers and Ordinances, Parliament's composition changed from ministers and judges to lords and peers.[504] The process of petitions remained a parliamentary function, expanding from private judicial complaints to common taxation, accountability, and other political matters. As an instrument with several uses, the petition was a hallmark of the English constitution.[505]

In the early part of the fourteenth century, petitions were brought by individuals but also by representatives. By the year of Isabella and Mortimer, knights and burgesses began to assume the identity of the petitioner petitioning the Lords and Peers of Par-

---

502 *Supra* Chapter VI secs. B–C. By the mid-fourteenth century, the Commons, likely at the crown's discretion, were summoned to Parliament along with the Lords. PRESTWICH, *supra* note 406, at 185–87 (commenting that the early fourteenth century was a transition period in Parliament's function and composition); *see also* MAY MCKISACK, THE FOURTEENTH CENTURY 1307–1399, at 187–91 (1959).

503 *Supra* Chapter V sec. C.

504 *Supra* notes 462–470.

505 HARDING, *supra* note 49, at 81, 86–88, 121.

liament on behalf of the community.[506] Petitions that implicated the state or a large subset of common men became known as "common petitions."[507] Petitioning individuals, groups, and communities sought to have the knights and burgesses, the Commons, endorse their petitions to become Commons' petitions.[508] Jolliffe explained that if only one community petitioned the king on an individual matter, his grant was like a charter or privilege to that community. If all the communities petitioned the king or the matter were common, his grant was a law or statute by the authority of King in Parliament.[509]

By Edward III's reign, the Commons regularly petitioned Parliament, initiating legislation on national issues and authorizing fiscal grants. The Lords judged petitions. Sayles added that the conception of Lords as peers in the early to mid-fourteenth century contributed to the role of Commons as petitioners. When peers were on the Council for adjudication of petitions, they served as the judges. Because a common maxim held that the petitioner could not also be a judge, Commons petitioned and Lords judged.[510] A bicameralism developed. Once put into form by the professionals of the Council and approved by the Lords and the

---

[506] HARRISS, KING & PARLIAMENT, *supra* note 36, at 118-127; SAYLES, KING'S PARLIAMENT, *supra* note 112, at 106-07; MCKISACK, *supra* note 502, at 104 (highlighting the importance of Parliament's function as well as the Commons' presence within Parliament; sixteen Commons' petitions in 1330 became statutes).

[507] DODD, *supra* note 14, at 128-55, 254-58.

[508] W. Mark Ormrod, *Murmur, Clamour and Noise: Voicing Complaint and Remedy in Petitions to the English Crown, c.1300-c.1460 in* MEDIEVAL PETITIONS, *supra* note 368, at 137; SAYLES, KING'S PARLIAMENT, *supra* note 112, at 118-19.

[509] JOLLIFFE, CONST. HIST., *supra* note 49, at 337.

[510] SAYLES, KING'S PARLIAMENT, *supra* note 112, at 106-07.

king's superior authority, the common petition became enacted statute.[511] With all this business and lords constituting the primary component of Parliament, its judicial function between individuals fell behind its new role as a tax-granting and legislative organ for important matters such as confirmation and modification of the common law.[512] Individual petitions before Parliament were channeled off to other departments.[513]

Edward III's reign marked the rise of the Commons' position in the form and initiation of the statute.[514] The Commons' petition became a regular component of Parliament's statute-making process and a source of the law.[515] The reforms of 1258 had failed because the community of barons attempted reform within the king's Council.[516] Fourteenth-century reforms were more invasive and operating in Parliament at arm's length from the king. Law from below—legislation by petition—became a normal process. Sayles commented that statute based on petition

---

[511] JOLLIFFE, CONST. HIST., *supra* note 49, at 372-74, 377-81; DODD, *supra* note 14, at 141-55.

[512] Sayles noted that thirteenth-century barons, lay and ecclesiastic, felt they were above most judicial work. SAYLES, KING'S PARLIAMENT, *supra* note 112, at 26-27. When they joined Parliament, it's natural that Parliament delegated most judicial work to others. *Id.*

[513] SAYLES, KING'S PARLIAMENT, *supra* note 112, at 109-111; *supra* note 382.

[514] HARRISS, KING & PARLIAMENT, *supra* note 36, at 118-27; JOLLIFFE, CONST. HIST., *supra* note 49, at 377-80; MUSSON & ORMROD, EVOLUTION OF ENG. JUSTICE, *supra* note 162, at 146; SAYLES, KING'S PARLIAMENT, *supra* note 112, at 115; 2 HOLDSWORTH, *supra* note 113, at 435.

[515] HARRISS, KING & PARLIAMENT, *supra* note 36, at 356-75. Elected knights and burgesses that were present in Commons scheduled a time to address common petitions. Ormrod, *Murmur, Clamour and Noise in* MEDIEVAL PETITIONS, *supra* note 368, at 136.

[516] *Supra* notes 353-358.

transformed the significance of statute from a kingly declaration of law to a resolution of justice owed to the community who brought the petition or on whose behalf the petition was introduced.[517]

In the years of Edward III, the Commons made many petitions but only a few were true statutes affecting new matters. The Commons, perhaps immature and unsophisticated, had a large presence in petitioning but a much more minor role in actual statute-law creation. Sayles observed that many Commons' petitions did not become statutes and those that did were declaratory of existing law, haphazard, and otherwise not controversial.[518] Even in this period of heightened activity by the Commons, the king and Council were the professionals and thus a powerful element of government and legislation.[519]

Contrary to today's concept of statute, the king's acceptance of a common petition was a judgment acknowledging a grievance rather than a sacred, binding text.[520] If it came down to a controversial matter, the will of the king overcame the will of the Commons and the Lords. Sayles wrote that the medieval king did not feel bound by statutes.[521] He could alter, dispense, or an-

---

[517] SAYLES, KING'S PARLIAMENT, *supra* note 112, at 86.

[518] *Id.* at 115-16; *see also* JOLLIFFE, CONST. HIST., *supra* note 49, at 449.

[519] Petitions were edited by the Council's professionals. G.L. Harriss, *The Formation of Parliament 1272-1377 in* DAVIES & DENTON, ENG. PARL. IN THE MIDDLE AGES, *supra* note 335, at 46-47.

[520] *Supra* notes 448-456 (contrasting Edwardian statutes and ordinances with later statutes adopted by Parliament's commonalty).

[521] SAYLES, KING'S PARLIAMENT, *supra* note 112, at 86, 116-17.

nul them as he saw necessary.[522] But the permanent change taking place in Edward III's reign was the legitimacy of the Commons and Lords as a source of the law. By the end of the fourteenth century, the ordinance of King in Council became disassociated with Parliament and generally subordinate to the statute.[523]

E. The King's Council and Common Law

The rise of the Commons and Commons' petition illuminated a problem in the competing sources of the law. As the Lords and Commons became a permanent presence in governance, they resented actions contrary to the common law, which put them in conflict with the Council's traditional powers.

The Council was an important part of fourteenth-century governance. During the reigns of Edward I and Edward II, the Council held a delegated judicial role in entertaining petitions at Parliament.[524] With more and more reliance on the Council's functions, its actions were scrutinized. Though at times Parliament recognized the Council's useful methods, Lords and Com-

---

522 *Supra* notes 64-67, 195-198, 393-397. The king's power to annul, suspend, or dispense with the law was part of his power as king and the protector of the welfare of the realm. *Supra* notes 20-24, 32-36 (common utility and law of necessity).

523 Harriss, *The Formation of Parliament in* DAVIES & DENTON, ENG. PARL. IN THE MIDDLE AGES, *supra* note 335, at 48-60 (describing Parliament's transformation from a center for petitions and judicial grievances to a source of government); RICHARDSON & SAYLES, *Early Statutes*, (XXV), *in* ENGLISH PARLIAMENT, *supra* note 331, at 31-47 (commenting on the difficulty of distinguishing between statute and ordinance and describing the changes to the fourteenth-century meaning of statute). The statute's significance likewise increased as the Magna Carta, statute, and common law merged under the binding authority of Lords, Commons, and the king in Parliament. THOMPSON, *supra* note 304, at 60-61.

524 WILKINSON, STUDIES, *supra* note 314, at 128.

mons resisted conciliar governance conflicting with the common law. Judicial and legislative action by the Council was not a satisfactory substitute.

Legislatively, there was concern that the Council would extend and amend acts of Parliament when Parliament was not in session.[525] The Council had a large role in editing, shaping, and formulating legislation before and after a session of Parliament.[526] Parliamentary procedure was weak, and the Council was likely able to overshadow the Commons' competence and influence. With all of the work on private petitions being done by the Council or by a committee of hearers, there were complaints that the common law or law of the land was adversely affected. Toward the end of Edward III's reign, the Commons did not want the hearers determining points of law affecting the law of the land outside of Parliament.[527] The Commons petitioned that no article of a statute be repealed by the Council and that neither the Council nor the chancellor make any ordinance against the common law after Parliament has ended.[528] It was declared in 1377 that a

---

[525] *Id.* at 127-28.

[526] Baldwin, KING'S COUNCIL, *supra* note 154, at 138, 318-20 (Council amended or altered statutes outside of Parliament; tallages, impositions, or loans instituted by Council without Parliament; ordinances passed by king and Council in derogation of common law).

[527] *Id.* at 325-26 (forbidding judgments contrary to law of the land unless by Parliament); 1 HOLDSWORTH, *supra* note 113, at 359 (baronial hearers of petitions rather than professionals).

[528] WILKINSON, STUDIES, *supra* note 314, at 127-28.

statute granted in Parliament could only be annulled in Parliament.[529]

From a judicial perspective, the protections of common-law process were well regarded; however, the tedious rules and requirements prevented effective justice.[530] Hence, the Council, with general approval, was adapting its special jurisdiction, as the chancellor and Council were not confined to common-law procedure and thus were seen as a method for summary disposition without delay.[531] The Council's judicial role was clearly acknowledged in 1346 when the chancellor, treasurer, and councilors were given expanded jurisdiction over complaints against sheriffs and officers.[532] The king could intervene in litigation and have the matter affecting the king brought to Council for trial.[533]

James F. Baldwin recounted that the Council's jurisdiction, though referred to as extraordinary, was really the original jurisdiction of the king.[534] He always had an exception to the law be-

---

[529] Harriss, *The Formation of Parliament in* DAVIES & DENTON, ENG. PARL. IN THE MIDDLE AGES, *supra* note 335, at 48; *supra* note 501 (importance of community in law-making); *supra* notes 517, 523 (importance of statute).

[530] *Supra* notes 338-342 (importance of petitions in the 1258 reforms); *supra* notes 363-383 (Edward I and petitions); *supra* notes 444-447 (Edward II and petitions in Parliament); *supra* Chapter VI sec. D (the "common petition").

[531] I.S. LEADAM & J.F. BALDWIN, SELECT CASES BEFORE THE KING'S COUNCIL 1243-1482, at xviii (1918) (hereinafter LEADAM & BALDWIN, SELECT CASES) (noting that petitions to Council served as an alternative to petitions in Parliament, which were backlogged); *see also supra* note 376 (petitions of grace).

[532] BALDWIN, KING'S COUNCIL, *supra* note 154, at 243.

[533] LEADAM & BALDWIN, SELECT CASES, *supra* note 531, at xxvii.

[534] BALDWIN, KING'S COUNCIL, *supra* note 154, at 262.

cause he had a divine right of kingship from God. The Council retained the power and status of the undivided *curia* and thus held the power of the king's justice and equity.[535] Baldwin noted that conciliar judgment was not bound by precedent nor was it intended to create precedent.[536] The older jurisdiction of the *curia* was intertwined with ecclesiastic authority and Roman civil law.[537] Many of the councilors were ecclesiastics. The Council, with its equity and the king's grace, was able to proceed by conscience and reason, though following the common law when applicable.[538]

The judicial work of the Council caused many grievances and complaints by the Commons.[539] The Council could hear

---

535 JOLLIFFE, CONST. HIST., *supra* note 49, at 338.

536 BALDWIN, KING'S COUNCIL, *supra* note 154, at 225. Because it was by the force of reason, the Council's equitable adjudication was not meant to serve as a precedent but was built upon an exception. *Id.*

537 *Id.* at 280.

538 3 WILKINSON, CONST. HIST., *supra* note 149, at 126–27; BALDWIN, KING'S COUNCIL, *supra* note 154, at 222, 225, 281; *supra* note 376 (petition of grace permitting common-law actions). The Council's, and later the Chancellor's, equity was an important source of justice and hence the law before the rule of law. Divine justice and royal equity were forms of quasi-positive law that could dispense with the letter of statute before the battle between equity and the rule of law—the rule of law here being the common law and Parliament. MILSOM, *supra* note 339, at 82; *supra* note 397. Milsom clarified that English equity in the medieval and Tudor period under the Chancellor was not defiance of statute or controlling Parliament's authority but rather interpreting justice in an age before Parliament was supreme over the royal prerogative of divine justice. MILSOM, *supra*, at 92; *see also* JEFFREY GOLDSWORTHY, THE SOVEREIGNTY OF PARLIAMENT: HISTORY AND PHILOSOPHY 45 (1999) (medieval interpretation of the law not a precedent for modern concept of judicial review).

539 Faith Thompson discussed several fourteenth-century statutes that expanded upon Chapter 39's meaning and were relied upon heavily in the seventeenth-century understanding of "due process of law" and "law of the land." THOMPSON, *supra* note 304, at 86–97; *infra* notes 686–698.

complaints by petition or bill.[540] It could arrest and put defendants on trial on the basis of an informer's public or private "information" or "suggestion" alone without indictment or presentment, without the common-law writ or appeal.[541] The Council could order the arrest of an individual by summary writs that varied significantly from the corresponding procedures at common law.[542] The conciliar process was secret. Parties brought before the Council were forced to submit to its jurisdiction and agree to honor its decision. Contrary to the common-law process, the criminal defendant was not necessarily informed of the charge, and if the matter were a felony, the defendant was not permitted the aid of an attorney and was not able to confront his accusers.[543] Conciliar fact-finding took place by commission or by inquisition and was considered intimidating and self-incriminating.[544]

The seventeenth-century understanding in turn heavily influenced American judicial use of "due process of law." *Infra* Chapter X.

540 LEADAM & BALDWIN, SELECT CASES, *supra* note 531, at xxxv; BALDWIN, KING'S COUNCIL, *supra* note 154, at 281-84; *supra* notes 367-370.

541 LEADAM & BALDWIN, SELECT CASES, *supra* note 531, at xxxvi-vii. For appeal of felony, see Margaret H. Kerr, *Angevin Reform of the Appeal of Felony*, 13 LAW & HIST. REV. 351 (1995); BAKER, *supra* note 88, at 57-59 (appeal of felony did not require an original writ but was typically accompanied by a writ of attachment to produce the defendant).

542 LEADAM & BALDWIN, SELECT CASES, *supra* note 531, at xxxviii-xl (writs issued to arrest and bring defendants before the Council for certain causes [*quibusdam certis de causis*] under penalty [*sub poena*]); BALDWIN, KING'S COUNCIL, *supra* note 154, at 288-91 (comparing conciliar procedure with common-law procedure).

543 LEADAM & BALDWIN, SELECT CASES, *supra* note 531, at xlii-xliv; BALDWIN, KING'S COUNCIL, *supra* note 154, at 288-89, 297-98.

544 LEADAM & BALDWIN, SELECT CASES, *supra* note 531, at xlii-xliv.

As early as Edward I's reign, it was argued that if the common law were applicable (that is, the king was not at issue), then the matter should not be heard at the Exchequer or Council.[545] Similar complaints had been made against the use of the Privy Seal in a manner contrary to the common law.[546] The Commons wanted all personal actions between private parties tried by common law and not by Council.[547]

In 1351 or 1352, the Commons prayed that the common law be kept for property, life, and limb.[548]

> Whereas it is contained in the great charter of the franchises of England, that none shall be imprisoned nor put out of Freehold, nor of his Franchises nor free custom, unless it be by the Law of the Land; it is accorded, assented, and [e]stablished, That from henceforth none shall be taken by Petition or Suggestion made to our Lord the King, or to his Council, unless it be by Indictment or Presentment of good and lawful People of the same Neighborhood where such Deeds be done, in due manner, or by Process made by Writ original at the Common Law; nor that none be out of his Franchises, nor of his Freeholds, unless he be duly brought into An-

---

545 BALDWIN, KING'S COUNCIL, *supra* note 154, at 218, 279 (citing statutes forbidding conciliar process in derogation of the Charter and the law of the land).

546 J.F. Baldwin, *The King's Council in* 1 ENG. GOV. AT WORK, *supra* note 392, at 154 (Privy Seal being used for arbitrary arrest and imprisonment); *supra* note 458 (complaints in *Articuli* and the Ordinances against the Privy Seal's use).

547 BALDWIN, KING'S COUNCIL, *supra* note 154, at 144.

548 The Council could imprison and pillory but did not exercise the power to inflict punishment of life and limb. LEADAM & BALDWIN, SELECT CASES, *supra* note 531, at xxvi, xlv-xlvi; BALDWIN, KING'S COUNCIL, *supra* note 154, at 304.

> swer, and forejudged of the same by the Course of the Law.[549]

A similar statute of 1354:

> That no man of what Estate or Condition that he be, shall be put out of Land or Tenement, nor take, nor imprisoned, nor disinherited, nor put to Death, without being brought in Answer by due Process of Law.[550]

One injustice generating grievances with the Commons was the failure of conciliar judicial process to root out false information. The Council's summary proceedings and secrecy removed safeguards. The Commons alleged that individuals, when confronted with legal proceedings against them, made spiteful false suggestions against others.[551] The Commons grieved that individuals were suffering criminal sanctions initiated by false suggestions and were deprived of judicial protections long ago secured at common law and through the Magna Carta.[552] In 1363, it was argued that petitioners proceeding by suggestion or information should seek surety to give proof to their claims.

> [T]hough that it be contained in the Great Charter, that no man be taken nor imprisoned, nor

---

[549] 25 Edw. III, Stat. 5, ch. 4 (1351/1352); *see also* THOMPSON, *supra* note 304, at 91; Keith Jurow, *Untimely Thoughts: A Reconsideration of the Origins of Due Process of Law*, 19 AM. J. OF LEGAL HIST. 265, 268 (1975); LEADAM & BALDWIN, SELECT CASES, *supra* note 531, at xxxvii; BALDWIN, KING'S COUNCIL, *supra* note 154, at 279.

[550] 28 Edw. III ch. 3 (1354); *see also* THOMPSON, *supra* note 304, at 92; Jurow, *supra* note 549, at 266-68.

[551] BALDWIN, KING'S COUNCIL, *supra* note 154, at 286, 340; LEADAM & BALDWIN, SELECT CASES, *supra* note 531, at xxxvii-viii.

[552] LEADAM & BALDWIN, SELECT CASES, *supra* note 531, at xxxvi-viii.

> put out of his freehold, without process of the law; nevertheless divers people make false suggestions to the King himself, as well for malice as otherwise, whereof the King is often grieved, and divers of the realm put in damage, against the form of the same charter: wherefore it is ordained, That all they that make such suggestions, be sent with the suggestions before the chancellor, treasurer and his council, and that they there find surety to pursue their suggestions, and incur the same pain that the other should have had if he were attainted, in case that his suggestion be found evil. And that then, at that time, process of the law be made against them, without being taken or imprisoned against the form of the said charter and other statutes.[553]

For simplicity, the several "due process of law" grievances, petitions, and statutes of the fourteenth century sought to curb the Council's jurisdiction which did not operate with common-law process.[554] The Commons and Parliament sought to protect the

---

[553] 37 Edw. III ch. 18 (1363); *see also* 42 Edw. III ch. 3 (Commons petitioned that "no man be put to answer without presentment before the justices, or matter of record, or by due process and original writ, according to the old law of the land"). *See generally* BALDWIN, KING'S COUNCIL, *supra* note 154, at 243–44; LEADAM & BALDWIN, SELECT CASES, *supra* note 531, at xxxvii; PLUCKNETT, CONST. HIST., *supra* note 59, at 114–16.

[554] For a summary of fourteenth-century due-process-of-law statutes, see THOMPSON, *supra* note 304, at 86–97; Powicke, *Per Judicium Parium vel Per Legem Terrae*, *in* MAGNA CARTA COMM. ESSAYS, *supra* note 238, at 116 (equating the phrase "due process of law" with indictment and presentment of the county and hundred); CAM, MAGNA CARTA, *supra* note 453, at 19. Plucknett hypothesized that the Commons used the phrase "due process of law" to characterize several processes that had hitherto been invoked inconsistently by the Commons. PLUCKNETT, STUDIES, VIII, *supra* note 274, at 154 n.1.

law of the land or at least a certain character of the law of the land.[555]

While Parliament might not have trusted the Council's methods *in toto*, they recognized and took advantage of conciliar processes for certain cases. The king acknowledged the protection of the common-law courts for several matters but with a saving clause that allowed the Council to handle matters where justice required.[556] The common law was considered ineffective on alien, maritime, and commercial matters as well as for serious crimes like fraud, riots, and contempt in which the parties refused to obey common-law processes.[557] Conciliar justice was more effective when one party was poor and powerless but the other was wealthy and powerful.[558] During the Tudors and Stuarts, the Council's jurisdiction grew into the infamous Star Chamber before being abolished in the seventeenth century.[559]

F. Archbishop Stratford and *Judicium Parium*

In addition to disputing the Council's legislative and judicial powers, the Lords and Commons also engaged in a mid-

---

555 *Supra* note 191 (discussing common law and law of the land). For the dispute on common law versus law of the land in the seventeenth century, see Chapter VIII. For this dispute in the early nineteenth century, see Chapter X sec. A.

556 BALDWIN, KING'S COUNCIL, *supra* note 154, at 144, 279-80.

557 *Id.* at 219-24, 265-78, 339; LEADAM & BALDWIN, SELECT CASES, *supra* note 531, at xxvi-vii, xxx-xxxi, xxxvii (Council appropriate forum to judge king's officers, aliens, powerful lords, foreign litigants, rioters, and those in contumacious disregard of legal process).

558 *Supra* note 557.

559 G.R. ELTON, THE TUDOR CONSTITUTION: DOCUMENTS AND COMMENTARY 163-86 (2d ed. 1982); 6 HOLDSWORTH, *supra* note 113, at 112; *infra* note 713.

fourteenth-century confrontation with the king, which brought about a temporary reform effort resembling the Ordinances of 1311.

In the late 1330s, Edward III was having trouble collecting money for his war with France.[560] By 1340, knights and burgesses, who had been present in the parleys and Great Councils to date, viewed themselves as a required element for granting taxation.[561] Mirroring thirteenth-century concessions, the Commons agreed to grant money conditioned upon the king's reception of their petition.[562] The Commons petitioned for the Charters' confirmation and a parliamentary inquiry into the king's spending so that future taxes would be more wisely spent for their designated purpose. Repeating frequently sought reforms, the Commons' demanded restraint on purveyances, parliamentary taxation, and accountability for maladministration.[563] Edward agreed to several demands in exchange for finances. These petitions became the statutes of 1340 securing the abolition of evil customs and requiring parliamentary consent of Lords and Commons for taxation.[564]

The collection of revenue proceeded unsuccessfully while Edward was away at war. John Stratford was a Lancastrian leader and Archbishop of Canterbury.[565] Stratford, along with other

---

[560] PRESTWICH, *supra* note 406, at 269-72. Edward's war with France was the beginning of the Hundred Years' War.

[561] *Supra* notes 334, 484; *supra* Chapter VI sec. D.

[562] HARRISS, KING & PARLIAMENT, *supra* note 36, at 255-69.

[563] *Id.* at 180-85, 255-69. *See also supra* notes 407-409, 434 (earlier instances of barons advocating for "common profit" in spending and governance).

[564] MCKISACK, *supra* note 502, at 162-63.

[565] *Id.* at 153. Other Stratfords also served in office.

ministers, was held responsible for the failed collection process.[566] In response, Edward III removed several officers.[567] The king felt that his ministers were responsible to him alone and were able to be dismissed by him alone.[568] But this was controversial, as Stratford was a peer and Archbishop. He attempted to insulate himself and others by invoking the Magna Carta and threatening excommunication of those who violate its provisions.[569] Stratford's grandstanding successfully shifted the focus from malfeasance of office to defense of the Magna Carta.[570] The king's attempt to hold ministers accountable was frustrated.

Stratford was eventually charged with contempt of the king's orders.[571] Stratford answered that he, as a peer, should be judged only in full and open Parliament by judgment of peers.[572] The previous century of reform had been slowly encroaching on the king's control over ministers. Barons and the community wanted appointment powers, and appointment and dismissal were two sides of the same coin. Reform efforts had made Par-

---

[566] The council-regency and collection effort depended on Stratford's administration. HARRISS, KING & PARLIAMENT, *supra* note 36, at 261-64, 273-87, 290.

[567] MCKISACK, *supra* note 502, at 166-69.

[568] Edward set up commissions to inquire into the conduct of ministers. The commissions expanded into unpopular general inquiries of local officials and communities. HARRISS, KING & PARLIAMENT, *supra* note 36, at 283-88.

[569] MCKISACK, *supra* note 502, at 170, 173, 174.

[570] MAUDE VIOLET CLARKE, FOURTEENTH CENTURY STUDIES 251 (L.S. Sutherland & M. McKisack eds. 1937).

[571] MCKISACK, *supra* note 502, at 170.

[572] HARRISS, KING & PARLIAMENT, *supra* note 36, at 294-95; MCKISACK, *supra* note 502, at 173.

liament a source of accountability for ministers in order to effect removal. Now Parliament's role and *judicium parium* were being invoked defensively against removal.[573]

Stratford's invocation of the Charter and *judicium parium* put pressure on royal authority and gained some leverage with the barons, clergy, Londoners, and others who were frustrated with Edward's invasive commissions.[574] Several important factions of supporters appealed to the king in favor of Stratford.[575] Petitions asked for confirmation of several protections: to appoint ministers; to maintain compliance with the Charters and other issues in Parliament; to secure privileges of peers in office; and to secure the privileges of Londoners from Edward's offending inquiries.[576] The king was forced to compromise.

The result of the Parliament of 1341 was a baronial-reform statute resembling the Ordinances. The king agreed to confirm the Charters and other laws and provided that anything done against them would be dealt with in Parliament.[577] Ministers were to be held accountable by judgment of peers for violations of the

---

[573] Removal of Justiciar Hubert de Burgh also caused a controversy. *Supra* Chapter V sec. A.

[574] HARRISS, KING & PARLIAMENT, *supra* note 36, at 297-300; MCKISACK, *supra* note 502, at 173-74; *supra* note 568.

[575] LAPSLEY, *supra* note 485, at 250.

[576] *Id.* at 251; PRESTWICH, *supra* note 406, at 276-77.

[577] 2 WILKINSON, CONST. HIST., *supra* note 149, at 200-02. Parliament was the natural choice for determining what the law of the land was and violations thereof. *Supra* Chapter VI secs. B-C (Parliament's rise to power in the Ordinances and thereafter). Lords and Commons also wanted power to interpret the Magna Carta's questionable parts as well as to amend certain sections. *Cf. supra* note 456 (Similar demand by Ordainers).

Magna Carta or the laws of the land.[578] The statute of 1341 contained Magna Carta's due process statement in the form of both due process before execution or enforcement of law as well as what would later be parliamentary privilege: no peer or officer shall be brought to judgment or lose lands, or be imprisoned, outlawed, exiled, arrested for anything because of his duties of office or other cause without a judgment by the peers of land.[579] The Statute of 1341, 15 Edw. III:

> Also, whereas before this time peers of the land have been arrested and imprisoned, and their temporalities, lands and tenements, goods and chattels have been seized into the king's hands, and some have been put to death without judgment of their peers, it is accorded and assented that no peer of the land, either officer or other, shall be brought to judgment, to lose his temporalities, lands, tenements, goods or chattels, or be arrested imprisoned outlawed or exiled, or be forejudged or put to answer, or be judged, because of his office, or because of things touching his office, or for any other cause, except by award of the said peers of parliament. Saving always to our sovereign lord the king and to his heirs, in other cases, the laws rightfully used by due process, and saving the suit of parties. . . .
>
> Also, because the points of the Magna Carta are blemished in several ways, and are not so well observed as they ought to be, to the great peril and slander of the king and to the damage of his people, especially since clerks, peers of the land,

---

[578] 2 WILKINSON, CONST. HIST., *supra* note 149, at 37, 182–84; HARRISS, KING & PARLIAMENT, *supra* note 36, at 298 (accountability in Parliament by *judicium parium*).

[579] Previous decades had witnessed several executive arrests, exiles, and even executions without common-law process or judgment of peers. *Supra* Chapter VI secs. B–C (Gaveston, Lancaster, Despensers, others).

> and other free men, are arrested and imprisoned and deprived of their goods and chattels without being appealed or indicted and against whom no suit of party has been affirmed, it is agreed and assented that in future such things shall not be done. And if any minister of the king, or any other person . . . proceed[s] against any point of the Magna Charta, or against other statutes or laws of the land, he shall answer in parliament, either at the king's suit or at the suit of the party. . . [notwithstanding if he acted by the king's commission or with the authority of previous law that is now annulled].[580]

The forum for grievances against royal officials was Parliament and *judicium parium*.[581]

With the Statute of 1341, we briefly see Lords and Commons recapturing the Ordainers' energy and demonstrating power of opposition to Edward III. Similar to the baronial demands of 1258, the Ordainers had attempted to secure baronial governance in Council and Parliament. The reform effort of 1341 followed suit, seeking to make the council-regency a permanent feature of governance rather than a temporary council when the king was away or a minor.[582]

The 1341 statute, however, followed the common fate of previous reform efforts.[583] The king soon repealed the Statute of 1341 as being against the prerogatives of the king and contrary to the laws and customs of the realm. The statute "shall be entirely

---

[580] 2 WILKINSON, CONST. HIST., *supra* note 149, at 201-02.

[581] HARRISS, KING & PARLIAMENT, *supra* note 36, at 298, 300-01.

[582] *Id.* at 300-01, 304; *cf. supra* note 355 (Henry III noting that he was being treated as ward and minor).

[583] 2 WILKINSON, CONST. HIST., *supra* note 149, at 184-85, 203.

repealed and annulled and shall lose the name of statute, as being prejudicial and contrary to the laws and usages of the realm and to the rights and prerogatives of our lord the king."[584] The king deemed other provisions "reasonable and in accord with law and right."

Despite efforts to have "reason and right" be baronial matters or under baronial supervision, by the mid-fourteenth century it was still the king who was to determine what was reasonable—for the king was bound only by conscience but little else.[585] Baronial-reform efforts had used the coronation oath as a lever for shared governance emerging from feudalism's common counsel.[586] To the extent that his coronation oath bound him to the law of the land, it was the king's place to determine whether his actions were in conformity or not.[587] Once again, we are reminded that the medieval king was still the king and the primary source of governance. External factors of rebellion and deposition were present but likely did not influence Edward III after the Stratford incident. Parliamentary authority and statute had appeal, and the king had Parliament confirm the repeal in 1343. In comparison to the reigns of Edward II before and Richard II after, Edward III's reign was uneventful.

G. Richard II and Impeachment

---

[584] *Id.* at 203.

[585] *Supra* Chapter I; *supra* notes 64-67, 195-198, 263, 393-397, 408, 448, 519-523.

[586] *Supra* Chapter VI secs. A-C.

[587] LAPSLEY, *supra* note 485, at 262; HOLT, MAGNA CARTA, *supra* note 207, at 92-93.

Parliamentary accountability and *judicium parium* touched upon in the Statute of 1341 resurfaced later in the fourteenth century.[588] Impeachment as a function of the High Court of Parliament became a key ideal and reform goal and was volleyed back and forth during fourteenth-century political controversies.

In the 1370s, several in close confidence of the king were abusing their office with inside dealings and corruption.[589] The Commons asserted the right to inquire into the crown's actions and impeach the king's corrupt ministers. The Commons, by the clamor of the community, impeached Lord William Latimer (Chamberlain), Lord John Neville (Steward), Richard Lyons (wealthy sheriff and financier), and others in the "Good Parliament" of 1376 for financial self-dealing and maladministration.[590] Latimer tried to claim defect of common-law process, that he was not arraigned and was not able to answer an accuser, but to no avail. The clamor of the Commons served as a substitute for legal process.[591] The judgment of Lords satisfied *judicium parium.*

---

[588] LAPSLEY, *supra* note 485, at 269.

[589] PLUCKNETT, CONST. HIST., *supra* note 59, at 164–65.

[590] GEORGE HOLMES, THE GOOD PARLIAMENT 108–10 (1975); *see also* 3 TOUT, CHAPTERS, *supra* note 332, at 286–302; COLIN G.C. TITE, IMPEACHMENT AND PARLIAMENTARY JUDICATURE IN EARLY STUART ENGLAND 5–23 (1974).

[591] PLUCKNETT, STUDIES, VIII, *supra* note 274, at 157–161 (Commons served as "grand inquest"); *cf. supra* note 481 (Lancaster's execution); *supra* Chapter VI sec. E (claims for due process of law vis-à-vis conciliar justice).

Due process in the beginning of the fourteenth century was not confined to indictment and presentment. Criminals caught red-handed deserved no further process. PLUCKNETT, STUDIES, VI, *supra*, at 548; *supra* note 92. Acts that were notoriously known by the king, the community, or prominent legal figures needed no further action. The king could convict a traitor by his record of the acts. PLUCKNETT, STUDIES, VI, *supra*, at 547; *supra* note 481 (execution of Thomas of Lancaster). Justices of the peace, coroners, and other legal officers could also make record that would suffice for judgment and conviction. The law man's record was actually a protection from defects in presentment and indictment—fear

Nonetheless, a short time later the political winds had shifted and the previous impeachment was declared illegal and reversed.[592]

Edward III died shortly after the Good Parliament. Richard II, Edward's ten-year-old grandson, assumed the reign as a minor. By Richard II's reign, the changes in Parliament—Lords and Commons and Commons' petition—were strong enough to provide precedent for the incoming king. Each generation had added substance to the foundation. Eventually, participation, representation, and accountability became practices that did not need to be fought for but something that was assumed.[593] The Commons had secured to a greater degree their right to participate in taxation, their right to assent to laws, their right to question the administration of the realm, and eventually the right to impeach the king's ministers if sufficient grounds were met.

---

among the grand jurors of retaliation by the accused-but-powerful rioters. PLUCKNETT, STUDIES, VI, *supra*, at 547-48 & n.1; *see also* 3 WILKINSON, CONST. HIST., *supra* note 149, at 180 (similar concern in 1285 statute); CAM, HUNDRED ROLLS, *supra* note 362, at 43, 71, 80. These substitutes for presentment and indictment stand in the face of the fourteenth-century claims for common-law processes. PLUCKNETT, STUDIES, VI, *supra*, at 557; *cf. infra* note 605 (Parliament rejecting common-law procedure in favor of its own parliamentary procedure in the Merciless Parliament's impeachments of 1388).

During Edward III's reign, the acceptance of noncommon-law process was changing. Convictions were overturned. It was argued that any subject in time of peace ought to be arraigned, have the opportunity to answer, and be convicted by process of law. PLUCKNETT, STUDIES, VI, *supra*, at 549-50; *supra* note 481 (Henry of Lancaster successfully appealed his brother's prosecution and murder). Roger Mortimer was indicted by the king's record but convicted by *judicium parium* in 1330. *Supra* note 498. In 1354, Parliament reversed Mortimer's conviction. *Id.*

[592] NIGEL SAUL, RICHARD II 17, 20-21 (1997); MCKISACK, *supra* note 502, at 394-95; 3 TOUT, CHAPTERS, *supra* note 332, at 308-10.

[593] *Supra* notes 296-299, 398-403, 499-501.

The fact that Richard II was a minor at accession helped reform efforts as continual councils of magnates, similar to council-regencies, had control of the realm.[594] As Richard approached majority, relations soured. In 1383, the Lords complained that Richard had ignored the barons and taken advice from unworthy counsel.[595] In 1385, the Commons, who were unhappy with Chancellor de la Pole, Earl of Suffolk, the progress of the war, and the financial state of the realm, petitioned for reform.[596] In 1386, de la Pole called for an exorbitant taxation, and the Commons and Lords responded by calling for his impeachment.[597] The king refused to remove de la Pole and thus began the impeachment controversies of Richard II's reign. Pressure prevailed as Richard succumbed and removed de la Pole. Over the king's objection, the Commons proceeded to impeach Chancellor de la Pole for financial incompetence against the profit of the realm.[598] But unlike other instances of impeachment, de la Pole's was against the king's wishes. Impeachment against the king's will was not an accepted procedure in the fourteenth century and resembled rebellion and treason.

Parliament in 1386 also resolved to take government from Richard II and rule by a continual council for a year.[599] The con-

---

[594] SAUL, *supra* note 592, at 28-29.

[595] *Id.* at 109-12.

[596] *Id.* at 140-47, 157.

[597] *Id.* at 157.

[598] *Id.* at 158-61; 4 A.R. MYERS, ENG. HIST. DOCS., *supra* note 3, at 150-52.

[599] SAUL, *supra* note 592, at 161-66; GERALD HARRISS, SHAPING THE NATION: ENGLAND 1360-1461, at 457-60 (2005) (hereinafter HARRISS, SHAPING THE NATION); *see also* 4 MYERS, ENG. HIST. DOCS., *supra* note 3, at 151-52 (contemporaneous account referencing the 1308 Baronial Declaration, *supra* note 426, which advocated displacing the king who refused to reform evil

tinual council or commission had several powers. It was to inquire about causes and complaints throughout the land. Royal expenses and ministers were under its purview.[600] This group would later be known as Lords Appellant.

Richard, displaced by the Appellants, sought to challenge both the commission and impeachment of royal officials against the wishes of the king.[601] The legality of impeachment by the Commons and Lords was one of the questions Richard privately put to several royal judges in 1387.[602] The judges declared the actions of Commons and Lords illegal and punishable as traitors.

The Lords Appellant continued their prosecutions of royal officials by a different type of legal procedure, the appeal.[603] By 1388, the Appellants sought to impeach numerous individuals, including the judges who had declared their proceedings illegal. The Lords Appellant were advised that the appeal of individuals in Parliament for treason in their absence was not permitted at common or civil law.[604] The Lords Appellant, however, declared that the High Court of Parliament was above the common and civil

---

counsel). Placing governance with council that resembled council-regents when the king was minor or absent was a reoccurring baronial goal. *Supra* notes 320-323 (Paper Constitution); *supra* note 329 (baronial committee and Council of Fifteen in 1258); *supra* Chapter VI secs. A-C (Ordainers); *supra* Chapter VI sec. F (baronial-reform Statute of 1341). Technically, Richard was still a minor in 1386.

600 4 MYERS, ENG. HIST. DOCS., *supra* note 3, at 152.

601 SAUL, *supra* note 592, at 170-75; HARRISS, SHAPING THE NATION, *supra* note 599, at 462-64.

602 PLUCKNETT, CONST. HIST., *supra* note 59, at 171; SAUL, *supra* note 592, at 173-75.

603 Rogers, *supra* note 498; SAUL, *supra* note 592, at 176-95.

604 SAUL, *supra* note 592, at 191-93.

law and could adopt its own procedure.[605] Thus, the Lords Appellant were able to effectively control Parliament and the realm, and a trial of officials took place in their absence.[606] Finding the accused, including the Chief Judge who had answered Richard's questions, guilty, the Lords Appellant and the Merciless Parliament of 1388 executed several over the king's personal plea for mercy.[607]

The Merciless Parliament's actions silenced disputes, for a time. Richard II and the Appellants feigned peace as the king swore a second coronation oath.[608] But the controversies of Richard II's reign continued. Richard assumed full majority and conflict resurfaced as he regained the prerogative and powers of kingship that had been subdued by the Appellants.[609] Richard replaced Appellants' officials with his own officers.[610] He had the Commons declare that his prerogative was as strong as that of his predecessors.[611] Breaching the peace, Richard II took revenge on reformers and the Lords Appellant. In 1397, Richard arrested Appellants for extortions and oppressions.[612] Appellants were

---

605 Rogers, *supra* note 498, at 108-11; SAUL, *supra* note 592, at 191-94; *see also* PLUCKNETT, STUDIES, IX, *supra* note 274 (discussing impeachment's use during Richard II's reign).

606 Rogers, *supra* note 498, at 107-08, 111; SAUL, *supra* note 592, at 191-94.

607 HARRISS, SHAPING THE NATION, *supra* note 599, at 464-66.

608 SAUL, *supra* note 592, at 195.

609 *Id.* at 203, 235-69.

610 *Id.* at 249-50.

611 *Id.* at 255-56.

612 *Id.* at 366-67; HARRISS, SHAPING THE NATION, *supra* note 599, at 479-80.

executed or sentenced to life imprisonment.[613] Petitions sought reform, but Richard was having none of it. Thomas Haxey, the clerk who merely delivered a reform petition in 1397, was tried for treason but later pardoned.[614]

History remembers Richard in the last years of his reign as a tyrant accused of arbitrary acts.[615] His behavior generated enemies. Duke Henry, Henry IV, invaded England in 1399 with the intent of ousting Richard II. Richard stood accused of violating his coronation oath, ignoring statutes, and shirking obligations to share governance with Parliament.[616] He denied the charges and claimed that his divine kingship could not be impeached or deposed and that he was fit for rule.[617] Facing insurmountable opposition, Richard finally yielded the throne.[618]

Henry IV supported the Parliament that Richard II suppressed.[619] In light of the events of Richard II's reign, Henry IV promised to give the Commons more authority. One might be tempted to state that the Lords and Commons succeeded in bind-

---

[613] SAUL, *supra* note 592, at 366.

[614] *Id.* at 369. The right to petition the king was a late seventeenth-century grievance and component of the English Bill of Rights. *Infra* notes 719, 725.

[615] 2 WILKINSON, CONST. HIST., *supra* note 149, at 293-94.

[616] 4 MYERS, ENG. HIST. DOCS., *supra* note 3, at 407-14; 2 WILKINSON, CONST. HIST., *supra* note 149, at 293.

[617] SAUL, *supra* note 592, at 420-22.

[618] *Id.*; *see also* MUSSON & ORMROD, EVOLUTION OF ENG. JUSTICE, *supra* note 162, at 109.

[619] THOMPSON, *supra* note 304, at 18 (citing Henry IV's formulaic confirmation of the Charters and "good" ordinances and statutes in contrast to Richard's absolutist approach to Parliament).

ing the king to the law. During the Tudors' reign, however, the Commons lost most of their power and would not regain it until the late sixteenth and seventeenth centuries.[620] The institution of impeachment also would wait until the seventeenth century.[621]

Wilkinson opined that Richard II's deposition marked the transition from absolute monarchy to a type of limited monarchy.[622] Richard's reign, however, was not a time for the development of the English Constitution as nothing was settled in the back and forth between Parliament and the king.

---

620 SAYLES, KING'S PARLIAMENT, *supra* note 112, at 134-36.

621 WILKINSON, STUDIES, *supra* note 314, at 106-07.

622 2 WILKINSON, CONST. HIST., *supra* note 149, at 298.

VII

Summary of the Medieval Period: The High Court of Parliament

The Angevin king, by his own will, disseized, outlawed, and imprisoned men without judgment of peers or other legal process.[623] In the twelfth century, there was little formal restraint on royal executive action. The king swore in his coronation oath to protect the good laws and abolish the bad laws and customs. He had a moral duty to the law—a duty to serve the common welfare and natural law—but from an enforcement perspective, he was above the law.[624] If the king did wrong, writs and process did not issue against the king in his courts unless he gave

623 *Supra* Chapter III.

624 *Supra* notes 32-36, 64-67.

permission.[625] The king modified existing law, made new law, and dispensed with the law if necessity required it.[626]

The theocratic power of kings often conflicted with feudal *consilium* as the two competed over good government.[627] The barons obtained a foothold against arbitrary kingship with the Magna Carta's promises. Chapter 12 established that, except for the three common aids at reasonable rates, no scutage or aid should be raised but by the common counsel of the realm.[628] Chapter 39 promised that the king shall not take, imprison, disseize, outlaw, exile, or destroy without judgment of his peers or by the law of the land.[629] The Magna Carta aimed to restrain the king's extraordinary executive action, leaving executive action in accordance with the law of the land. Chapter 61 attempted to enforce the Magna Carta's promise by providing a means for a council to distrain the king's castles and possessions if he violated the Charter's provisions.[630]

With the Magna Carta, the barons established themselves as a community capable of opposing the king. The barons were determined to maintain their ground. Each demand for the Charter's reissuance or confirmation was a further step in this direction. When the king needed taxes, the barons demanded conces-

---

[625] *Supra* notes 263-265, 312, 372-377, 424.

[626] *Supra* notes 32-36, 64-67, 195-198, 263, 393-397, 408, 432, 448, 519-523, 585, 587.

[627] *Supra* Chapter VI secs. A-C.

[628] *Supra* Chapter IV sec. A.

[629] *Supra* Chapter IV sec. B.

[630] *Supra* Chapter IV sec. C.

sions and confirmations.[631] The Magna Carta was a bargaining chip and symbol of the back-and-forth political relationship between the barons and the king.

During the thirteenth century, there were several examples of baronial uprisings challenging the king. Chapter 61's effort to distrain the king for violating the charter was omitted in reissues. By 1244, barons were considering insertion into the king's council to counsel erring rule.[632] Conservators of liberty could be put directly into the king's administration on a permanent basis rather than as an ad hoc group managing distraint after the fact.[633] The 1244 plan was never implemented.

But these considerations were put into effect in 1258. The baronial-reform plan of 1258, evolving upstream from Chapter 61's distraint, was a type of administrative rebellion as barons sought to control the king's Council. The kingship was placed in a shared committee and council not unlike the council-regency when the king was away or a minor.[634]

Though ultimately unsuccessful, the gains of the baronial reform of 1258, for a time, added a building block to the Magna Carta's spirit, serving as the new ideal that the barons sought to obtain and secure. After the king regained power, the barons went back to seeking promises and confirmations. Reform was lost but not forgotten.

---

631 *Supra* Chapter V sec. A.

632 *Supra* notes 320-323.

633 *Supra* Chapter V.

634 *Id.*

One area of continuity between the reform period of 1258 and Edward I's reign was the petition. The petition served many needs: it was a grievance, a judicial process, a preliminary to impeachment, and a preliminary to statute. Parliament served as a court for the many petitions encouraged by Edward I. His inquiry into ministerial corruption and use of committees of Parliament to investigate petitions was a foundation of the fourteenth century's High Court of Parliament.[635]

Edward I, with his statutes and efforts at accountability, was a reformer. But he also had his fight with the barons over taxes. In exchange for funds, he confirmed the Charters in 1297 and again three years later in the *Articuli super Cartas*.[636] Each of these promises expanded upon the Magna Carta's promise. The king, of course, frequently confirmed that he would abide by the Charters, but his oath was mostly for his own conscience as he was not held accountable at law.[637] Like John and Henry III before him, Edward in 1305 sought a papal release of his oath and promise.

The papal release and the end of Edward I's reign influenced Edward II's reign.[638] The barons were determined to make this reign different from others. In 1308, the barons sought that the king swear, in his most sacred coronation oath, to abide by laws chosen by the commonalty. In a Declaration shortly thereafter, several barons separated the king's person from the crown and swore allegiance to the latter over the former.

---

[635] *Supra* notes 402-403.

[636] *Supra* note 410.

[637] *Supra* notes 38, 263-265, 372-377, 519-523.

[638] *Supra* Chapter VI sec. A.

The thirteenth century had demonstrated that promises, confirmations, excommunication, and distraint did not work. The barons had tried controlling the Council, but this was superficial. The barons had to find some lasting enforcement role against the king and his ministers.

The answer was shared governance in Parliament. The Ordainers revived the reforms of 1258 but went further into the king's household. The Ordainers sought to remove evil councilors and share decision-making power on matters such as war, appointment of ministers, and accountability by a committee of Parliament. The barons were substituting for royal administration and seeking a partnership with the king at all levels. The relationship might be described as a change in sovereignty "from God to king" to "from God to king and community" as the barons assumed a role of evaluating the king's divine "right and reason," "common profit," "necessity," and general principles of good government. The barons were grasping at the idea that their law served God's justice, not the king's sword.[639] National law and justice were rights of the subject rather than obligations the king owed to his subjects.[640]

Wilkinson described the fourteenth century as an expansion both of the role that the nation played in government (Parliament vis-à-vis the king) as well as an expansion of the classes of the nation participating in government (the Commons joining the

639 *Supra* Chapter VI secs. B-C.

640 *Supra* note 500 (people's voice gave authority to the rule of law).

barons).[641] The king and the community formed a partnership and "the community eventually became the dominant partner."[642]

> These changes effected, or perhaps more truly reflected, a change in the centre of political gravity. . . . From lying in the hands of the ruler, the centre of political gravity continued its long movement, imperceptibly and for the most part unrecognized, into the hands of the people. Parliament, which had begun as mainly the instrument of the former, began, tentatively and uncertainly, to be the instrument of the latter.[643]

The end of Edward II's reign was stained with rebellion and violence. The barons' exiling and holding royal officials accountable initiated a transformation in the relationship between king and subject.[644] But like the reform of 1258, the king defeated the competition and reclaimed his prerogative. When the king regained control, summary executions followed.

The struggles of Edward II's reign shaped the reform efforts for the remainder of the fourteenth century. The relationship between the barons and the king changed with each reform. Each controversy set the bar one step further and communicated the English Constitution to the realm. Succession often saw a conciliatory or accepting attitude to the controversy of the former reign—especially succession of minor kings.[645] The radical gain of one rebellion or crisis became the ideal of the next generation until it became accepted nature and civil process. The baronial

---

[641] 2 WILKINSON, CONST. HIST., *supra* note 149, at 5.

[642] *Id.* at 6.

[643] *Id.* at 6-7.

[644] *Id.*

[645] *Supra* notes 296-299, 399-400, 499-501, 593.

reform of 1258 leveraged the Magna Carta and added to its spirit of reform. Ordainers took up where the barons of 1258 left off. The royalists regained their footing in 1322 only to have Edward II deposed in 1327. His reign was probably the most violent one discussed; Edward III's reign was probably the least controversial.

Whether or not knights and burgesses were a significant part of Parliament in the early part of the fourteenth century, by the middle of the fourteenth century, the boroughs and shires held the title of "community of the realm." Legislation, a short time into Edward III's reign, would be through Commons' petition with Lords and king assenting and enacting.[646] The Commons' petition paved the way for the English Constitution's growth and eventually became a means of initiating legislation. The petition substituted parliamentary grievance resolution for the violence and rebellion of former reigns.[647]

Unlike previous reform efforts, Parliament's authority to make the law came with the enforcement power of accountability and impeachment. Communities and Commons acted as an accusing body and, through petition and indictment, brought the matter before the Lords and the High Court of Parliament.[648] The Lords gave judgment, satisfying *judicium parium*.[649] Impeachment and the Commons' petition were characterized as transforming the petition from the king's favor and grace to a matter

[646] *Supra* Chapter VI sec. D.

[647] *Id.*

[648] *Id.*

[649] *Supra* Chapter VI secs. F–G.

of law, an assertion or petition of right.[650] Judgment was not by the king or the King in Council but by the Lords and Commons in Parliament.

The king still confirmed the Magna Carta in the fourteenth century, but it was less important and coupled with confirmation of and adherence to additional legislation.[651] The theory that emerged is that when Parliament was strong, the Lords and Commons were no longer content with assent, no longer asking for the king to promise, no longer seeking a confirmation of the Charter. Fourteenth-century England no longer needed *diffidatio*.[652] Lords and Commons were demanding the right to ordain and enforce their own good government with statute, accountability, and impeachment.[653] In theory, they could make the law of the land, new Magna Cartas.[654] The function of rebellion and diffidation had evolved into several different law-making and enforcement components of Parliament and the English Constitution. The era of the Magna Carta and confirmations had passed;

---

[650] 2 WILKINSON, CONST. HIST., *supra* note 149, at 206, *citing* CLARKE, *supra* note 570, at 265.

[651] *Supra* notes 577-578; *infra* note 655; *see also* CAM, MAGNA CARTA, *supra* note 453, at 19-20 (noting that Confirmations and charges of violations become less frequent as the Magna Carta merged into statutory and common law).

[652] JOLLIFFE, CONST. HIST., *supra* note 49, at 404-05; 2 WILKINSON, CONST. HIST., *supra* note 149, at 207-08, 212-13 (collective power of petition and impeachment replaced ancient right of feudal resistance).

[653] *Supra* Chapter VI.

[654] *Supra* notes 317, 448-456.

the Magna Carta was a statute in late fourteenth-century Parliament.[655] Richardson and Sayles wrote:

> [The Charter] became a symbol and assumed mystic properties. It became the symbol of the rule of law, the vindication of the right of the barons to maintain the law and to be consulted on changes in the law. The mystical aura surrounding the Charter was the result of the attitude of the kings from John to Edward I. To John the Charter was a shameful invasion of his rights. To Henry III it was a boon, to be sold for money, or granted, as it was to Ireland, as a reward for good behaviour. In Edward's excited imagination it was a fetter from which he must free himself. It was not until the reign of Edward II that the Charter was unfeignedly accepted, by which time it had become so integrated into the statutory law that it would have been impossible to undo it, though its undoing had been conceived by the failing intelligence of the king's father.[656]

The High Court of Parliament sought to transfer sovereignty from the court of the King in Council to the court of Lords and Commons. Parliament was a place for Lords and Commons to participate in national governance in key areas such as war, appointment of officials, taxation; a place for petitions and statute-making; a court of appeals for judicial matters and justice; and a center of accountability for impeachment and *judicium parium*.

---

[655] Harriss noted a change in the Common Petition of 1340 in which the Charter's confirmation was minimized. Parliament provided a forum for enforcement. HARRISS, KING & PARLIAMENT, *supra* note 36, at 260-61; *supra* notes 577-578.

[656] RICHARDSON & SAYLES, GOVERNANCE, *supra* note 49, at 391 (footnotes omitted).

Parliament's functionality ensured its role as forum for enforcing good government. Lords and Commons succeeded, at least briefly, in placing the king not only under natural law but also under their law, which was the law of the land because of their participation.[657] Lords and Commons became a source of the law. Law came from below, *legislatio.*

The rise of Lords and Commons in Parliament prompted jealous protection of the common law.[658] During reform movements, and especially in the fourteenth century, the barons and Commons frequently grieved nonparliamentary encroachment upon the common law. Grievances included protecting against unauthorized expansion of original writs, criticizing the use of the Privy Seal, and critiquing the Council's judicial and legislative processes in derogation of the law of the land. The Commons wanted due process of law protected from arbitrary judicial and legislative action by the king and Council unless with Parliament's blessing and common consent.[659]

Wilkinson described the fourteenth century as a clash of sovereignties.[660] While we see glimpses of parliamentary sovereignty in the fourteenth century, the description of the High Court of Parliament as a partnership with the king is mostly theory and exaggeration except for times of crisis when baronial reform was at its peak. True parliamentary sovereignty would wait until the end of the seventeenth century. Though impeachment made a debut in the fourteenth century, the process as an institution subsided during the strong reign of the Tudors. It, like other four-

---

[657] *Supra* Chapter VI.

[658] *Supra* Chapter VI sec. E.

[659] *Id.*

[660] 2 WILKINSON, CONST. HIST., *supra* note 149, at 4.

teenth-century reforms, rekindled in the seventeenth century. Sayles reminded us that while the Commons had tasted sovereignty in the fourteenth century and Parliament had shifted the political center of gravity, both were not seen as constitutional requirements and the King in Council initiated legislation and enacted laws without Parliament in the fifteenth and sixteenth centuries.[661] Though fourteenth-century legislation might seem to bind the king's acts, the king retained the prerogative to decline enforcement or to do away with legislative reform.[662]

---

661 SAYLES, KING'S PARLIAMENT, *supra* note 112, at 133-36.

662 *Supra* notes 32-36, 38, 195-198, 263-265, 372-377, 393-397, 519-523, 624-629.

VIII

The Seventeenth Century and Reason of State

THE SEVENTEENTH CENTURY'S RICH DETAIL and contribution to the English Constitution is beyond the scope of this book other than a few brief observations to complete the story of king and Parliament.

The seventeenth century witnessed another civil war and successive constitutional controversies ultimately transforming the English form of government. Though the realm evolved greatly in the intervening centuries, the seventeenth century was not much different in its main theme and character from the baronial-reform periods of the thirteenth and fourteenth centuries. The thirteenth-century baron fought against the king over extraordinary taxation and common consent.[663] The fourteenth century added the Commons and shifted the political center of gravity to Lords and Commons.[664] After Richard II's deposition, the Lords and Commons would likely describe the realm as mixed-

---

[663] *Supra* Chapters IV, V.

[664] *Supra* Chapter VI.

monarchy. The Tudors, however, were largely autocratic and the fourteenth century's parliamentary gains receded.

Reform efforts reignited in the seventeenth century.[665] During the 1620s, the Commons challenged all or nearly all aspects of the king's prerogative. Sir Edward Coke, a learned jurist of the early seventeenth century, was a leader of the 1620s Commons. Coke's contemporaries struggled to keep up with his intellectual prowess. His knowledge, however, was an instrument for his advocacy rather than for historical truth. He glossed ancient texts out of context and manipulated precedents to serve his interests. For this reason, Coke was removed from his judicial duties but ultimately found a place in Parliament.

Coke's advocacy was effective against the king but left those who relied upon his writings with much to be corrected. Stephen D. White wrote:

> Coke was peculiarly skillful and eloquent when it came to giving "reasons" for the House's positions on these subjects. In performing this task, he could not only call on his vast knowledge of precedent and earlier English history and his four decades of personal experience in English government; he was also able to exploit his singular capacity for formulating abstruse legal arguments in simple terms, and his highly developed skill at quoting or inventing aphorisms, maxims, figures, etymologies, and parables. By using these skills, he was apparently able to convince his listeners that his views were completely consistent with not only the common

---

[665] PLUCKNETT, CONST. HIST., *supra* note 59, at 331-37. *See generally* J.P. KENYON, THE STUART CONSTITUTION 1603-1688: DOCUMENTS AND COMMENTARY (2d ed. 1986).

> law, but also natural reason and traditional wisdom.[666]

Coke, for example, argued that the divine right of kings established that the king could do no wrong because he was the lieutenant of God.[667] Coke manipulated this to mean that because the king had done wrong in a grant to an individual, the grant must be judicially undone by the court itself because the king could do no wrong.[668] Coke repeatedly claimed that royal acts were done "against reason" but provided no definition or context for "reason." Only he seemed to know what "reason" meant.[669] Coke denied the king's divine authority of natural reason. For Coke, "reason" was artificial and, together with the laws of the realm, bound the king.[670] The king was not educated in the laws of the realm

---

[666] STEPHEN D. WHITE, SIR EDWARD COKE AND "THE GRIEVANCES OF THE COMMONWEALTH," 1621-1628, at 226 (1979).

[667] *Supra* Chapter II sec. A (divine right and vicar of God).

[668] 2 COMMONS DEBATES, 1621, at 253 (Wallace Notestein, Frances Helen Relf, Hartley Simpson eds. 1935) (March 21, 1621); 5 *id.* 59; *see also* 2 COMMONS DEBATES, 1628, at 201, 204, 207, 209 (Robert C. Johnson, Mary F. Keeler, Maija J. Cole, William B. Bidwell, eds. 1977-78) (March 29, 1628) (the king cannot do what is against the good of the people, and going against such fundamental statutes is against the king's prerogative); WHITE, *supra* note 666, at 122, 155, 232. For a better description of the equitable rule that Coke glossed, see William S. Holdsworth, *The History of Remedies Against the Crown II*, 38 LAW Q. REV. 280, 281, 293 (1922) (courts presuming that the king would extend equity against his interests in the same manner that he or royal courts would for a common person).

[669] WHITE, *supra* note 666, at 80 n., 231-32, 237-41, 247.

[670] Coke's Report:

> Then the King said, that he thought the Law was founded upon reason, and that he and others had reason, as well as the Judges: To which it was answered by me, that true it was, that God had endowed his Majesty with excellent Science and great endowments of nature, but his Majesty was not learned in the Lawes of his Realm of *England*,

and thus unable to wield "reason." Citing Bracton, Coke popularized the notion that the king was under the law, under ordinary law.[671]

Seventeenth-century reformers agreed that the king in Parliament was more powerful than the king out of Parliament.[672] We saw above that barons invoked the king's two bodies and separate capacities in the beginning of the fourteenth century.[673] These arguments resurfaced in the seventeenth century. Once the king's powers were subject to separation, arguments against the prerogative and divine right of kings followed.

James I's reign was a period of transition. In the beginning of his reign, we find the king's divine right supported; the king

---

> and causes which concerne the life, or inheritance, or goods, or fortunes of his Subjects; they are not to be decided by naturall reason, but by the artificiall reason and judgment of Law, which Law is an art which requires long study and experience, before that a man can attain to the cognizance of it; And that the Law was the golden metwand and measure to try the Causes of the Subjects; and which protected his Majesty in safety and peace: With which the King was greatly offended, and said, that then he should be under the Law, which was Treason to affirm, as he said; To which I said, that *Bracton* saith, *Quod Rex non debet esse sub homine, sed sub Deo & Lege* (The king ought not to be under man but under God and the law).

Coke reporting on the case Prohibitions del Roy, *reprinted in* 1 JOYCE LEE MALCOLM, THE STRUGGLE FOR SOVEREIGNTY 18 (1999), *available at* http://oll.libertyfund.org/pages/1658-coke-prohibitions-del-roy-pamphlet.

[671] For discussion of Bracton's statement, *see supra* notes 36-45.

[672] MARGARET ATWOOD JUDSON, THE CRISIS OF THE CONSTITUTION: AN ESSAY IN CONSTITUTIONAL AND POLITICAL THOUGHT IN ENGLAND 1603-1645, at 83, 86-87 (1949); KENYON, STUART CONSTITUTION, *supra* note 665, at 60-62.

[673] *Supra* Chapter VI secs. A-C.

justified acts in the name of necessity.[674] Parliament, however, came to resent the king's justification of necessity.[675] By the mid-seventeenth century, the Commons argued that the king's power was limited; the Commons competed with the king for the realm's common welfare and the liberty of both Parliament and the subject.[676] Specifically, the Commons argued that the king's prerogative did not permit him to interfere with vested property interests and other injuries to the subject.[677] The Commons connected an-

---

[674] JUDSON, *supra* note 672, at 10, 17-30.

[675] CONRAD RUSSELL, THE FALL OF THE BRITISH MONARCHIES 1637-1642, at 481-82 (1991) (hereinafter RUSSELL, FALL OF MONARCHIES) (king arguing for power of necessity; parliamentary privilege to declare what the law was); *id.* at 505-08, 510 (king attempting to protect his royal judges with prerogative; Parliament claiming that kingship separate from the king's body and allegiance owed to public authority not the king's person); JUDSON, *supra* note 672, at 152-53, 163-67, 240-43, 272, 364 (Parliament argued that royal claims of necessity were just another means of taking property without consent).

[676] JUDSON, *supra* note 672, at 28-43, 61-65, 113-15, 130-132, 141-47 (welfare for the people).

[677] *Id.* at 34-43, 86-87, 163-70 (landed interests grew and sought to protect their property rights even against the king's prerogative without their consent, especially against royal monopoly powers and prerogative argument of necessity). Vested property interests would not control Parliament, though courts would do their best to construe acts within the confines of the law, equity, and reason. Blackstone wrote in the late eighteenth century:

> [I]f the parliament will positively enact a thing to be done which is unreasonable, I know of no power in the ordinary forms of the constitution, that is vested with authority to control it: and the examples usually alleged in support of this sense of the rule do none of them prove, that, where the main object of a statute is unreasonable, the judges are at liberty to reject it; for that were to set the judicial power above that of the legislature, which would be subversive of all government.

1 SIR WILLIAM BLACKSTONE, COMMENTARIES ON THE LAWS OF ENGLAND 158-59, **91-92 (William Carey Jones ed. 1915) (rejecting the implication of Sir Edward Coke's *dicta* in Dr. Bonham's Case, 8 Coke Rep. 113b, 77 Eng. Rep. 646, 652-54 (1610), that the common law controls Parliament and

cient rights concerning taxation with property interests; the king was limited in his ability to tax or take property without Parliament's consent.[678]

The seventeenth century can be characterized as a struggle between the belief that king's will was absolute law and the maxim that the "*salus populi suprema lex*," welfare of the people is supreme law.[679] The Commons faced off against the king's prerogative on multiple fronts: monopoly powers, forced loans, habeas corpus, nonparliamentary taxation, and suspending and dispensing powers.[680] The institution of impeachment reappeared, and attacks against the king's evil councilors were a significant component of Stuart conflict.[681] The Common's use of impeach-

finding such a preference or construction in favor of the common law appropriate for ambiguous parliamentary text but emphasizing that statute controls common law); *infra* note 694 (Parliament controls common law).

[678] JUDSON, *supra* note 672, at 71-72, 229-30, 234, 243-47, 252, 260-61, 277, 305-10 (the Commons connected taxation with property interest; king limited in ability to tax or take property without Parliament without consent); GOLDSWORTHY, *supra* note 538, at 31 (Parliament's acts represent consent of community).

[679] JUDSON, *supra* note 672, at 28-29, 61-65, 112-14, 136, 143-48, 171-218, 249-51, 283, 292, 300-01.

[680] 4 HOLDSWORTH, *supra* note 113, at 348-54 (monopoly powers); FRANCES HELEN RELF, THE PETITION OF RIGHT 1, 23, 29 (1917) (discussing nonparliamentary taxation); 6 HOLDSWORTH, *supra* note 113, at 27-28 (taxation); LOIS G. SCHWOERER, THE DECLARATION OF RIGHTS, 1689, at 59-64 (1981) (describing seventeenth-century views on limiting or prohibiting the king's suspending and dispensing power); 6 HOLDSWORTH, *supra* note 113, at 217-25 (suspending and dispensing power).

[681] TITE, *supra* note 590 (impeachment's revival in 1620s Parliaments); CLAYTON ROBERTS, THE GROWTH OF RESPONSIBLE GOVERNMENT IN STUART ENGLAND (1966) (surveying the seventeenth century through the lens of impeachment and the king's prerogative to appoint and maintain his officers); WHITE, *supra* note 666, at 142-64, 213-14.

ment naturally brought out the question of the king's prerogative to appoint and maintain his ministers.

One particular controversy characterized the early Stuart period. To pay for military needs, Charles I reverted to a former Tudor practice of forced loans.[682] Forced loans or benevolences were loans to the king that were intended to be repaid.[683] The forced-loans controversy erupted when five knights refused to pay loans and were arrested. During the seventeenth century, the king arrested those who defied his commands—for example, did not pay forced loans. Thereafter, the question arose in Darnel's Case, or the Five Knights Case, whether the king's special command was sufficient for arrest and detention.[684] The prisoners petitioned for a writ of habeas corpus to be released pending trial. The writ of habeas corpus was a royal writ directed to the prison warden to bring the prisoner to a common-law court with the cause of his commitment so that the court could review the cause and detention.[685] Ultimately, the judges in Darnel's Case refused to challenge the king's power to commit without cause.

---

682 Conrad Russell, The Crisis of Parliaments: English History 1509-1660, at 304-310 (1971) (hereinafter Russell, Crisis); *see also* 9 Holdsworth, *supra* note 113, at 112-25.

683 Schwoerer, *supra* note 680, at 67; Plucknett, Const. Hist., *supra* note 59, at 185-86, 347.

684 White, *supra* note 666, at 213-276 (1628 debates focusing largely on the king's prerogative to arrest and detain without cause); Relf, *supra* note 680, at 1-26 (discussing Darnel's Case and habeas corpus); Judson, *supra* note 672, at 117-22, 167 (noting that Stuart kings permitted issues of prerogative to be judged in the common-law courts out of grace and respect for the law; pragmatically, the king had to appear to abide by the law for support and harmony). Seventeenth-century practice was consistent with medieval practice. *Supra* notes 312, 376.

685 Relf, *supra* note 680, at 24-25.

The Magna Carta or the spirit of the Magna Carta, as a venerated instrument of the past and inroad against the king, was invoked throughout the 1620s as the Commons advocated that several royal actions were done against the Magna Carta and the law of the land.[686] It was argued that because due process, indictment, presentment, and law of the land were being used interchangeably in several fourteenth-century statutes, they were all equivalent. In the context of binding the king, ancient statutory use of "law of the land" meant due process, presentment, and indictment.[687] The crown was forbidden from several inconsistent prerogative actions as not law of the land.[688] Members of the Commons specifically equated Magna Carta's "law of the land" with statutory "process by law."[689] For the Commons, "law of the

---

[686] WHITE, *supra* note 666, at 213-76 (analyzing 1628 Commons debates); THOMPSON, *supra* note 304, at 294-353 (highlighting the Magna Carta's use during the Stuarts; seventeenth-century advocates cited and expanded upon the Magna Carta and several fourteenth-century statutes, *supra* Chapter VI sec. E, to challenge a host of royal prerogatives).

[687] 2 COMMONS DEBATES, 1628, *supra* note 668, at 335-38 (April 7, 1628) (Littleton listed Edward III's statutes and petitions, *supra* Chapter VI sec. E, and reasoned that because "law of the land" was stated to include presentment and indictment, "law of the land" must be limited to presentment and indictment per Edward III's statutes); RELF, *supra* note 680, at 12-13.

[688] The Commons deflected royalists' arguments that the prerogative itself was also fundamental law and law of the land. JUDSON, *supra* note 672, at 121-24, 134, 246-47. But the king could cite many precedents for royal supremacy and the prerogative as fundamental law. *Id.* at 46, 126-70.

[689] 2 COMMONS DEBATES, 1628, *supra* note 668, at 335-38 (April 7, 1628) (finding that the cited statutes made specified common-law processes part of "the law of the land" as used in this context against the king but distinguishing other customs not addressed by the cited statutes as other "laws of the land" not covered in this context); 3 *id.* 216, 221, 228 (May 2, 1628), *citing* 37 Edw. III c.18. ("[T]hough that it be contained in the

land" was law generally, but in certain supporting statutes, it meant that royal action could not deprive one without the "common law" presentment and indictment or due process of law.[690] The Commons emphatically argued that the king could not commit without cause.

In the seventeenth century and medieval times, "law of the land" and "due process of law" had meaning only against the king or other arbitrary actors. Later generations, however, interpreted this to mean that legislative acts were not "law of the land" or "due process of law." It is corrupt transposition to attribute to Coke or the Commons that Parliament could not alter the common law or that the law of the land did not also include acts of Parliament.[691] For Coke, the several fourteenth-century statutes, in the context of binding the king, provided for "due process of

---

Great Charter, that no man be taken nor imprisoned, nor put out of his freehold, without process of the law"). *See also supra* note 553.

[690] 2 COMMONS DEBATES, 1628, *supra* note 668, at 335-38 (April 7, 1628); 3 *id.* 94-95, 100, 104, 117 (April 26, 1628); WHITE, *supra* note 666, at 254 (arguing that Magna Carta's "law of the land" means "common law"); 1 SIR EDWARD COKE, SECOND PART OF THE INSTITUTES OF THE LAWS OF ENGLAND 45-55 (Clarke & Sons, ed. 1817). *But see* 2 COMMONS DEBATES, 1628, *supra* note 668, at 527-531 (April 17, 1628) (citing other forms of law of the land that were not common law); WHITE, *supra*, at 248-49 (same); *supra* notes 556-559 (fourteenth-century conciliar process was preferred to common law for some situations because common law was insufficient).

[691] Elsewhere, Coke cited statutory law as the law of the land. 1 COKE'S SECOND PART INSTITUTES, *supra* note 690, at 46 ("no man may be taken or imprisoned, but *per legem terrae*—that is, by the common law, statute law, or custom of England"), *cited in* Robert E. Riggs, *Substantive Due Process in 1791*, 1990 WISC. L. REV. 941, 960 (1990). *See also* 1 COKE'S SECOND PART INSTITUTES, *supra*, at 47 ("By the law of the land no man can be exiled, or banished out of his native country, but either by authority of parliament, or in case of abjuration for felony by the common law"); GOLDSWORTHY, *supra* note 538, at 112.

law . . . according to the law of the land."[692] While the Commons defined "arbitrary" as the king's commitment without cause, that criticism did not apply to commitment by Parliament. In seventeenth-century terms, Parliament created the "process of law" along with the other "law of the land." Coke himself reported: "no free man ought to be confined by any command of the King, the Privy Council, or any other, unless it be by act of parliament or by other due course or warrant of law."[693] Coke, the Commons, and contemporaneous pamphleteers emphasized that Parliament's law was the law of the land and due process of law.[694] Parliament spoke for the welfare of the nation.[695]

During the Commons' debates, Coke also cited 42 Edward III for the position that statutes against the Magna Carta were void and the Commons could not alter the Magna Carta.[696] As noted

---

[692] 1 COKE'S SECOND PART INSTITUTES, *supra* note 690, at 52 ("Now seeing that no man can be taken, arrested, attached, or imprisoned but by due process of law, and according to the law of the land, these conclusions hereupon doe follow . . . .").

[693] 2 COMMONS DEBATES, 1628, *supra* note 668, at 279, 286, 292 (April 3, 1628). The Petition of Right capped the 1628 debates. In the Petition, the King, Lords, and Commons relied extensively on Parliament's law. *Infra* note 705. Parliament was not the focus of reform. Parliament was clearly a source of the law and the law of the land. Coke and the Commons would not agree that "law of the land" was separate from Parliament's acts.

[694] JUDSON, *supra* note 672, at 134-36, 243-49, 257, 367-69, 400-01, 428-30 ("*lex terrae*" in the Stuart reign); 2 COMMONS DEBATES, 1628, *supra* note 668, at 335 (statutes change the fundamental law); JUDSON, *supra*, at 367-68 (Parliament alters the common law. Seventeenth-century acknowledgement that the "Common law . . . is not superior to our Statute law, and by consequence, not unalterable.").

[695] *Supra* notes 672-681; JUDSON, *supra* note 672, at 274-310.

[696] 2 COMMONS DEBATES, 1628, *supra* note 668, at 47, 64 (March 21-22, 1628); 3 *id.* 100 (April 26, 1628); WHITE, *supra* note 666, at 255. Parlia-

above, Coke was not the bastion of legal accuracy, just legal advocacy. To the extent that Coke believed that the Magna Carta was unalterable, that position was not consistent with medieval history and was not shared by others.[697] But challenging Parliament was not the theme of 1620s; rather it was challenging the king's power. In this fight, the Commons grounded their efforts in the Magna Carta and several fourteenth-century confirming statutes.[698] The point of 1620s reform efforts was to bridle the king with the law of the land, Parliament's law.[699] Parliament removed

---

ment fought for the right to declare the common law against contrary views of royal judges under the king's personal influence. As mentioned above, medieval judges and statesmen attributed different meanings to the notion of statute. *Supra* notes 448-454. Statutes could be declarations of right for the subject and realm; but statutes could also reflect royal judgments amenable to equitable interpretation consistent with other law. JUDSON, *supra* note 672, at 92-106; *supra* note 538 (Chancellor's equity before the age of rule of law and Parliamentary supremacy). Parliament understood that the power of royal judges to interpret or declare a law was the power to create the law. RUSSELL, FALL OF MONARCHIES, *supra* note 675, at 482-83. In this latter sense, reforms sought to limit the king, royal judges, and royal officers in the dispensation or equitable interpretation of statute. *Supra* notes 317, 386, 397, 449-456, 520-523, 539, 555, 651-657 (High Court of Parliament developed authority of statute; statute transitioned from king's act in Council to subject's right; Lords and Commons no longer sought confirmations of Magna Carta; Lords and Commons could make their own law, their own Magna Cartas). During the seventeenth century, Lords and Commons advocated to move away from judicial interpretation in favor of statute law because of the role of royal judges in judicial interpretation. GOLDSWORTHY, *supra* note 538, at 108.

[697] *Supra* Chapter V sec. C (Edward I's statutes); *supra* notes 317, 448-454 (modifying law and Magna Carta's promises).

[698] 3 COMMONS DEBATES, 1628, *supra* note 668, at 495, 497, 503, 505 (May 20, 1628); *see also* 2 *id.* at 292 (April 3, 1628); 2 *id.* at 342, 356 (April 7, 1628); *supra* notes 686-694.

[699] JUDSON, *supra* note 672, at 76-80 (importance of statute and law of the land to 1620s reformers).

tyranny and arbitrariness and provided a competing source for right and reason, utility, and necessity—for reason of state.[700]

By the end of the 1620s, the grievances had culminated in the famous Petition of Right—a set of demands the Commons attempted to force upon the king. The Petition of Right's grievances included forced loans, billeting troops, martial law, arbitrary commitment by the king, and denial of habeas corpus.[701] Many wanted the remedy in the form of a law. The king informed the Commons that he would disallow a law enforcing new laws against his prerogative but would allow a confirmation of existing law, referring to the Magna Carta and the famous six statutes.[702] Coke and several members advocated that they proceed by petition instead of bill or law because the king could suspend and dispense with the law.[703] The petition would bind the king's promise, heart, and oath to the matter.[704] Ultimately, the Commons pursued their grievances in the form of a petition, the Petition of Right. It sought to bind the king to the law of the land and acts of Parliament. The Petition provided:

---

[700] GOLDSWORTHY, *supra* note 538, at 99, 105, 118 (discussing seventeenth-century pamphlets); CHARLES HERLE, A FULLER ANSWER TO A TREATISE, *reprinted in* 1 MALCOLM, *supra* note 670, at 234-36, 242, 245, 247.

[701] PETITION OF RIGHT, 3 Car. I ch. 1 (1628), *reprinted* KENYON, STUART CONSTITUTION, *supra* note 665, at 68-71; WHITE, *supra* note 666, at 216-17, 223, 264; RUSSELL, CRISIS, *supra* note 682, at 304-10.

[702] WHITE, *supra* note 666, at 259-63; RELF, *supra* note 680, at 34, Elizabeth Read Foster, *Petitions and the Petition of Right*, 14 THE J. OF BRITISH STUD. 26 (1974).

[703] RELF, *supra* note 680, at 27-29, 31; Foster, *supra* note 702, at 21, 26-27.

[704] RELF, *supra* note 680, at 27-29.

[I]t is declared and enacted by a statute made in the time of the reign of King Edward I . . . that no tallage or aid should be laid or levied by the king or his heirs in this realm without the good will and assent of [Parliament]. . . ; and by authority of parliament [in 25 Edw. III]. . ., it is declared and enacted, that from henceforth no person should be compelled to make any loans to the king against his will because such loans were against reason and the franchise of the land, and by other laws of this realm it is provided, that none should be charged by any charge or imposition called a benevolence nor by such like charge, by which the statutes before mentioned and other the good laws and statutes of this realm your subjects have inherited this freedom, that they should not be compelled to contribute to any tax, tallage, aid, or other like charge not set by common consent, in parliament. . . .

III. And where also by the statute called The Great Charter of the Liberties of England it is declared and enacted, that no freeman may be taken or imprisoned or be disseized of his freehold or liberties or his free customs or be outlawed or exiled or in any manner destroyed, but by the lawful judgment of his peers or by the law of the land.

IV. And in [28 Edw. III], it was declared and enacted by authority of parliament, that no man, of what estate or condition that he be, should be put out of his land or tenement, nor taken, nor imprisoned, nor disinherited, nor put to death without being brought to answer by due process of law.

V. Nevertheless against the tenor of the said statutes and other the good laws and statutes of your realm to that end provided, divers of your subjects have of late been imprisoned without any cause shown. . . .

> VII. And whereas also by authority of parliament, in [25 Edw. III], it is declared and enacted that no man should be forejudged of life and limb against the form of the Great Charter and the law of the land; and by the said Great Charter, and other the laws and statutes of this your realm, no man ought to be adjudged to death but by the laws established in this your realm, either by the customs of the same realm, or by act of parliament. . . .
>
> VIII. They do therefore humbly pray your most excellent Majesty that no man hereafter be compelled to make or yield any gift, loan, benevolence, tax, or such like charge without common consent by act of parliament, and that none be called to make answer or take such oath or to give attendance or be confined or otherwise molested or disquieted concerning the same or for refusal thereof. . . .
>
> All which they most humbly pray of your most excellent Majesty as their rights and liberties according to the laws and statutes of this realm. . . .[705]

Throughout the Petition, statutes and participatory government were the check against the king's acts.

Sayles noted that the Petition of Right, as that term was used in the seventeenth century, did not exist in the medieval era. All petitions were petitions of grace in which the king permitted the action against his interests.[706] The seventeenth-century hope

[705] PETITION OF RIGHT, 3 Car. I ch. 1 (1628), *reprinted* KENYON, STUART CONSTITUTION, *supra* note 665, at 68-71.

[706] *Supra* note 376; *see also* RELF, *supra* note 680, at 36; Foster, *supra* note 702, at 32-35, 37, 43 (evolution of petition of right).

was that the Petition of Right, accepted by both houses and the king, would bind the king in the courts.[707]

Sir Edward Coke and the 1620s Commons were mostly successful at reform efforts. Charles I, who was always in need of money, agreed to the Petition in June 1628. However, the Commons soon lost support of the Lords, who sided with Charles.[708] Charles I regained his footing and ignored the Petition's reforms.[709] During an eleven-year period without Parliament, 1629-1640, Charles ruled freely and generated many grievances challenging his arbitrary royal governance.[710]

Charles's conflict with Scotland required taxation and he was forced to call a Parliament. A Parliament meant concessions in exchange for taxation. The Parliaments that followed enacted several reforms.[711] In the 1641 triennial act, Parliament demanded that the king summon frequent parliaments. But because the king could ignore the demand, Parliament wanted to substitute for the king's power in case he refused to summon them. Thus,

---

[707] WHITE, *supra* note 666, at 262-63, 269-70 (noting that debate on legal effect of Petition of Right was inconclusive); RELF, *supra* note 680, at 36, 40-46, 48-50, 56-58 (citing contemporaneous accounts comparing the Petition of Right to the Magna Carta and noting that the Petition was largely unenforceable but achieved the effect of putting the king's oath on record); KENYON, STUART CONSTITUTION, *supra* note 665, at 89; JUDSON, *supra* note 672, at 257-73.

[708] KENYON, STUART CONSTITUTION, *supra* note 665, at 53-54.

[709] *Id.* at 89-90; JUDSON, *supra* note 672, at 266-67 (noting that while the Petition was formally ignored, it succeeded in putting the king on record to parliamentary reforms).

[710] RUSSELL, CRISIS, *supra* note 682, at 330, 337-38 (listing the grievances that had accumulated during eleven years since the Petition of Right); Foster, *supra* note 702, at 44; JUDSON, *supra* note 672, at 269-73.

[711] JUDSON, *supra* note 672, at 350-51.

Lords and Commons secured a share of executive power, not unlike the barons in 1258 and 1311.[712] The Lords and Commons also enacted the famous Habeas Corpus Act, which abolished the Council's noncommon-law jurisdiction in the infamous Star Chamber.[713] Shortly thereafter, England entered into another civil war.[714] Charles I was executed, and England fell into interregnum during the 1650s.[715]

Charles's son, Charles II, restored the monarchy in 1660.[716] Charles II ruled for more than two decades before his brother, James II's, reign in 1685. The end of the Stuarts' reign maintained the characteristic Stuart volatility. James II was Catholic, and anti-Catholic views flourished in seventeenth-century England. A great dispute arose over James's 1687 Declaration of Indulgence or Liberty of Conscience, which dispensed and suspended several laws against Roman Catholics.[717] James's suspension and dispensation and its aftermath were a major component of the Glorious Revolution.[718] Several bishops petitioned James that his suspension and dispensation were illegal. James II had the petitioners arrested and tried for seditious libel. But the real

---

[712] RUSSELL, CRISIS, *supra* note 682, at 330; JUDSON, *supra* note 672, at 220-21; KENYON, STUART CONSTITUTION, *supra* note 665, at 179, 197.

[713] KENYON, STUART CONSTITUTION, *supra* note 665, at 104, 204.

[714] RUSSELL, CRISIS, *supra* note 682, at 339-41, 353.

[715] PLUCKNETT, CONST. HIST., *supra* note 59, at 415.

[716] 6 HOLDSWORTH, *supra* note 113, at 163-65.

[717] MAURICE ASHLEY, THE GLORIOUS REVOLUTION OF 1688, at 199 (1966) (reproducing 1687 Declaration for Liberty of Conscience).

[718] MAURICE ASHLEY, JAMES II, at 183-236 (1977).

issue was the bishops' right to petition the king.[719] The jury found the bishops not guilty. The peaceful but significant Glorious Revolution followed in 1688-1689, and James II was forced to flee the realm.[720]

As we saw above, the king's power of suspending and dispensing with the law was a feature of the king ruling by the grace of God.[721] But late seventeenth-century Parliament was vehemently opposed to such a power and its end was Parliament's primary objective. One of the main components of the Declaration of Rights was to prevent the king's suspending and dispensing power.[722]

Lois G. Schwoerer noted that the term "declaration" was used interchangeably with "petition" and "address" but likely carried a stronger connotation than "petition" after the Petition of Right's failure to secure lasting reform.[723] Seventeenth-century

---

719 KENYON, STUART CONSTITUTION, *supra* note 665, at 406-411; ASHLEY, GLORIOUS REVOLUTION, *supra* note 717, at 116-20; *id.* at 200-01; *cf. supra* note 614 (Richard II's punishment of Haxey for delivering a controversial petition).

720 ASHLEY, JAMES II, *supra* note 718, at 249-63.

721 As noted above, the suspending and dispensing power had a long history as a prerogative of the king. *Supra* notes 64-67, 195-198, 393-397, 448, 519-523. The king's power to annul, suspend, or dispense with the law was part of his power as king and the protector of the realm's welfare. *Supra* notes 20-24, 32-36 (common utility and necessity).

722 February 12, 1689 Declaration of Rights in SCHWOERER, *supra* note 680, at 295-98.

723 SCHWOERER, *supra* note 680, at 14-17, 256.

reformers equated the Petition and Declaration to binding law, a statute.[724]

To avoid any ambiguity on that point, the Declaration was modified some and put into statutory form in the 1689 Bill of Rights.[725] The English Bill of Rights addressed the king's suspending and dispensing power as well as the king's *non obstante* power.

> That the pretended power of suspending of laws or the execution of laws by regal authority without consent of Parliament is illegal;
>
> That the pretended power of dispensing with laws or the execution of laws by regal authority, as it hath been assumed and exercised of late, is illegal; . . .
>
> And be it further declared and enacted by the authority aforesaid, that from and after this present session of Parliament no dispensation by *non obstante* of or to any statute or any part thereof shall be allowed, but that the same shall be held void and of no effect, except a dispensation be allowed of in such statute, and except in such cases as shall be specially provided for by

---

[724] *Id.* at 15-17, 235, 267; *supra* note 707. The fight to enforce the Petition continued into the Civil War. RUSSELL, FALL OF MONARCHIES, *supra* note 675, at 211-12, 214, 355.

[725] 8 ANDREW BROWNING, ENG. HIST. DOCS. (1660-1714), *supra* note 3, at 122-28. The Declaration was signed into law as the Bill of Rights on December 16, 1689, but with several major changes including specifying the established and preferred religion of future monarchs. SCHWOERER, *supra* note 680, at 27-28, 269-72.

> one or more bill or bills to be passed during this present session of Parliament.[726]

Shortly after the Glorious Revolution, England entered into an era of permanent parliamentary sovereignty.[727] For the Lords and Commons at the end of the Glorious Revolution, the king's role in affairs was not necessary. The Commons had transformed the divine rights of king from sovereignty, to "ay" or "no" on matters, and finally to optional.[728] In the preface to the English Bill of Rights, the Lords and Commons implied that sovereignty rests with the Lords and the Commons and that the king was not a required "estate" of the realm. "Whereas the Lords Spiritual and Temporal and Commons assembled at Westminster, lawfully, fully and freely representing all the estates of the people of this realm. . . ."[729]

In a sense, the seventeenth century's achievements can be viewed as a continuation and completion of the thirteenth- and fourteenth-century efforts, moving toward participatory government in fact rather than in theory. The successive political struggles forming the English Constitution can be paraphrased as promoting common consent against the king's arbitrary power. We know from Petrinacy that the king was the vicar of God, a sword

---

726 8 BROWNING, ENG. HIST. DOCS., *supra* note 3, at 123, 128.

727 6 HOLDSWORTH, *supra* note 113, at 209, 230–42. On this subject, see JEFFREY GOLDSWORTHY, PARLIAMENTARY SOVEREIGNTY: CONTEMPORARY DEBATES (2010); GOLDSWORTHY, *supra* note 538.

728 PLUCKNETT, CONST. HIST., *supra* note 59, at 331–32 (Commons sought to reverse the medieval policy of relegating the Commons' input to "ay" or "no" and apply that rule to the king).

729 8 BROWNING, ENG. HIST. DOCS., *supra* note 3, at 122; *see also* SCHWOERER, *supra* note 680, at 28, 268.

bearer.[730] Divine justice came from God, then went to the king, and then to community. The fourteenth century planted the seeds of parliamentary sovereignty as barons sought a partnership "from God to king and community."[731] The seventeenth century harvested the fruit, effecting a change to "from God to community to king."[732] The community governed the common utility and welfare of the people (commonwealth).[733] John Locke, a famous seventeenth-century philosopher, published in 1689:

> [I]n a constituted commonwealth, standing upon its own basis, and acting according to its own nature, that is, acting for the preservation of the community, there can be but one supreme power, which is the legislative, to which all the rest are and must be subordinate; yet the legislative being only a fiduciary power to act for certain ends, there remains still "in the people a supreme power to remove or alter the legislative," when they find the legislative act contrary to the trust reposed in them: for all power given with trust for the attaining an end, being limited by that end; whenever that end is manifestly neglected or opposed, the trust must necessarily be forfeited, and the power devolve into the hands of those that gave it, who may place it anew where they shall think best for their safety and security. And thus the community perpetually retains a supreme power of saving themselves from the attempts and designs of any body, even of their legislators, whenever they

---

730 *Supra* Chapter II sec. A.

731 *Supra* Chapter VI secs. A-C.

732 SCHWOERER, *supra* note 680, at 61.

733 2 JOHN LOCKE, TWO TREATISES OF GOVERNMENT (Hollis ed. 1764), *available at* http://oll.libertyfund.org/titles/222; *see also* SCHWOERER, *supra* note 680, at 153; *supra* notes 674-681.

> shall be so foolish, or so wicked, as to lay and carry on designs against the liberties and properties of the subject.[734]

The Lords and Commons completed in the seventeenth century what had begun in the thirteenth century with the Magna Carta.

[734] 2 LOCKE, *supra* note 733, at § 149 (minor formatting added).

IX

The American Constitution

A. Independence, the Articles of Confederation, and Amendments to the Articles

THE AMERICAN COLONIES, too, suffered under monarchical absolutism.[735] American colonists celebrated the "liberties of the Englishmen" and considered it a birthright notwithstanding their status as colonists.[736] Colonial governance, however, varied from English politics in one central feature. The English Constitution's beacon—common consent and parliamentary representation—did not shine its light across the Atlantic.

The lack of representation in Parliament was the center of a late eighteenth-century taxation dispute. Colonists perceived parliamentary taxation and several other aspects of English gov-

---

[735] DAVID S. LOVEJOY, THE GLORIOUS REVOLUTION IN AMERICA (1972).

[736] 3 HERBERT L. OSGOOD, THE AMERICAN COLONIES IN THE SEVENTEENTH CENTURY 11-12 (1907); Burrell, *Story of Privileges and Immunities*, *supra* note 85, at Part V.

ernance without their consent as arbitrary, similar to the baronial grievances underlying the Magna Carta and medieval era.

In the 1774 Declaration and Resolves, a "colonial bill of rights," the colonists proclaimed:

> 1. That they are entitled to life, liberty, and property, and they have never ceded to any sovereign power whatever, a right to dispose of either without their consent.
>
> 2. That our ancestors, who first settled these colonies, were at the time of their emigration from the mother country, entitled to all the rights, liberties, and immunities of free and natural born subjects within the realm of England.
>
> 3. That by such emigration they by no means forfeited, surrendered, or lost any of those rights, but that they were, and their descendants now are, entitled to the exercise and enjoyment of all such of them, as their local and other circumstances enable them to exercise and enjoy.
>
> 4. That the foundation of English liberty, and of all free government, is a right in the people to participate in their legislative council: and as the English colonists are not represented, and from their local and other circumstances, cannot properly be represented in the British parliament, they are entitled to a free and exclusive power of legislation in their several provincial legislatures, where their right of representation can alone be preserved, in all cases of taxation and internal polity, subject only to the negative of their sovereign, in such manner as has been heretofore used and accustomed. But, from the necessity of the case, and a regard to the mutual interest of both countries, we cheerfully consent to the operation of such acts of the British parliament, as are bona fide, restrained to the regulation of our external commerce, for the pur-

pose of securing the commercial advantages of the whole empire to the mother country, and the commercial benefits of its respective members; excluding every idea of taxation, internal or external, for raising a revenue on the subjects in America without their consent.

5. That the respective colonies are entitled to the common law of England, and more especially to the great and inestimable privilege of being tried by their peers of the vicinage, according to the course of that law.

6. That they are entitled to the benefit of such of the English statutes, as existed at the time of their colonization; and which they have, by experience, respectively found to be applicable to their several local and other circumstances.

7. That these, his majesty's colonies, are likewise entitled to all the immunities and privileges granted and confirmed to them by royal charters, or secured by their several codes of provincial laws.

8. That they have a right peaceably to assemble, consider of their grievances, and petition the King; and that all prosecutions, prohibitory proclamations, and commitments for the same, are illegal.

9. That the keeping of a Standing army in these colonies, in times of peace, without the consent of the legislature of that colony, in which such army is kept, is against law.

10. It is indispensably necessary to good government, and rendered essential by the English constitution, that the constituent branches of the legislature be independent of each other; that, therefore, the exercise of legislative power in several colonies, by a council appointed, dur-

> ing pleasure, by the crown, is unconstitutional, dangerous, and destructive to the freedom of American legislation.[737]

Attempts to resolve the dispute with Great Britain failed. On July 4, 1776, the colonies declared independence. Following independence, the former colonies were encouraged to form their own governments.[738] To substitute for English authority in the colonies, many states adopted a constitution.[739]

Replacing perceptions of English imperialism, state constitutions emphasized representative government in several ways. States provided for republican principles, separation of powers, term limits, bicameralism, and various other components from their English and colonial heritage. Several state constitutions were accompanied by bills of rights of varying length and subject matter.[740]

The last part of the colonial era left the former colonies with a firm belief in local government, except for some external

---

[737] October 14, 1774 Declarations and Resolves, in 1 JOURNALS OF THE CONTINENTAL CONGRESS 1774-1789, at 63-73 (Worthington Chauncey Ford ed. 1904) (hereinafter JOURNALS).

[738] May 10, 1776 Resolves, in 4 JOURNALS, *supra* note 737, at 341-42 (suggestion for states to form their own governments); *id.* at 357-58 (May 15, 1776).

[739] *See generally* FRANCIS NEWTON THORPE, THE FEDERAL AND STATE CONSTITUTIONS, COLONIAL CHARTERS, AND OTHER ORGANIC LAWS OF THE STATES, TERRITORIES, AND COLONIES NOW OR HERETOFORE FORMING THE UNITED STATES OF AMERICA (1909).

[740] THORPE, *supra* note 739; Riggs, *supra* note 691, at 973-75; Ryan C. Williams, *The One and Only Substantive Due Process Clause*, 120 YALE L.J. 408, 437-39 (2010).

matters for which local government would not work.[741] Accordingly, state constitutions regulated internal concerns, but foreign concerns and interstate matters required collective governance. At the same time that the states were forming state governments, the Continental Congress was creating a compact or confederation among the states. The Articles of Confederation replaced English regulation and provided an initial framework for a limited confederation in areas of trade, revenue, and collective defense of the states.[742] Prior to this, England and English citizenship had served this function.[743]

The Articles of Confederation suffered many defects, primarily due to a lack of enforcement concerning western land boundaries, commerce, and national revenue.[744] During its short life, the Confederation Congress struggled to regulate commerce and to raise revenue from the too-sovereign states.[745] Compliance with the Articles was considered mostly voluntary. In 1780, before the Articles were ratified, Congress sought power to collect its own revenue through duties on specified imports. The effort became an amendment to the Articles after they were ratified in

---

741 RICHARD BLAND, THE COLONEL DISMOUNTED (1764), *reprinted in* 1 PAMPHLETS OF THE AMERICAN REVOLUTION 1750-1776, at 301, 320-21 (Bernard Bailyn ed., 1965); *see also supra* note 737.

742 Burrell, *Journey*, *supra* note 60, at Part II.C.

743 *Id.* at Part II.

744 JACK N. RAKOVE, THE BEGINNINGS OF NATIONAL POLITICS: AN INTERPRETIVE HISTORY OF THE CONTINENTAL CONGRESS 288-90 (1979); MERRILL JENSEN, THE NEW NATION: A HISTORY OF THE UNITED STATES DURING THE CONFEDERATION 1781-1789, at 1-27 (3d prtg. 1962) (hereinafter JENSEN, NEW NATION).

745 1 THE DOCUMENTARY HISTORY OF THE RATIFICATION OF THE CONSTITUTION, CONSTITUTIONAL DOCUMENTS AND RECORDS, 1776-1787, at 140-74 (Merrill Jensen ed. 1976) (hereinafter DOC. HIST. OF RATIF. CONST.); Burrell, *Journey*, *supra* note 60, at 229-34.

March 1781. Each state except Rhode Island agreed, so the amendment to collect revenue failed as amendments required unanimity.[746]

Within weeks of the Articles' adoption, a Committee including James Varnum, James Madison, and James Duane was formed to propose a plan to enforce the Articles.[747] The Committee proposed:

> It is understood & hereby declared that in case any one or more of the Confederated States shall refuse or neglect to abide by the determinations of the United States in Congress assembled or to observe all the articles of the Confederation as required in the 13th Article, the said United States in Congress assembled are fully authorized to employ the force of the United States as well by sea as by land to compel such State or States to fulfill their federal engagements, and particularly to make distraint on any of the effects Vessels and Merchandizes of such State or States or of any of the Citizens thereof wherever found, and to prohibit and prevent their trade and intercourse as well with any other of the United states and the Citizens thereof, as with any foreign State, and as well by land as by sea, until full compensation or compliance be obtained with respect to all Requisitions made by the United States in Congress assembled in pursuance of the Articles of Confederation.
>
> And it is to be understood, and is hereby agreed and conceded that this Article shall be fully and absolutely binding and conclusive when all the

---

746 1 DOC. HIST. OF RATIF. CONST., *supra* note 745, at 140.

747 *Id.* at 141.

> States not actually in the Possession of the Enemy, shall enact the same.[748]

Under the proposal, the Confederation would be able to coerce and distrain a noncomplying state. But military coercion was considered harsh. A less forceful report followed which proposed to give Congress several legislative powers to carry out and enforce the Articles. The committee enumerated over two dozen powers necessary for federal government.[749] But the committee felt the effort was frustrated because it could not name all the needed enforcement powers.

The end of the war with England in 1783 introduced international trade problems as the states fought English restrictions in the Caribbean colonies.[750] States were flouting Confederation regulation and violating federal treaties.[751] Similar problems occurred between the states on matters of interstate trade. Divisions between North and South and between large and small states permeated the conflict.[752]

---

[748] *Id.* at 142-43.

[749] *Id.* at 144-45. In this we can see the germ of what would soon become congressional enforcement powers found in the Constitution's Article I, Section 8.

[750] JENSEN, NEW NATION, *supra* note 744, at 401; 1 DOC. HIST. OF RATIF. CONST., *supra* note 745, at 153.

[751] JENSEN, NEW NATION, *supra* note 744, at 280-81, 297; RAKOVE, *supra* note 744, at 343; Burrell, *Journey*, *supra* note 60, at 231.

[752] JENSEN, NEW NATION, *supra* note 744, at 404-06 (southern commercial interests varied from northern commercial interests); 1 DOC. HIST. OF RATIF. CONST., *supra* note 745, at 155; Burrell, *Journey*, *supra* note 60, at 229.

Congress needed a means of authorizing and enforcing national needs and national legislation.[753] A proposed 1785 amendment would have bolstered the Confederation Congress's interstate and foreign commerce authority.

> The United States in Congress Assembled shall have the sole and exclusive right and power of determining, on peace and war, except in the cases mentioned in the sixth Article[;] of sending and receiving Ambassadors[;] entering into treaties and alliances[;] of regulating the trade of the States as well with foreign Nations, as with each other[;] and of laying such imposts and duties, upon imports and exports as may be necessary for the purpose; provided that the Citizens of the States, shall in no instance be subject to pay higher imposts and duties, than those imposed on the subjects of foreign powers; provided also that the Legislative power of the several States shall not be restrained from prohibiting the importation or exportation of any species of goods or commodities whatsoever, provided also that all such duties as may be imposed, shall be collected under the authority and accrue to the use of the State in which the same shall be payable. And provided lastly that every Act of Congress for the above purpose shall have the assent of nine States in Congress assembled. . . .[754]

The 1785 proposal was not sent to the states as it generated significant controversy in Congress.[755]

Piecemeal attempts at amending the Articles were not working. Leading statesmen sought more comprehensive reform.

---

[753] 1 DOC. HIST. OF RATIF. CONST., *supra* note 745, at 153-54.

[754] *Id.* at 156.

[755] JENSEN, NEW NATION, *supra* note 744, at 404-06.

In July of 1786, a Grand Committee of the Confederation Congress was formed to collect grievances and amend the Articles.[756] The Committee proposed several amendments. Article 14 resembled the 1785 proposal; it provided authority for the Confederation Congress to more fully regulate interstate and foreign commerce:

> The United States in Congress Assembled shall have the sole and exclusive power of Regulating the trade of the States as well with foreign Nations as with each other and of laying such prohibitions, and such Imposts and duties upon imports, and exports, as may be Necessary for the purpose; provided the Citizens of the States shall in no instance be subjected to pay higher duties and Imposts than those imposed on the subjects of foreign powers, provided also, that all such duties as may be imposed shall be collected under such Regulations as the United States in Congress Assembled shall establish consistent with the Constitutions of the States Respectively and to accrue to the use of the State in which the same Shall be payable; provided also that the Legislative power of the several States shall not be restrained from laying embargoes in times of Scarcity And provided lastly that every Act of Congress for the above purpose shall have the assent of Nine States in Congress Assembled, and in that proportion when there shall be more than thirteen in the Union.[757]

Under the Articles, requests for revenue had been ignored. In proposed Article 15, states, upon receipt of federal requests, were to adopt resolutions acknowledging and implementing Con-

---

[756] 1 DOC. HIST. OF RATIF. CONST., *supra* note 745, at 163.

[757] *Id.* at 163-64.

federation requisitions for financial and military aid. States would be fined for noncompliance. Proposed Article 16, like earlier efforts, attempted to provide a means for enforcing Confederation taxation. If states did not comply with federal requests, then the federal government and federal officers would step into the shoes of state officials and collect the funds by the same process by which states collect funds from its own citizens. Proposed Article 19 provided for a federal judiciary.

> The United States in Congress Assembled shall have the Sole and exclusive power of declaring what offences against the United States [constitute] treason and what Offences against the same [constitute] Misprision of treason, and what Offences shall be deemed piracy or felonies on the high Seas[;] to annex suitable punishments to all the Offences aforesaid respectively and power to institute a federal Judicial Court for trying and punishing all Officers appointed by Congress for all crimes, offences, and misbehavior in their Offices[.] [A]n Appeal Shall be allowed from the Judicial Courts of the several States, in all Causes wherein questions Shall arise on the meaning and construction of Treaties entered into by the United States with any foreign power, or on the Law of Nations, or wherein any Question shall arise respecting any Regulations that may hereafter be made by Congress Relative to trade and Commerce, or the Collection of federal Revenues pursuant to powers that shall be vested in that body, or wherein questions of importance may arise, and the United States shall be a party—provided that the trial of the fact by Jury shall ever be held sacred, and also the benefits of the writ of *Habeas Corpus;* provided also that no member of Congress or Officer holding any other Office under the United States shall be a Judge of said Court, and the said Court shall consist of Seven Judges, to be appointed from the different parts of the Union to wit, one from New Hampshire, Rhode is-

> land and Connecticut, one from Massachusetts, one from New-York and New Jersey, one from Pensylvania, one from Delaware and Maryland, one from Virginia, and one from North Carolina, South Carolina, and Georgia, and four of whom shall be a quorum to do business.[758]

The federal tribunal would have jurisdiction over crimes by federal officers and appellate jurisdiction over state tribunals concerning (1) interpretations of federal treaties with foreign nations; (2) congressional regulations concerning taxation and trade and commerce; and (3) any other great cause of great interest (where the U.S. is a party).

From the beginning, the Confederation was having problems enforcing sovereignty over interstate and national matters. The amendments proposed from 1781-1786 would have expanded congressional power and given substance to the initial 1781 proposal to exercise distraint and coercion against noncomplying states. The Confederation Congress would have jurisdiction over and pass national law regulating interstate and foreign commerce. A federal tribunal would have power to interpret national law. Federal officers would enforce national law. In a sense, the rise of congressional sovereignty resembled the ascent of parliamentary sovereignty and the High Court of Parliament—moving from promises and distraint after the fact to supreme legislation in order to enforce national will.

In the opinion of several states, the Grand Committee Report created too strong a central government. It did not go far before a Convention was called, the Constitutional Convention in Philadelphia.

---

[758] *Id.* at 166-67.

B. The United States Constitution and the Fifth Amendment

The Philadelphia Convention of 1787 was initially formed to consider amendments to the Articles. After many failed attempts at amending the Articles, however, the leading founders decided to propose a new constitution with congressional sovereignty to legislate in enumerated areas. The new national government would be in large part "national" rather than "federal" like the Articles of Confederation.[759] One of the Framers' primary goals was to build a government based on the people rather than on the states.

The Constitution's provisions were debated during the summer of 1787.[760] In September, the Convention agreed to the Constitution. From there, it was sent to the Confederation Congress to approve and send to the states for ratification.

In many ways, the Constitution inherited aspects of the English Constitution as viewed through the colonial experience. The Constitution provides for three independent and supreme branches of government. Throughout, the Framers were highly sensitive to establishing and safeguarding participatory government. The Constitution apportioned taxation and representation among the people of the states—common consent.[761] The Constitution has several checks and balances, many drawn from the Eng-

---

759 1 THE RECORDS OF THE FEDERAL CONVENTION OF 1787, at 37 (Max Farrand rev. ed. 1966) (hereinafter FARRAND).

760 For discussion, see the three volumes by Max Farrand, *supra* note 759.

761 U.S. CONST. art. I. § 2 (1789).

lish Constitution, to ensure against abuse.[762] Copying baronial demands for frequent Parliaments, the Constitution requires that Congress meet at least once a year. While the legislature can abuse its station, the executive veto was deemed a very important check against the abuse of majorities in the national legislature.[763]

> We must introduce the Checks, which will destroy the measures of an interested majority—in this view a negative in the [executive] is not only necessary for its own safety, but for the safety of a minority in Danger of oppression from an unjust and interested majority[.] The independent condition of the [executive] who has the Eyes of all Nations on him will render him a just Judge—add the Judiciary and you increase the respectability.[764]

But because the executive itself can abuse power, the office is held to four-year terms and Congress can override an executive veto.[765]

To diffuse power, the Constitution established a bicameral system of representatives. The Senate is in office for six years and was intended to represent the merchants and higher classes (House of Lords). The House is in office for two years and was designed to be a more direct connection with the people (House of

---

[762] *See, e.g.*, U.S. CONST. art. I §§ 2, 3 (staggered bicameralism, impeachment), § 7 (veto power, overriding presidential veto); *id.*, Art. II, §§ 1, 2 (frequent elections, apportionment, advise and consent); *see also* Burrell, *Journey*, *supra* note 60 at 238. For state constitutions, see generally THORPE, *supra* note 739.

[763] U.S. CONST. art. I. § 7.

[764] 1 FARRAND, *supra* note 759, at 108. Madison supported adding judicial officers to the executive veto to make a Council of Revision. Madison advocated for this throughout the Convention, but it failed to secure a place in the final draft.

[765] U.S. CONST. art. I. § 7.

Commons). The House is able to impeach officers, like the Commons and Commons' Petition.[766] The Senate tries impeachments, like the Lords and *judicium parium*.[767]

The Constitution also provides for miscellaneous qualifications, establishes term limits, requires oaths of office, and requires advice and consent for executive appointments. Each power is checked with a countervailing power, and the people are the ultimate arbiters through frequent elections.[768] The Constitution became fundamental law for the states.

For many, the United States Constitution did not resolve the problem. Fears spread over the unknown powers of the national government, which would threaten state and local government.[769] Congress's proposed Necessary and Proper Clause was a frequent focus of concern. It reads:

> To make all laws which shall be necessary and proper for carrying into Execution the foregoing powers, and all other Powers vested by this Constitution in the Government of the United States, or in any Department or Officer thereof.[770]

Antifederalists felt that the Necessary and Proper Clause gave Congress too much discretion. George Mason and other Antifederalists objected to the Constitution because it did not, among

---

766 U.S. CONST. art. I. § 2.

767 U.S. CONST. art. I. § 3.

768 *See generally* FEDERALIST PAPERS.

769 *See generally* HERBERT J. STORING, THE COMPLETE ANTI-FEDERALIST (1981) (reproducing Antifederalist literature).

770 U.S. CONST. art. I, § 8, cl. 18.

other things, include a federal Bill of Rights.[771] Mason was worried that without a Bill of Rights, the federal government would swallow up state governments and state bills of rights.

The debates over the Constitution and Bill of Rights continued from the end of the Convention through the state-ratifying conventions.[772] In 1789, the states ratified the Constitution. During the ratification controversy, several states demanded a national bill of rights.

Following the Constitution's ratification, to appease Antifederalists, the 1st Congress proposed, and in 1791 the states ratified, the United States Bill of Rights to limit the federal government in favor of state and local government.[773] The national Bill of Rights largely copied from state bills of rights and both drew from the English Bill of Rights and English law to various degrees.

Several comparisons between the United States Bill of Rights and English legal history can be made. For purposes of this discussion, we focus on the Fifth Amendment. The Fifth Amendment provided:

---

[771] George Mason, *Objections to the Constitution of Government Formed by the Convention*, *in* 2 STORING, *supra* note 769, at 9-14; *see also* 1 STORING, *supra*, at 64-70.

[772] For the ratification debates, see the volumes in DOC. HIST. OF RATIF. CONST., *supra* note 745.

[773] The 1st Congress debated the proposed amendments from June through September 1789. A majority of the debates can be found in JOSEPH GALES, THE DEBATES AND PROCEEDINGS IN THE CONGRESS OF THE UNITED STATES, 1st Cong., 1st. Sess. 440-809 (1834) (hereinafter ANNALS OF CONGRESS). The ANNALS OF CONGRESS can be found online at http://memory.loc.gov/ammem/amlaw/lwac.html.

> No person shall be held to answer for a capital, or otherwise infamous crime, unless on a presentment or indictment of a grand jury, except in cases arising in the land or naval forces, or in the militia, when in actual service in time of war or public danger; nor shall any person be subject for the same offense to be twice put in jeopardy of life or limb; nor shall be compelled in any criminal case to be a witness against himself, nor be deprived of life, liberty, or property, without due process of law; nor shall private property be taken for public use, without just compensation.[774]

The Fifth Amendment's central features were not new. It borrowed from English custom and common law, some of which we saw in Henry II's assizes.[775] The plain language of the Amendment clearly requires presentment and indictment for specified crimes. In a separate clause, the Fifth Amendment, adopted by the 1st Congress without substantive discussion, paraphrased Chapter 39 and fourteenth-century statutes by prohibiting the deprivation of life, liberty, or property without due process of law.[776] Chapter 39 of the Magna Carta provided:

> No freemen shall be taken or imprisoned or disseised or exiled or in any way destroyed, nor

---

[774] U.S. CONST. amend. V. For state law-of-the-land clauses and bills of rights similar in form and content to the Fifth Amendment, see Williams, *supra* note 740, at 437–39 and the citations therein.

[775] *Supra* Chapter III sec. C. The Northwest Ordinance of 1787 may have been a template for the Fifth Amendment. *Infra* note 884; Williams, *supra* note 740, at 446 n.156.

[776] 1 ANNALS OF CONGRESS, *supra* note 773, 1st Cong., 1st. Sess. 781 (August 17, 1789); *see also supra* Chapter IV sec. B; Frank H. Easterbrook, *Substance and Due Process*, 1982 SUP. CT. REV. 85, 97 (1982) (commenting that the due process provision came from New York's recommendation and that it did not receive significant debate in the New York Assembly either); Williams, *supra* note 740, at 445–46.

> will we go upon him nor send upon him, except by the lawful judgment of his peers or by the law of the land.[777]

In separate language, the Amendment also provided other express guaranties against double jeopardy, self-incrimination, and takings without compensation.

Recall that the principles of judgment before execution and participation in taxation were central features of feudal justice and the Magna Carta.[778] Due process of law was the opposite of Angevin monarchy *per voluntatem*—the opposite of the abuses generating the Magna Carta: arbitrary arresting, imprisoning, exiling, and disseisin. By the mid-fourteenth century, the Lords and Commons were jealous of conciliar encroachments upon the common law.[779] Due process of law was shorthand for legal procedure such as indictment and presentment, which were components of the common law or law of the land.[780] Royal and conciliar actions were arbitrary because they did not follow the law. The Lords and Commons of Parliament could extend, modify, or repeal the common law when prudence called.[781] Due process of law and law of the land were not what the law ought to be but what it was. In its proper context, "due process of law" had meaning against the king and other arbitrary actors, never against the

---

777 MAGNA CARTA ch. 39 (1215) *in* 3 ROTHWELL, ENG. HIST. DOCS., *supra* note 3, at 320.

778 *Supra* Chapter IV.

779 *Supra* Chapter VI sec. E.

780 *Supra* notes 539, 554.

781 *Supra* Chapters V sec. C, VI sec. D; *supra* notes 317, 449-456, 517-522, 694.

common consent of the Lords and Commons.[782] Such an application would turn common consent's essential nature against itself, a perversion creating arbitrary from participatory.[783]

But this concept of due process struggled to cross the Atlantic with the language. A leading member of the founding generation and a Federalist did not appear to agree with this medieval understanding of the due process concept. Alexander Hamilton, in a February 1787 debate on a state legislative matter, commented that "law of the land" meant the process of presentment and indictment, but not legislation:

> In one article of it, it is said no man shall be disfranchised or deprived of any right he enjoys under the constitution, but by the *law of the land,* or the judgment of his peers. Some gentlemen hold that the law of the land will include an act of the legislature. But Lord Coke, that great luminary of the law, in his comment upon a similar clause, in Magna Charta, interprets the law of the land to mean presentment and indictment, and process of outlawry, as contradistinguished from trial by jury. But if there were any doubt upon the constitution, the bill of rights enacted in this very session removes it. It

---

[782] *Supra* notes 690-705.

[783] Blackstone wrote:

> It were endless to enumerate all the *affirmative* acts of parliament, wherein justice is directed to be done according to the law of the land; and what that law is every subject knows, or may know, if he pleases; for it depends not upon the arbitrary will of any judge, but is permanent, fixed, and unchangeable, unless by authority of parliament.

1 BLACKSTONE, COMMENTARIES, *supra* note 677, at 243-44 (*141-42). *See also* Williams, *supra* note 740, at 433-43 (citing the Blackstone passage and supporting evidence for the understanding that law of the land meant positive law; Parliament updated and modified common law); Riggs, *supra* note 691, at 971-73.

> is there declared that, no man shall be disfranchised or deprived of any right, but by *due process of law,* or the judgment of his peers. The words "*due process*" have a precise technical import, and are only applicable to the process and proceedings of the courts of justice; they can never be referred to an act of legislature.[784]

Hamilton relied forcefully on his perception of Coke.[785] Coke is often criticized and does not provide a reliable source for legal history.[786] But even for him, the statement that the "law of

[784] 4 THE PAPERS OF ALEXANDER HAMILTON 35 (Harold C. Syrett, Jacob E. Cooke eds. 1962), *cited in* Easterbrook, *supra* note 776, at 98 n.35. We have no indication that Hamilton's understanding was widely shared. Modern commentators make that assumption but further research may well show that Hamilton's views were not representative, especially in light of the larger concern over participatory government. For example, William Penn used the terms "due process of law" and "law of the land" interchangeably in his 1687 commentary on the Magna Carta.

> [Chapter 39 means first that] no man be taken or imprisoned but by *per legem terrae*; that is, by the common-law, statute-law, or custom of England; . . . . Secondly. No man shall be disseised . . . unless it be by the lawful judgment . . . of his equals . . . or by the law of the land, that is (to speak it once for all) by the due course and process of law.

WILLIAM PENN, THE EXCELLENT PRIVILEDGE OF LIBERTY & PROPERTY BEING THE BIRTH-RIGHT OF THE FREE-BORN SUBJECTS OF ENGLAND 23-24 (1687) (minor formatting added); *see also id.* at 29. Penn's understanding comports with English history. During the seventeenth century, the Commons sought to secure due process of law according to the law of the land. When considered in light of the king and royal judges, the point was to curb the king in favor of the law, Parliament's law. *Supra* Chapter VIII. The terms were consistently used in favor of legislation against forces denying the law and legislation.

[785] *See also* Nathan S. Chapman & Michael W. McConnell, *Due Process as Separation of Powers*, 121 YALE L.J. 1671, 1713-17 (2012).

[786] *Supra* notes 666-669, 696.

the land" was not Parliament's law of the land would be fiction.[787] Coke's advocacy for the common law against royal action was based largely on specific statutes that were read along with the Magna Carta. The entire context for Coke's statements is that the Magna Carta and several statutes made the king's arbitrary confinement contrary to statute law because royal confinement was without presentment and indictment as provided for in the statute. Moreover, confinement by Parliament was accepted.[788] Coke recognized that Parliament updates, modifies, and repeals the common law. While Coke can also be found stating that statutes against the Magna Carta were void, Parliament was not the focus of the 1620s debates on the Petition of Right.[789] What must be remembered is that these English debates, clauses, and treatises were, in root and stem, discussions in light of the king and arbitrary royal action.[790] For Coke and the Commons, the Magna Carta and confirming statutes were fundamental law and limited the king.

Contrary to Hamilton's apparent position, colonists understood that their law-of-the-land provisions meant their own law or English statute and common law as modified by their local law. Before Hamilton's observation in 1787, the New York Colonists incorporated a version of the Due Process Clause from the Magna Carta in the 1683 New York Charter of Liberties:

---

[787] *Supra* notes 690-705. The confusion is likely attributed to myopic consideration of text from the Commons' debates or Coke's INSTITUTES without appreciating the broader context of arbitrary royal government and the underlying effort of limiting **the king** *in favor of* Parliament.

[788] *Supra* notes 686-699.

[789] *Supra* notes 697-698.

[790] *Infra* notes 824, 847.

> No freeman shall be taken and imprisoned or be disseized of his freehold or Liberty of free Customs or be outlawed or Exiled or any other ways destroyed nor shall be passed upon adjudged or condemned But by the Lawful Judgment of his peers and by the Law of this province.[791]

Other colonial laws demonstrate a similar understanding.[792]

Alexander Hamilton's misunderstanding of "due process of law" may have been limited to a pre-Constitution misconception. The Framers did not share this confusion. The Constitution clearly provides that federal law is the "supreme Law of the land." The Supremacy Clause of Article VI:

> This Constitution, and the Laws of the United States which shall be made in Pursuance thereof; and all Treaties made, or which shall be made, under the Authority of the United States, shall be the supreme Law of the Land; and the Judges in every State shall be bound thereby, any Thing in the Constitution or Laws of any State to the Contrary notwithstanding.[793]

After the Convention, Hamilton showed no hesitation in referring to congressional laws as the "Supreme Law of the Land."[794] None-

---

[791] New York Charter of Liberties 1683, *available at* http://oll.libertyfund.org/pages/1683-charter-of-liberties-and-privileges-new-york (minor formatting added).

[792] Raoul Berger, *"Law of the Land" Reconsidered*, 74 NW. U. L. REV. 1, 8–10 (1979); Riggs, *supra* note 691, at 963–65.

[793] U.S. CONST. art. VI.

[794] Hamilton on the power to constitute a national bank. http://founders.archives.gov/documents/Hamilton/01-08-02-0060-0002.

theless, the confusion was a sign of what was to come with judicial interpretation of the Due Process Clause.

X

The Judiciary and Due Process of Law: Substantive Due Process

A. Due Process of Law, Law of the Land, and Constitutional Common Law

THE IMPLICATION IN HAMILTON'S STATEMENT—that due process of law is not controlled by positive law and legislation—confused the first seventy-five years of law-of-the-land and due-process-of-law adjudication. Did the "law of the land" provision in state constitutions mean deprivation only by a fixed judicial action such that the constitutions prohibited the legislature from abrogating the common law or associated judicial procedure? Or did "law of the land" and "due process of law" create a restriction against arbitrary actions by branches other than the legislature such that the state's positive law together with or expressly abrogating the common law creates the "law of the land"?

As demonstrated above, England's law of the land included various procedures of which presentment and indictment were legislatively a part, not the whole. Madison seemed to have clearly understood this when he proposed the Fifth Amendment.[795] The Amendment expressly constitutionalizes several guaranties. In separate language, the Amendment includes the Due Process Clause. A plain-language construction reveals that "due process of law" meant something other than the "common law" guaranties of indictment, presentment, and just compensation, which were expressly provided for in the same paragraph in separate language.[796]

Former colonists assumed before and after independence that the common law was part of the law of the state unless modified by the state legislature or state constitution.[797] New York's adoption of the common law:

> And this convention doth further, in the name and by the authority of the good people of this State, ordain, determine, and declare that such parts of the common law of England, and of the statute law of England and Great Britain, and of the acts of the legislature of the colony of New York, as together did form the law of the said colony on the 19th day of April, in the year of our Lord one thousand seven hundred and sev-

---

[795] *Supra* notes 773-777.

> No person shall be held to answer for a capital, or otherwise infamous crime, unless on a presentment or indictment of a grand jury, except in cases arising in the land or naval forces, or in the militia, when in actual service in time of war or public danger; nor shall any person be subject for the same offense to be twice put in jeopardy of life or limb; nor shall be compelled in any criminal case to be a witness against himself, nor be deprived of life, liberty, or property, without due process of law; nor shall private property be taken for public use, without just compensation.

U.S. CONST. amend. V.

[796] *Supra* notes 774-783.

[797] *Supra* notes 791-792; 1774 Declaration of Grievances, *supra* note 737; *infra* note 814 (constitutional common law and trial by jury).

> enty-five, shall be and continue the law of this State, subject to such alterations and provisions as the legislature of this State shall, from time to time, make concerning the same.[798]

Any ambiguity in positive law was to be construed consistent with the common law.[799] To construe legislation or constitutional provisions with the common law[800] or English heritage for definition or meaning is not controversial.[801] It becomes controversial when a judge elevates the common law above the state's positive legislation to the contrary. And this was the fight fought in the first seventy-five years of the Republic.

The early lines were drawn by state courts. State judges recognized the positive-law aspect of due process of law and law of the land. The traditional view, based on English heritage and colonial understanding, was that the state's "law of the land" was the constitution, state positive law, and common law in that order.[802]

In the North Carolina opinion *State v. ----*, the issue before the court was whether the North Carolina Constitution's "law of

---

[798] Sect. XXXV of New York's 1777 Constitution, 5 THORPE, *supra* note 739, at 2635; *cf. supra* Chapters V sec. C, VI sec. D; *supra* notes 651-656, 676, 694 (Parliament updates and alters common law).

[799] 2 JAMES KENT'S COMMENTARIES ON AMERICAN LAW, Part IV, § 24 at 53-54 n.7 (William M. Lacy, 9th ed. 1889) (noting "trial by jury" provision in state bills of rights but citing state statutes providing for nonjury trial deprivations).

[800] The term "common law" was used loosely in the seventeenth century and by the colonists. The common law included English custom as well as ancient statute law.

[801] The common-law definition was understood when drafters, for example, used terms such as "*ex post facto*" or "bills of attainder."

[802] *Supra* notes 791-792, 797.

the land" and "trial by jury" provisions prohibited the legislature from allowing the Attorney General to obtain judgments against delinquent recipients of public money without trial, their delinquencies being sufficient notice.[803] Judge Williams opined that because the provisions were in the North Carolina Constitution and common law controlled "law of the land," legislation deemed contrary to the common law—the Constitution—was void. For Williams, the state's action against delinquents required judicial procedure and trial by jury, and the legislature could not pass a law to the contrary.

Attorney General Haywood clarified his position in light of Williams's concerns. Haywood's position, as reported, deserves quoting at length.

> Next day at the sitting of the court, Haywood, the Attorney General, moved the subject again, as follows:—The clauses of the constitution that are [cited for invalidating] this act[804] are decla-

---

[803] 2 N.C. (1 Hayw.) 50 (1794). The North Carolina Declaration of Rights:

> I. That all political power is vested in and derived from the people only.
>
> II. That the people of this State ought to have the sole and exclusive right of regulating the internal government and police thereof. . . .
>
> V. That all powers of suspending laws, or the execution of laws, by any authority, without consent of the Representatives of the people, is injurious to their rights, and ought not to be exercised. . . .
>
> XII. That no freeman ought to be taken, imprisoned, or disseized of his freehold, liberties or privileges, or outlawed, or exiled, or in any manner destroyed, or deprived of his life, liberty, or property, but by the law of the land.
>
> XIV. That in all controversies at law, respecting property, the ancient mode of trial, by jury, is one of the best securities of the rights of the people, and ought to remain sacred and inviolable.

N.C. Const. 1776, 5 THORPE, *supra* note 739, at 2787-88.

[804] *Supra* note 803.

rations the people thought proper to make of their rights; not against a power they supposed their own representatives might usurp, but against oppression and usurpation in general. The second clause, for instance, could not be intended as a restraint upon the Legislature; it could not be supposed the Legislature would ever attempt to oppose the right of the people to regulate their internal government; it was intended to assert the right of the people against the power of the British King and Parliament, and against all other foreign powers, who hereafter might claim a right under any pretence whatever, of interfering with the affairs of this government[.] [It also] serve[d] as a standing and perpetual memento to posterity that the least intermeddling by any foreign power with the internal policy of this government is an invasion of their privileges. Such also is the manifest meaning of the fifth section. Who were the Convention suspicious of when they declared, "That all power of suspending laws or the execution of laws, by any authority, without the consent of the representatives of the people, is injurious to their rights and ought not to be exercised"? This is not a restraint upon the legislative power of the Assembly. From the experience of what had happened in older governments, they apprehend that in the vicissitudes of human affairs, some ambitious men might usurp the power of dispensing with laws, or claim the right of exercising such a power. It had been frequently done in that government which they were the most intimately acquainted with, to the great oppression of the people. . . . This I take to be the true meaning of the Declaration of Rights; and if we attend to the 12th clause, we shall find it was copied almost *verbatim* from the 29th chap. of *Magna Charta*,[805] and of the occasion of which our Bill of Rights

[805] Chapter 39 became Chapter 29 in the 1225 reissue.

were very similar—the struggle of the people against oppression. This clause in both has nearly the same meaning—and then the spirit of this clause is in exact unison with the other clauses, not intended to restrain the Legislature from making the law of the land, but a declaration only, that the people are to be governed by no other than the law of the land[.] [*P*]*er legem terrae* were words used in the charters granted by Henry I, Stephen, Henry II, John, and Henry III, whose confirmation seemed finally to give stability to this charter . . . .

In these times therefore, the term *lex terrae* meant the English law. . . . [A]nd in like manner in our Constitution, where the Convention are declaring the rights of the people, and use the words of the *Magna Charta* of England, they mean to assert in general, that the people of North Carolina have a right to be governed by their own laws, and not to be subject to laws made by any foreign power upon earth; in like manner, as in the 2nd clause, they declare that the people of this state ought to have the sole and exclusive right of regulating the internal government and police thereof—by all which they mean to vindicate the sovereignty of this country, and the inherent right of the people thereof to govern themselves[.] [T]he term *lex terrae*, in the times of King John and Henry III, began to have a meaning additional to what it had in the former reigns: these princes were guilty of great abuses under the pretence of prerogative—they had confiscated the estates of many of their subjects—they had exiled and destroyed many also by the power of prerogative. . . . [A]nd thus the term *law of the land* is to be understood in our constitution, beside the meaning already ascribed to it, to declare that the people of this State are not to be deprived of liberty, property, the benefit of the law, nor exiled from their country, by any power whatsoever; acting without or contrary to the established law of the country, or by any proceeding not directed or authorised by that law. The meaning of the words *lex terrae* may therefore be thus shortly defined—a law for the people of North Carolina, made or adopted by themselves by the intervention of their own Legislature. This definition excludes the idea of foreign legislation, of royal or executive prerogative, and of usurped power, and leaves the power of inflicting punishments, or rather of passing laws for that purpose, in their own Legislature only. In this sense, the *lex terrae* of North Carolina at present is the whole body of law, composed partly of the common law, partly of customs, partly of the acts of the British Parliament received and enforced here, and partly of the acts passed by our own Legislature. [Citation to Sir Edward Coke's INSTITUTES, *supra* note 690, at 46.] If this body of laws is not the *lex terrae* designated in our Bill of Rights, but the common law only, then the common law is immutable, and the Assembly can not alter it by any legislative act. Should the Assembly in any instance attempt to alter any rule of property with respect to its transmission, descent, &c. so as to entitle any other person to it than is entitled by the common law, he that is entitled by the rule of the common law may say no man is to be deprived of his property or rights but according to the law of the land, or the common law. If an act not punishable by the common law, or punishable only in a smaller degree, should be rendered penal, or more penal than it was by the common law, by any legislative act, the party to be affected by it might say, I am not to be imprisoned, or exiled, or disseised of my freehold, or in any manner destroyed, but according to the law of the land, or in other words, the common law. It is easy to see into what a labyrinth of confusion this would lead us[.] [I]t would contradict the very spirit of the constitution, which in establishing a Republican form of Government, must have been inevitably led [them] to foresee the great alteration which the new state of things would make necessary in the great fabric of the common law; they must have intended such changes therein by the legislative power, as would more perfectly adapt it to the genius of that species of government—many of the maxims of which are so diametrically opposed to all those of the common law, which ha[s] [a] view towards the support of the kingly power, or that of the nobles. Such a construction would destroy all legislative power whatsoever, except that of making laws in addition to the common law, and for cases not provided for by that law. It would lop off the whole body of the statute law at one stroke, and leave us in the most miserable condition that can well be imagined[.] [A]ll capital punishments ordained by the statute law for murder, rape, arson, &c. would be done away, and every malignant passion of the human heart let loose to roam through the land, unbridled by fear, and free from all manner of restraint, except those very ineffectual ones the common law imposes. This cannot, therefore, be the true meaning of the term *law of the land*, made use of in the Bill of Rights; it must be that which I have already contended for, or something very similar to it; and if that be the true meaning of the term, then how do these words at all imply that the Legislature have not a right to pass such an act as that which is the subject of our present discussion? Do they not, on the other hand, prove that as this is neither the act of any foreign Legislature, nor the arbitrary edict of any usurped power acting independent of the people, but the act of their representatives assembled for the purposes of legislation, . . . consult[ing] together for the public welfare[, it] ought to be respected? Does it follow, because the Constitution hath declared the right of the people to be exempted from all foreign jurisdiction and from all power acting independently of the laws, that their own representatives cannot make a law which is useful and necessary for the public good? There is no part of this Constitution that directs the process by which a suit

> shall be instituted, or carried on, and the Legislature are, therefore, free to direct what mode of proceeding in Courts they think proper . . . .[806]

Upon Haywood's re-argument, Judge Williams adhered to his opinion of the day before. Judge Ashe and Judge McCay allowed the Attorney General's judgments to proceed contrary to Judge Williams's opinion. Therefore, the opinion that the law of the land was based on positive law prevailed.[807] The view that "law of the land" elevated English common law above the positive law or that the provision for trial by jury was absolute was narrowly set aside.

In a similar opinion, Chief Judge Richardson in *Mayo v. Wilson* held that state law is "due process of law."[808] Richardson rejected the position that New Hampshire's law-of-the-land provision included and elevated specific common-law procedure above state positive law.

> The question then is what are we to understand by due process of law? The plaintiff contends that the writs of duly constituted courts and warrants, under the hand and seal of magistrates, are the only due process of law by which an arrest can be made within the meaning of the constitution. If this be the true construction of the constitution, the law in question is most clearly invalid, for it certainly purports to authorize an arrest without writ and without warrant from a magistrate.

---

[806] 2 N.C. (1 Hayw.), at 52-57 (minor formatting added).

[807] *Id. See also* Williams, *supra* note 740, at 449-50, 454-55 (discussing case and citing early nineteenth-century treatise commenting that due process of law would be application consistent with constitutional and legislative law).

[808] Mayo v. Wilson, 1 N.H. 53 (1817).

On the part of the defendants, it is contended that the meaning of the constitution is not to be thus restricted, but that an arrest without writ and without warrant, if authorized by the common or statute law of the land, is an arrest by due process of law and an arrest by the law of the land within the meaning of the constitution, as much as an arrest made by virtue of a warrant from a magistrate. . . .

It seems clear that an arrest, if authorized by the statute or common law, though without writ or warrant in deed, has always been considered in England as warranted *per legem terrae*, by due process of law, within the meaning of magna carta, and we have no doubt that any arrest here authorized by our common or statute law must be considered an arrest by the law of the land, by due process, within the meaning of our constitution. We think that the 15th article in our bill of rights [the Law of the Land provision, similar to Chapter 39] was not intended to abridge the power of the legislature, but to assert the right of every citizen to be secure from all arrests not warranted by law. . . .

But further to elucidate this, it may be necessary to take a broader view of the constitution.

The second article of the bill of rights declares that all men have certain natural, essential, inherent rights, among which are enjoying and defending life and liberty, and acquiring, possessing and defending property; but the third article declares that when men enter into a state of society, they surrender up some of their natural rights to that society. All society is founded upon the principle that each individual shall submit to the will of the whole. When we become members of society then, we surrender our natural right to be governed by our own wills in every case where our own wills would lead us counter to the general will. We agree to conform our actions to the rules prescribed by the whole, and we agree to pay the forfeiture, which the general will may impose upon the violation of those rules, whether it be the loss of property, of liberty, or of life. Upon this agreement rests all legitimate government, and the general will duly expressed is alone law. The people of this state have formed a constitution in which they have agreed upon the manner in which the public will shall be expressed, and upon the extent to which individuals shall surrender their natural rights; and the people being the fountain of all power, and the constitution their will duly expressed, it is clear that the constitution is a part of the law of the land paramount to all other laws.

By the constitution, the power to declare the general will is confided to a general court.[809] "Full power and authority are hereby given and granted to said general court from time to time to make, ordain and establish all manner of wholesome and reasonable laws, statutes, ordinances, directions and instructions, either with penalties or without, so as the same be not repugnant or contrary to this constitution." The people of this state seem to have been extremely anxious that their natural rights should be surrendered only to the will of the whole or, in other words, to the law. It is therefore declared in the 12th article of the bill of rights that the inhabitants of this state are not controlable by any other laws than those to which they or their representative body have given their assent. The constitution is a part of the law of the land, made by the people themselves, and the constitution having declared that all laws which had been adopted and approved, and usually practised on in the courts of law, should remain and be in force until altered by the legislature[.] [T]he common and statute law in force before

[809] The "General Court" in New Hampshire refers to the legislative body.

> the adoption of the constitution may be considered as adopted and made by the people themselves. It is clear then that the people of this state are controlable only by the constitution, by the common and statute law adopted by the constitution and not altered, and by laws made by the general court in pursuance of the constitution. The last clause in the 15th article of the bill of rights only asserts the same thing. No subject shall be arrested, &c. but by the judgment of his peers or the law of the land. This clause may be thus analized. 1. No subject shall be arrested but by the law of the land; that is, by due process of law warranted by the constitution, by the common law adopted by the constitution and not altered, or by statutes made in pursuance of the constitution. Thus if the house of representatives were to commit or arrest a person for a contempt in their presence, it would be by process of law expressly warranted by the constitution. If this court were to arrest a person for a contempt in its presence, it would be by process of law warranted by the common law adopted by the constitution. When an individual is arrested for travelling on Sunday, it is by process warranted by a statute made in pursuance of the constitution.[810]

For several state judges in the early Republic, "law of the land" meant the laws of the state. And the state's constitution and other positive law modified, updated, or repealed the common law.

Commentators have described these views quoted above as the "dying view" of Blackstonian legislative supremacy.[811] The basis for this assertion is the supremacy of written constitu-

---

810 *Mayo*, 1 N.H. 53 (minor formatting added).

811 Chapman & McConnell, *supra* note 785, at 1724-25.

tions.[812] Such "Blackstonian views" would eventually lose to a contrary opinion that merged several variables to the law-of-the-land and due-process-of-law language of state constitutions. These other state judges, like Hamilton, rejected the view that legislation was or created law of the land. They cited and quoted available literature on the Magna Carta and English common law and fixed the phrases "law of the land" and "due process of law" to those venerated procedures at common law—for example, presentment and indictment, to which was added trial by jury.[813] The "constitutional common law" doctrine was a set of premises strung together: the legislature is bound by the Constitution, which is supreme; the Constitution's "law of the land" provision mandates that deprivations follow judicial procedure and common law; hence, the state's positive legislation in conflict with the constitutional common law is unconstitutional.[814]

---

[812] But constitutional supremacy must assume some standard of repugnance—for example, repugnance beyond a reasonable doubt. *Infra* notes 848-849, 902, 912, 915 (repugnance standard discussed or developed in court decisions). Otherwise, you substitute the court for the legislature.

[813] *See infra* Chapter X sec. B (vested property interests as a vehicle for substantive due process).

[814] The ancient provision for trial by jury posed a vexing constitutional question for several early state courts. Did the laws and customs of the state require trial by jury even when there was no constitutional provision? Was trial by jury assumed as part of a state's common law or "law of the land" provision? When the words "trial by jury" were used without any definition, could the state allow for six-man juries? *See* Holmes v. Walton (New Jersey, 1780) (unreported) (finding that twelve-man juries were required even though no constitutional provision required twelve-man juries); Trevett v. Weeden (R.I. 1786), discussed in 1 THE BILL OF RIGHTS: A DOCUMENTARY HISTORY 417 (Bernard Schwartz ed. 1971) (finding trial by jury required without constitutional provision providing for trial by jury). For a discussion of constitutional common law on an international scale, see GOLDSWORTHY, PARLIAMENTARY SOVEREIGNTY, *supra* note 727, at 14-56.

Joining state court uncertainty, the United States Supreme Court also struggled with the due-process-of-law concept. The Court associated the Magna Carta not with arbitrary executive or judicial action without the rule of law but as a check against all government, even against enacted law. In an 1819 opinion, *Bank of Columbia v. Okely*, Justice Johnson wrote:

> As to the words from the Magna Carta, after volumes spoken and written with a view to their exposition, the good sense of mankind has at length settled down to this: that they were intended to secure the individual from the arbitrary exercise of the powers of government, unrestrained by the established principles of private right and distributive justice.[815]

Contemporaneous with the *Okely* case, Daniel Webster engaged in a different law-of-the-land argument in *Trustees of Dartmouth College v. Woodward*.[816] New Hampshire's Law of the Land Clause read:

> [N]o subject shall be arrested, imprisoned, despoiled, or deprived of his property, immunities, or privileges, put out of the protection of the law, exiled, or deprived of his life, liberty, or estate, but by the judgment of his peers or the law of the land.[817]

For Webster, the New Hampshire's Law of the Land Clause meant:

> By the law of the land, is most clearly intended, the general law; a law which hears before it condemns; which proceeds upon inquiry, and renders judgment only after trial. The meaning is that every citizen shall hold his life, liberty,

[815] Bank of Columbia v. Okely, 17 U.S. (4 Wheat.) 235, 244 (1819).

[816] 17 U.S. (4 Wheat.) 518, 561 (1819).

[817] 4 THORPE, *supra* note 739, at 2453–57.

> property, and immunities under the protection of the general rules which govern society. Everything which may pass under the form of an enactment is not, therefore, to be considered the law of the land. If this were so, acts of attainder, bills of pains and penalties, acts of confiscation, acts reversing judgments, and acts directly transferring one man's estate to another, legislative judgments, decrees and forfeitures, in all possible forms, would be the law of the land. Such a strange construction would render constitutional provisions, of the highest importance, completely inoperative and void. It would tend directly to establish the union of all powers in the legislature. There would be no general permanent law for courts to administer, or for men to live under. The administration of justice would be an empty form, an idle ceremony. Judges would sit to execute legislative judgments and decrees, not to declare the law, or to administer the justice of the country.[818]

Hamilton and state judges had limited "law of the land" to common law, presentment, indictment, and trial by jury.[819] Webster bootstrapped "law of the land" with a broader, unknown meaning by giving it an independent source of constitutional oversight reach. In so doing, Webster violently opened the door to an umbrella construction including principles of fairness and other generalities. His argument reads: laws that run afoul of constitutional commands such as prohibiting acts of attainder are not law of the land. Therefore, "law of the land" provides not for the rule of law but for a substantive review of the quality and character of legislation in order for that law to be law of the land.

---

[818] 17 U.S. (4 Wheat.) at 581-82. *See also* John Harrison, *Due Process and the Constitutional Text*, 83 VA. L. REV. 493, 528-29 (1997) (minor formatting added).

[819] *Supra* notes 784-794, 811-813; *infra* Chapter X sec. B (vested property interests).

Further, substantive review included fairness review among other generalities. Under this reading, law of the land was an undefined variable inclusive of the Constitution as well as general principles of fairness and justice.

The remarkable or incredulous point that Webster, Hamilton, and state judges offer is that "due process of law" and "law of the land" are processes by common law that *cannot be altered by legislation* but at the same time "due process of law" and "law of the land" remain open to various *judicial* interpretations, modifications, and discoveries which carry the force of constitutional law and supremacy. This is the exact reverse of western constitutionalism.[820] Whereas Parliament wrested the power and force of law from the divine right of kings and royal judges, Webster, Hamilton, and state judges—following a misperception of Coke—wrested the power of law from the legislatures to create the divine right of judges. "Due process of law" became a catchall and constitutional grab bag for the courts but a stone tablet for the people and their elected legislatures. Although there was uncertainty in the courts before Webster's advocacy, his opinion carried a great deal of weight into what became the substantive understanding of due process.[821]

---

[820] *Supra* notes 317, 386, 449-456, 520-523, 539, 555, 651-657, 798 (High Court of Parliament developed authority of statute; statute transitioned from king's act in Council to subject's right; Lords and Commons no longer sought confirmations of Magna Carta; Lords and Commons could make their own law, their own Magna Cartas).

[821] Williams, *supra* note 740, at 462-64, 491. Williams, crediting Webster, noted that judicial opinions supporting open-ended interpretations of due process and law of the land went from the law of three states to the law of at least eleven states within three decades. *Id.* The same period saw an increase in courts invalidating legislative acts. Charles Grove Haines, *Judicial Review of Legislation in the United States and the Doctrines of Vested Rights and of Implied Limitations on Legislatures*, 2 TEX. L. REV. 257, 271-72 (1924) (crediting reasonableness review and fairness readings of "higher law" doctrines, vested rights, and due process of law).

B. Vested Property Interests and Due Process of Law

One of the first classes of due-process-of-law cases involved protecting vested property rights. Early American courts stoutly defended vested interests, and their opinions provide the origins of American judicial activism.

In *Vanhorne's Lessee v. Dorrance*, Justice Paterson, riding circuit, addressed a Pennsylvania statute attempting to "quiet and confirm" disputed land grants.[822] The statute appointed a board to hear evidence and assign value to compensate for taken land. In an early opinion defending judicial review, Paterson gave a lengthy speech in his charge to the jury. He distinguished American law under a constitution from English law under Parliament. Paterson identified the principles of constitutional supremacy and declared that legislative acts repugnant to the constitution were void. He quoted the first, eighth, and eleventh provisions of the Pennsylvania Declaration of Rights:

> I. That all men are born equally free and independent, and have certain natural, inherent and inalienable rights, amongst which are, the enjoying and defending life and liberty, acquiring, possessing and protecting property, and pursuing and obtaining happiness and safety. . . .
>
> VIII. That every member of society hath a right to be protected in the enjoyment of life, liberty and property, and therefore is bound to contribute his proportion towards the expence of that protection, and yield his personal service when necessary, or an equivalent thereto: But no part of a man's property can be justly taken from him, or applied to public uses, without his own consent, or that of his legal representatives: Nor can any man who is conscientiously scrupu-

822 2 U.S. (Dall.) 304 (1795).

> lous of bearing arms, be justly compelled thereto, if he will pay such equivalent, nor are the people bound by any laws, but such as they have in like manner assented to, for their common good. . . .
>
> XI. That in controversies respecting property, and in suits between man and man, the parties have a right to trial by jury, which ought to be held sacred.[823]

With these provisions and constitutional supremacy, Paterson launched into a passionate natural-rights defense of property interests as fundamental law.[824] Yielding reluctantly to the notion that the legislature can take land when necessity requires,[825] Paterson supplied the additional constraint—by the "dictates of reason and the eternal principles of justice, as well as the sacred

---

[823] 5 THORPE, *supra* note 739, at 3082-83.

[824] 2 U.S. (Dall.) at 310-11. We discussed above that the divine king had an inalienable duty to protect the fisc and serve the welfare of the kingdom. *Supra* Chapter II. By the law of the necessity, the king was above positive law, even his own positive law. The king could undo grants and acts contrary to the welfare of the state when necessity required. *Supra* notes 52-54, 64-67. During the seventeenth century, Lords and Commons fought against arbitrary royal government. Parliament competed with the king over the standard of necessity. *Supra* notes 675-676. In a Republic, the state takes over the function of necessity and common welfare. *Supra* notes 732-734. When pointing to pre-Revolution sources citing grievances against parliamentary acts, it's important to keep in mind that the central grievance against Parliament's acts was that they were enacted without colonists' consent.

[825] Civil society requires surrendering some portion of liberty and property to the community for common good. *See, e.g.*, 2 LOCKE, *supra* note 733, at §§ 22 ("The liberty of man, in society, is to be under no other legislative power, but that established, by consent, in the commonwealth; nor under the dominion of any will, or restraint of any law, but what that legislative shall enact, according to the trust put in it."), 87-89, 95-99, 123-131. Western constitutionalism evolved from arbitrary rule and placed the power of determining the common good or common utility with legislative and representative processes. *See also supra* Chapters III-VIII; *supra* notes 500, 675-676.

principles of the social contract"—that such taking must be done with just compensation as determined by a jury or equivalent method.[826]

> The legislature, therefore, had no authority to make an act devesting one citizen of his freehold, and vesting it in another, without a just compensation. It is inconsistent with the principles of reason, justice, and moral rectitude; it is incompatible with the comfort, peace, and happiness of mankind; it is contrary to the principles of social alliance in every free government; and lastly, it is contrary both to the letter and spirit of the Constitution. In short, it is what everyone would think unreasonable and unjust in his own case.[827]

Contrary to the constitutional supremacy that Paterson touted, the Pennsylvania constitutional text that he cited and relied upon made no mention of compensation, only that such taking be done by individual or representative consent. Paterson relied upon natural-law principles and his personal opinion concerning social justice to invent and add the requirement to the Pennsylvania Constitution's text.[828] He continued:

> The interposition of a jury [to determine compensation] is, in such case, a constitutional guard upon property, and a necessary check to legislative authority. It is a barrier between the individual and the legislature, and ought never to be removed; as long as it is preserved, the rights of private property will be in no danger of.

---

[826] 2 U.S. (Dall.) at 312-13.

[827] *Id.* at 310-11.

[828] *Id.* at 313-16.

> violation, except in cases of absolute necessity, or great public utility.[829]

Paterson rejected the statute's use of a board to determine the value of compensation and declared the statute void.

Militating against Paterson's natural- and social-justice critique of the legislature, it seems that state takings provisions aimed to protect against arbitrary actions and not legislative ones. Pennsylvania's Constitution provided: "no part of a man's property can be justly taken from him, or applied to public uses, without his own consent, or that of his legal representatives."[830] Other states had similar provisions. Virginia's 1776 Constitution provided:

> all men, having sufficient evidence of permanent common interest with, and attachment to, the community, have the right of suffrage, and cannot be taxed or deprived of their property for public uses, without their own consent, or that of their representatives so elected, nor bound by any law to which they have not, in like manner, assembled, for the public good.[831]

Massachusetts:

> Each individual of the society has a right to be protected by it in the enjoyment of his life, liberty, and property, according to standing laws. He is obliged, consequently, to contribute his share to the expense of this protection; to give his personal service, or an equivalent, when nec-

---

[829] *Id.* at 315; *see also* Lindsay v. Commissioners, 2 S.C.L. (2 Bay) 38 (Ct. App. 1796), *infra* note 839.

[830] Art. 8, Pennsylvania Declaration of Rights 1776, 5 THORPE, *supra* note 739, at 3082-83.

[831] Sect. 6, Virginia Bill of Rights 1776, 7 THORPE, *supra* note 739, at 3813.

> essary: but no part of the property of any individual can, with justice, be taken from him, or applied to public uses, without his own consent, or that of the representative body of the people. In fine, the people of this commonwealth are not controllable by any other laws than those to which their constitutional representative body have given their consent. And whenever the public exigencies require that the property of any individual should be appropriated to public uses, he shall receive a reasonable compensation therefor.[832]

New Hampshire's 1784 Constitution:

> XII. Every member of the community has a right to be protected by it in the enjoyment of his life, liberty and property; he is therefore bound to contribute his share in the expence of such protection, and to yield his personal service when necessary, or an equivalent. But no part of a man's property shall be taken from him, or applied to public uses without his own consent, or that of the representative body of the people. Nor are the inhabitants of this state controllable by any other laws than those to which they or their representative body have given their consent.[833]

These provisions connect takings with broader representative principles. The taking language of Massachusetts, New Hampshire, and Virginia was grouped with principles such as election, taxation, and voting. No taxation or taking without representation; property and money were one and the same. Taxation and takings were connected by the common grievance against the king's nonparliamentary taking or taxation. "Consent" in the con-

---

[832] Sect. X, Massachusetts's 1780 Const., 3 THORPE, *supra* note 739, at 1891.

[833] 4 THORPE, *supra* note 739, at 2455.

stitutional provisions did not mean an individual's permission but the broader notion of representative consent as found in English history.[834] Consent and representative consent intuitively bypass the jury requirement, which aimed to curb nonrepresentative action. A jury of representatives trumps a jury of twelve neighbors. Certain state constitutions provided for just compensation, others did not. Paterson's passionate natural-rights insertion, from a constitutional perspective, was a slippery slope to judicial anarchy. His invention of constitutional text is equivalent to modern-day judicial activism.[835]

In *Calder v. Bull*, shortly after Paterson's opinion in *Vanhorne's Lessee*, the full Supreme Court discussed judicial review and commented on takings.[836] Justice Chase opined, in more reserved language than Paterson, that "a law that takes property from A. and gives it to B[.] is against all reason and justice . . . [and] cannot be presumed" to have been the legislative intent or the people's will.[837] Courts later declared that a law that transfers property from A to B is not due process of law (A-to-B laws). In *Davidson v. New Orleans*, the Court commented in more direct language:

---

834 *Supra* notes 675-678 (Commons applied Magna Carta's provisions preventing nonparliamentary taxation to other royal acts such as taking property without consent or Parliament).

835 By the same language and liberty that Paterson invoked to invent and graft compensation and jury to Pennsylvania's taking provision, a judge could invent the right to privacy. *See* Charles Grove Haines, *The Law of Nature in State and Federal Judicial Decisions*, 25 YALE L.J. 617, 634-35 (1916) (quoting a Georgia Supreme Court opinion discussing the "right to privacy" as a natural, immutable right); *see also infra* Chapter X secs. D-E (rise of judicial activism).

836 3 U.S. (3 Dall.) 386, 388 (1798).

837 *Id.* at 388; *see also* Wilkinson v. Leland, 27 U.S. (2 Pet.) 627, 658 (1829). A-to-B laws typically refer to a state's taking of private property and giving it to another private individual rather than a taking for a public purpose.

> It seems to us that a statute which declares in terms, and without more, that the full and exclusive title of a described piece of land, which is now in A., shall be and is hereby vested in B., would, if effectual, deprive A. of his property without due process of law, within the meaning of the constitutional provision.[838]

Paterson's jury charge criticizing the legislature and requiring trial by jury and just compensation in *Vanhorne's Lessee* influenced state courts as well. In *Lindsay v. Commissioners*, the South Carolina judges were equally divided as to whether the state's taking of private property was lawful according to a state statute which did not specify for compensation or whether the statute was unconstitutional by unwritten legal maxims similar to Paterson's reasoning in *Vanhorne's Lessee* because it failed to provide for just compensation.[839] The South Carolina legislative action in question was argued to be consistent with prior practice and previous legislation. Judges Grimke and Bay noted that the South Carolina legislature had exercised this power and authority from the first establishment of civil government to the present day. They, therefore, considered it as much a part of South Carolina's common law as any other part.

> [Legislative taking by statute] was neither against *magna charta*, nor the state constitution, but part of the *lex terrae*, which both meant to defend and protect. The so much celebrated *magna charta* of *Great Britain* was not a concession of rights and privileges, which had no previous existence but a *restoration* and *confirmation* of those, which had been usurped or

---

[838] Davidson v. New Orleans, 96 U.S. 97, 102 (1878). *See generally* Harrison, *supra* note 818, at 498, 507-12. One distinction between *Davidson* and *Calder* is that *Calder* seems to be discussing a presumption whereas *Davidson* firmly suggests a prohibition against A-to-B legislation.

[839] 2 S.C.L. (2 Bay) 38 (Ct. App. 1796) (minor formatting added).

> had fallen into disuse. It was therefore only declaratory of the well known and established laws of the kingdom.
>
> So, in like manner, the 2d section of the 9th article of our state constitution[840] confirms all the before-mentioned principles. It was not declaratory of any new law, but confirmed all the ancient rights and principles, which had been in use in the state, with the additional security that no bills of attainder, nor *ex post facto* laws, or laws impairing the obligation of contracts, should ever be passed in the state. They were therefore of opinion, that so far from interfering with or contradicting this high and important privilege of the legislature, in laying off highways, they both confirmed and secured it; consequently that none of the cases relied on by the counsel in favour of this motion had the least tendency to contradict or overturn these principles.[841]

Dividing the opinion, Judge Waties concurred with Judge Burke that the taking required just compensation.[842] Waties's opinion has been cited as support for substantive due process. For Waties, state legislation could not conflict with the constitu-

---

[840] S.C. Const. Art. IX, Sec. 2 (1790):

> No freeman of this State shall be taken, or imprisoned, or disseised, of his freeholds, liberties, or privileges, or outlawed, or exiled, or in any other manner destroyed, or deprived of his life, liberty, or property, but by judgment of his peers, or by the law of the land: nor shall any bill of attainder, ex post facto law, or law impairing the obligations of contracts ever be passed by the legislature of this state.

6 THORPE, *supra* note 739, at 3264.

[841] *Lindsay*, 2 S.C.L. (2 Bay), at 56-58 (minor formatting added).

[842] Burke felt that the state's taking required compensation and trial by jury to determine the amount of the proper compensation. *Cf.* Vanhorne's Lessee v. Dorrance, 2 U.S. (Dall.) 304 (1795), *supra* notes 826-829.

tion—an opinion with which most would agree. Waties, however, attributed the common law and legal maxims to the constitution's "law of the land" provision.[843] Thus, the central issue for Waties was whether the positive act of legislation was controlled by the common law—the constitutional common law.[844]

In *Trustees of the University of North Carolina v. Foy*, the North Carolina legislature in 1800 repealed a 1789 legislative grant of escheated land to the University of North Carolina. As land had already been transferred to the University, the issue for the Court was whether the state's repeal interfered with vested property interests and required judicial procedure to comply with the "law of the land" provision.[845] Judge Locke delivered the opinion of the Court.

> But one great and important reason which influences us in deciding this question is section 10 of the Bill of Rights, which declares "that no freeman ought to be taken, imprisoned, or disseized of his freehold, liberties or privileges, or outlawed or exiled, or in any manner destroyed or deprived of his life, liberty or property, but by the law of the land." It has been yielded on the part of the defendant that if the Legislature had vested an individual with the property in question [as opposed to a taking for public purpose], this section of the Bill of Rights would restrain them from depriving him of such right. . . . It is also insisted that the term "law of the land" does not impose any restrictions on the

[843] Waties's opinion extended his earlier 1794 opinion in *Zylstra v. Corp. of Charleston*, 1 S.C.L. (1 Bay) 382 (Ct. Com. Pl. 1794) (law of the land requires specified procedure).

[844] *Lindsay*, 2 S.C.L. (2 Bay), at 58-62.

[845] 5 N.C. (1 Mur.) 57 (1805). *See also* Williams, *supra* note 740, at 447-48.

Legislature, who are capable of making the law of the land, and was only intended to prevent abuses in the other branches of government. . . . It is evident the framers of the Constitution intended the provision as a restraint upon some branch of the Government, either the executive, legislative, or judicial. To suppose it applicable to the executive would be absurd on account of the limited powers conferred on that officer; and from the subjects enumerated in that clause, no danger could be apprehended from the Executive Department that being entrusted with the exercise of no powers by which the principles thereby intended to be secured could be affected. To apply it to the judiciary would, if possible, be still more idle, if the Legislature can make the "law of the land." *For the judiciary are only to expound and enforce the law, and have no discretionary powers enabling them to judge of the propriety or impropriety of laws. They are bound, whether agreeable to their ideas of justice or not, to carry into effect the acts of the Legislature as far as they are binding or do not contravene the Constitution. If, then, this clause is applicable to the Legislature alone, and was intended as a restraint on their acts (and to presume otherwise is to render this article a dead letter), let us next enquire what will be the operation which this clause will or ought to have on the present question.* It seems to us to warrant a belief that members of a corporation as well as individuals shall not be so deprived of their liberties or property, unless by a trial by Jury in a court of justice, according to the known and established rules of decision, derived from the common law and such acts of the Legislature as are consistent with the Constitution. Although the Trustees are a corporation established for public purposes, yet their property is as completely beyond the control of the Legislature, as

> the property of individuals or that of any other corporation.[846]

For Locke, the trustees were operating for public good, and University property was not subject to the "arbitrary will of the Legislature." Property interests can be taken only by judicial decisions in the usual and common form. We can see from Locke's description of "law of the land" as a "dead letter" if not applicable to the legislature that he had no idea of the history and origin of the language. Specifically, Locke stated that to apply "law of the land" to the executive would be "absurd on account of the limited powers conferred on that officer." Americans had lost appreciation for the concept of an arbitrary king or executive and cited and quoted constitutional text without appreciating its context.[847]

Attempting to provide some form of judicial restraint, Judge Hall disagreed with Locke:

> A question of more importance than that arising in this case cannot come before a court. It is nothing less than one branch of the Government undertaking to decide whether another branch of the same Government has or has not transcended its constitutional powers; a question which in its discussion should at all times command the best energies of the head and heart. When this shall be the case, although a difference of opinion may sometimes exist, it will be an honest one, and cannot fail to find its remedy in mutual tolerance and concession. But well convinced, indeed, ought one person to be of another's error of judgment before he passes sentence of condemnation on it, when he reflects that each has given the same pledges to

---

846 *Foy*, 5 N.C. (1 Mur.), at 62-63 (minor formatting and emphasis added).

847 *Supra* notes 784-790, 824; *infra* notes 855, 880.

> support the Constitution. Before a law enacted by the Legislature should be pronounced unconstitutional, it ought to appear to the Court to be palpably so. If an honest doubt can be entertained on the subject, we owe it to ourselves, as well as to the Legislature, to carry it into effect.[848]

Hall attempted to set a standard of repugnance, repugnant beyond a reasonable doubt, but to no avail.[849]

After these cases, vested property disputes in the state courts provided a key forum for the discussion of due process of law.[850] Under Sir Edward Coke's influence or perceptions thereof, law of the land and due process of law had been deemed judicial and mutually exclusive of law and legislation in itself.[851] Adding the principle of written constitutions and constitutional supremacy, legislative acts violating the common law, judicial procedures, or even perceived natural-law principles were violations of the states' law-of-the-land and due-process-of-law clauses.[852]

---

[848] *Foy*, 5 N.C. (1 Mur.), at 64.

[849] *Supra* note 812; *infra* notes 902, 912, 915.

[850] Several state opinions in the Republic's first seventy-five years developed their understanding of their respective due process clauses in the context of, among other issues, vested property interests. Trustees of the University of North Carolina v. Foy, 5 N.C. (1 Mur.) 57 (1805); Hoke v. Henderson, 15 N.C. (4 Dev.) 1 (1833); Taylor v. Porter, 4 Hill 140 (N.Y. Sup. Ct. 1843); Wynehamer v. People 13 N.Y. 378 (1856).

[851] *Supra* notes 784, 839-848.

[852] *Supra* Chapter X sec. A. As noted above, a plain-language construction of the Fifth Amendment strongly suggests that "due process of law" meant something other than indictment, presentment, just compensation, etc. Otherwise, "due process of law" is entirely redundant as the Amendment expressly provides for these guaranties. *Supra* notes 774-783.

All of these views were debated and discussed in the well-known New York case, *Wynehamer v. People*.[853] In *Wynehamer*, Justice Comstock of the New York Court of Appeals, summarizing state opinions and citing *Calder v. Bull*, connected vested property interests with due process of law.[854] The New York law against intemperance, pauperism, and crime at issue in *Wynehamer* affected vested property in intoxicating liquors because it not only affected future manufacture and sale of liquor but also applied to liquor or property owned before the law went into effect. Comstock and the state judges he cited believed that "law of the land" and "due process of law" unequivocally meant judicial procedure. Because these clauses required judicial procedure and legislatures were limited by the constitution, a legislative deprivation of property that did not utilize some or all of the perceived judicial procedure required by the language was unconstitutional. Justice George F. Comstock:

> To say, as has been suggested, that "the law of the land," or "due process of law," may mean the very act of legislation which deprives the citizen of his rights, privileges or property, leads to a simple absurdity.[855] The constitution would then mean that no person shall be deprived of his property or rights, unless the legislature shall pass a law to effectuate the wrong, and this would be throwing the restraint entirely away. The true interpretation of these constitutional phrases is that, where rights are acquired by the citizen under the existing law, there is no power in any branch of the government to take them away; but where they are held contrary to

---

853 Wynehamer v. People, 13 N.Y. 378 (1856). Wynehamer was reported with a sister case involving the same issue, *People v. Toynbee*.

854 Wynehamer, 13 N.Y. at 390-97.

855 *Supra* notes 784-790, 824, 847; *infra* note 880.

> the existing law, or are forfeited by its violation, then they may be taken from him—not by an act of the legislature, but in the due administration of the law itself, before the judicial tribunals of the state. The cause or occasion for depriving the citizen of his supposed rights must be found in the law as it is, or at least it cannot be *created* by a legislative act which aims at their destruction. Where rights of property are admitted to exist, the legislature cannot say they shall exist no longer; nor will it make any difference, although a process and a tribunal are appointed to execute the sentence. If this is the "law of the land," and "due process of law," within the meaning of the constitution, then the legislature is omnipotent. It may, under the same interpretation, pass a law to take away liberty or life without a preexisting cause, appointing judicial and executive agencies to execute its will. Property is placed by the constitution in the same category with liberty and life.[856]

Justices Alexander S. Johnson and Samuel L. Selden concurred with Comstock in *Wynehamer v. People* and shared the assumption that due process of law was a restraint against the legislature. But their concurring opinions were more conservative. Justice A.S. Johnson:

> I am not to judge of the wisdom of the laws under review, or of their reasonableness or abstract justice. Sitting in the exercise of mere judicial power, which is strictly limited to answering the question, what *is* the law, and has not been entrusted with saying what it ought to be, I have no authority to weigh the justice of legislation, and to allow or disallow it as I shall find the scale to turn. Certainly, that which the interest and welfare of the people required to be made law was proper to be enacted, and was

---

[856] Wynehamer, 13 N.Y. at 390-97 (minor formatting added).

> within the scope of legislative power, if no constitutional inhibition exists.
>
> If a court is to judge of such a question at all, it must go over the same field upon which the legislature has acted. It must consider the occasion of the law, the existence of the evil, the suitableness of the remedy. "A person exercising a judicial capacity is neither to apply to original justice, nor to a discretionary application of it. He goes to justice and discretion only at second hand, through the medium of some superiors. He is to work, neither upon his opinion of the one nor of the other, but upon a fixed rule, of which he has not the making, but singly and solely the application to the case." Whether a given action shall be prohibited, and under what penalty, whether loss of life, or liberty, or of fine, must depend upon an infinite variety of facts, and upon the consideration of the evil the action occasions or is likely to occasion to the people. What machinery has a court of justice, sitting to determine questions of law, with which to investigate such a question?[857]

Justice Johnson quoted a passage from *Cochran v. Van Surlay*, responding to the state's law-of-the-land provision.[858]

> "It is difficult, upon any general principles, to limit the omnipotence of the sovereign legislative power by judicial interposition, except so far as the express words of a written constitution give that authority. There are, indeed, many dicta, and some great authorities, holding that acts contrary to the first principles of right are void. The principle [of strict construction] is unquestionably sound, as the governing rule of a legislature in relation to its own acts, or even

[857] *Id.* at 411-12.

[858] 20 Wend. 365, 381-82 (1838).

> those of a preceding legislature. It affords a safe rule of construction for courts, in the interpretation of laws admitting of any doubtful construction, to presume that the legislature could not have intended an unequal and unjust operation of its statutes. Such a construction ought never to be given to legislative language, if it be susceptible of any other more conformable to justice; but if the words be positive and without ambiguity, I can find no authority for a court to vacate or repeal a statute on that ground alone. But it is only in express constitutional provisions, limiting legislative power and controlling the temporary will of a majority by a permanent and paramount law, settled by the deliberate wisdom of the nation, that I can find a safe and solid ground for the authority of courts of justice to declare void any legislative enactment."[859]

Justice Selden:

> It follows that if a society or people, wishing to form an organized government, should simply create the three essential departments, vesting the whole executive power in one, the legislative in another, and the judicial in a third, as the three departments combined would possess all the powers which belong to the people in their collective capacity, the legislative department could make any law which the people themselves could have made, arbitrary or otherwise; unless, under such a distribution of the governmental powers, some authority is vested in the judiciary, to pass upon the propriety or justice of the laws.
>
> But it is evident that this is a legislative and not a judicial power. It is necessarily to be exercised, in the first instance at least, when the law is passed, and obviously constitutes the most

---

859 *Wynehamer*, 13 N.Y. at 412-13, quoting *Cochran v. Van Surlay*.

essential portion of the duty of the legislature itself. To suppose the same power vested in the judiciary tends to confound the distinction between the two departments. Besides, when exercised by the latter, it becomes a supervisory and appellate power, and thus virtually subversive of all legislation. It is clear, therefore, in my judgment, that in a perfectly natural and simple distribution of the governmental powers, it is not within the province of the judiciary to pronounce any act of the legislature void. It may, however, acquire this right through an artificial distribution of those powers, by means of the organic law.

Let us look, then, at our state constitution. Section 1, art. 3, declares that, "The legislative power of this state shall be vested in a senate and assembly." This means, of course, the whole legislative power. The words are general and unlimited; nothing is reserved. . . .

Why, then, as it has been shown that the people could make any law, just or unjust, is not the legislature equally absolute? It is because, by other clauses in the constitution, hereafter to be noticed, a portion of this absolute power has been transferred to the judiciary. Not, it is true, in direct terms, but the constitution being the result of legislation by the people themselves, before parting with their power, is the paramount law. When, therefore, any law passed by the legislature conflicts with this, the judiciary pronounces between them, as it does between the acts of two successive legislatures, and the paramount law prevails. It will be seen that in this mode a restriction upon the power of the legislature is effected, without confounding the distinction between the two departments, as the judiciary continues to exercise only its appropriate judicial functions.

> To determine, then, the extent of the law-making power, we have only to look to the provisions of the constitution. It has, and can have, no other limit than such as is there prescribed; and the doctrine that there exists in the judiciary some vague, loose and undefined power to annul a law, because in its judgment it is "contrary to natural equity and justice," is in conflict with the first principles of government, and can never, I think, be maintained. I am aware that some eminent judges, when the question was not before them, have expressed a belief in the existence of such a power; but no court has ever, I believe, assumed to declare an explicit enactment of the legislature void on that ground.[860]

Despite these statements supporting the legislative function (except where directly repugnant to constitution), both Justices Johnson and Shelden ultimately supported the applicability of the due-process-of-law provision to the intemperance law because it infringed vested property interests.

The conservative streaks of Johnson's and Selden's concurrences were likely in anticipation of the persuasive aspects of the dissenting justices. Justice Thomas A. Johnson's dissent in *Wynehamer*:

> It is claimed that courts, independent of constitutional limitations upon legislative power, have the right to annul statutes and pronounce them void, whenever, in their judgment, they are in conflict with the fundamental principles of the government and tend to individual oppression, although not in conflict with any provision of the constitution of the United States or of the state. I know of no such power vested in the courts, and they should never attempt to usurp it. The limitations upon legislative power are

[860] *Id.* at 429-30 (minor formatting added).

> written in the fundamental law, and that is the standard by which all questions of power exercised by the legislature must be tried. To this extent, the question is a legitimate one for adjudication by the courts, as the construction of the fundamental law necessarily falls within their province. Nor does this involve the philosophical absurdity insisted upon by some writers of the inferior power annulling the acts of the superior; because, upon our theory of government, the legislature is powerless when it attempts to pass the limits prescribed by the constitution. To this extent, under a written constitution, this power may be safely and properly exercised by the courts, and, indeed, its exercise often becomes necessary to prevent the encroachments of power, and to protect rights shielded by the constitution.
>
> But, beyond this, such a power, exercised by the courts, would be a mere veto or dispensing power. No such power is conferred by the constitution, nor does it pertain to the judicial functions. . . . Indeed, without a written constitution, it has no foundation to stand upon.[861]

Johnson did not believe courts had the authority to void statutes merely on fundamental principles without express constitutional text. For T.A. Johnson, exercising judicial review based on ambiguous text would be equivalent to the judge "suspending and dispensing" with the law. T.A. Johnson continued:

> Should the time ever come when the courts, instead of promptly sustaining and enforcing the legislative will, become forward to thwart and defeat it, and assume to prescribe limits to its exercise other than those prescribed in the constitution; to substitute their discretion and notions of expediency for constitutional restraints;

[861] *Id.* at 476–78 (minor formatting added).

and to declare enactments void for want of conformity to such standards; or when, to defeat unpalatable acts, they shall habitually resort to subtleties and refinements and strained constructions to bring them into conflict with the constitution, the end of all just and salutary authority, judicial as well as legislative, will not be remote. When men, chafing under the restraints of particular statutes, and prompted by interest, passion, appetite or partizanship to disregard them and set their authority at defiance, once begin to expect from courts immunity and protection, instead of punishment, the judiciary will have lost, not only its claim to respect and confidence, but the power of enforcing general laws. Courts can only sustain their own authority and efficiency by vigilantly and fearlessly upholding and sustaining legislative enactments in all cases where they are not plainly and clearly in derogation of constitutional limitations. The people have a far more certain and reliable security and protection against mere impolitic, overstringent or uncalled-for legislation than courts can ever afford, in their reserved power of changing, annually and biennially, the representatives of their legislative sovereignty; and to that final and ultimate tribunal should all such errors and mistakes in legislation be referred for correction.

As there is nothing, therefore, in the constitution, either of this state or of the United States, which takes away or limits the rights of the legislature to make such regulations in regard to the traffic in property amongst the citizens of the state, and to impose such restrictions and prohibitions upon it as it shall deem necessary for the public good, this act, so far as it restricts and prohibits the sale of intoxicating drinks, must be pronounced a valid, constitutional act

> and entitled to obedience from every citizen of the state.[862]

Johnson emphasized strict construction of constitutional text when it came to voiding state legislation; the legislature should receive its due deference. Johnson did not find that the state statute violated the due-process-of-law provision. He warned that the court's liberal exercise of voiding statutes based on partisan and self-interested pursuits would reduce the authority and integrity of the courts; impolitic laws should be changed at the polls. Johnson continued:

> If the legislature shall determine that the occasion has arisen or that the necessity exists for the exercise of a more extended and stringent power than it has hitherto exercised, who shall decide to the contrary? What other tribunal is clothed with power to entertain an appeal and reverse such determination? The veto power given to the executive is the only authority the constitution has provided, and that must be exercised before legislation has ripened into statutes, and is then not necessarily conclusive. Whoever bestows the slightest reflection upon the nature and character of the judicial office will see that courts can entertain no such question; and any attempt on their part to take cognizance of it, and to draw it within their jurisdiction, would be a clear invasion of the legislative province and a usurpation of legislative power.
>
> The spectacle of a conflict between the representatives of the legislative and the judicial sovereignty of the people respecting a question of this character, upon any other than clear, undoubted, constitutional grounds, would, at this day, be at once novel and alarming. Every legis-

862 *Id.*

> lative act, when questioned, is to be brought to the test of the constitution, and if the power exercised is not there forbidden in express terms, or by clear and necessary implication, courts have no discretion, but are bound to pronounce it valid. The right of courts to declare legislative enactments, in derogation of the constitution, void is one which has been too long and steadily exercised in this country to be now doubted or questioned. It is, however, one of the highest and most delicate of all conservative powers, and is never to be exercised against the acts of the superior branch of the sovereignty in doubtful and questionable cases. The legislative department being naturally the superior, its authority is always presumed to have been rightfully exercised. And this presumption is to prevail until the contrary has been made clearly to appear, and has been determined by the courts.[863]

T.A. Johnson did not challenge the validity of judicial review, but he had a conservative standard: legislation should be presumed to be valid, and only in clear cases—beyond reasonable doubt—should the judge consider voiding a repugnant statute for unconstitutionality.

C. The Fifth Amendment, Substantive Due Process of Law, and Judicial Enforcement of the Bill of Rights

While "law of the land" and "due process of law" enjoyed a rich discussion in state courts under state constitutions, federal courts did not have much substantive discussion of the Fifth Amendment's due process language before the Civil War. One of the first formal Supreme Court interpretations of the Fifth

[863] *Id.* at 482-83 (*People v. Toynbee*) (minor formatting added).

Amendment's Due Process Clause occurred in 1856.[864] In *Murray v. Hoboken Land and Improvement Company*, Justice Curtis of the U.S. Supreme Court commented:

> That the warrant now in question is legal process is not denied. It was issued in conformity with an act of Congress. But is it "due process of law"? The constitution contains no description of those processes which it was intended to allow or forbid. It does not even declare what principles are to be applied to ascertain whether it be due process. It is manifest that it was not left to the legislative power to enact any process which might be devised. *The [Due Process Clause] is a restraint on the legislative as well as on the executive and judicial powers of the government, and cannot be so construed as to leave congress free to make any process 'due process of law' by its mere will.* To what principles, then, are we to resort to ascertain whether this process, enacted by congress, is due process? To this, the answer must be twofold. We must examine the constitution itself, to see whether this process be in conflict with any of its provisions. If not found to be so, we must look to those settled usages and modes of proceeding existing in the common and statute law of England, before the emigration of our ancestors, and which are shown not to have been unsuited to their civil and political condition by having been acted on by them after the settlement of this country.[865]

Justice Curtis, following state judges before him, began with an assumption that due process of law provided judicial discretion to review acts of Congress. For Curtis, United States con-

---

[864] For brief mention of due process in federal courts before *Murray's Lessee v. Hoboken Land & Improvement Co.*, see *Bloomer v. McQuewan*, 55 U.S. (14 How.) 539, 553 (1852).

[865] Murray v. Hoboken Land & Improvement Co., 59 U.S. (18 How.) 272, 276–77 (1856) (emphasis added).

gressional law was irrelevant to the question of due process of law and law of the land. Justice Curtis chose instead to apply the umbrella understanding of the Clause to incorporate ancient English custom and statute law as binding authority on the United States Congress.

Chief Justice Taney's majority opinion in *Scott v. Sanford* (*Dred Scott*) followed shortly after *Murray*.[866] Taney ruled:

> The powers of the Government and the rights and privileges of the citizen are regulated and plainly defined by the Constitution itself. . . . [T]he Federal Government can exercise no power over his person or property beyond what that instrument confers, nor lawfully deny any right which it has reserved. . . .
>
> For example, no one, we presume, will contend that Congress can make any law in a Territory respecting the establishment of religion, or the free exercise thereof, or abridging the freedom of speech or of the press, or the right of the people of the Territory peaceably to assemble, and to petition the Government for the redress of grievances.
>
> Nor can Congress deny to the people the right to keep and bear arms, nor the right to trial by jury, nor compel anyone to be a witness against himself in a criminal proceeding.
>
> These powers, and others, in relation to rights of person, which it is not necessary here to enumerate, are, in express and positive terms, denied to the General Government; and the rights of private property have been guarded with equal care. Thus the rights of property are united with the rights of person, and placed on the same ground by the Fifth Amendment to the

[866] Scott v. Sanford, 60 U. S. 339 (1857).

> Constitution, which provides that no person shall be deprived of life, liberty, and property, without due process of law. *And an act of Congress which deprives a citizen of the United States of his liberty or property, merely because he came himself or brought his property into a particular Territory of the United States, and who had committed no offence against the laws, could hardly be dignified with the name of due process of law.*[867]

Chase and Taney were following Webster's argument in *Dartmouth.* Taney implicitly bootstrapped the Due Process Clause with the Bill of Rights in the same manner that Webster did with miscellaneous other provisions.[868] Under the Webster-Taney umbrella theory, "due process of law" meant a host of variable qualities, including standards found in the Constitution, English law, fairness, and other general principles.[869]

Taney's *Dred Scott* opinion often receives the credit for developing "substantive due process." John Harrison noted that many coin "procedural due process" as (1) a pure rule-of-law application—that is, to an executive or judicial deprivation without any law, or (2) attach a body of legal procedures and fairness

---

867 *Scott*, 60 U.S. at 449-50 (emphasis added).

868 *Supra* notes 818-821.

869 *See infra* Chapter X sec. D; Hurtado v. California, 110 U.S. 516, 535-36 (1884) (reciting views similar to Webster's and adding that special, partial, and arbitrary exertions of power, among others, are not "due process of law"); Poe v. Ullman, 367 U.S. 497, 540-41 (1961) (Harlan, J., dissenting) (Due Process is a broader concept than procedural fairness. "Were due process merely a procedural safeguard it would fail to reach those situations where the deprivation of life, liberty or property was accomplished by legislation. . . . Thus the guaranties of due process, though having their roots in Magna Carta's '*per legem terram*' and considered as procedural safeguards 'against executive usurpation and tyranny,' have in this country 'become bulwarks also against arbitrary legislation.'").

principles to the Clause's meaning. Under this second construction, even validly enacted laws contrary to these legal procedures are not due process of law.[870] For Harrison, these are two types of procedural due process and all other use of the Clause is substantive due process.[871]

For purposes of this discussion, all use of the Due Process Clause against validly enacted legislation is substantive due process. As we saw above in the discussion of the English Constitution, even the most lauded procedure that formed the basis of "due process of law" was enacted law or the medieval equivalent.[872] Coke's fight against the king was based in large part on statute law.[873] Indeed, Coke and the Commons grieved the king's arbitrary commitment without cause, but Parliament's power to commit was supported.[874] "Law of the land" included Parliament's acts.[875] What constituted the law that formed due process of law was subject to change. Parliament frequently updated statute law, the common law, and even the Magna Carta.[876] The

---

[870] *Supra* Chapter X sec. A.

[871] Harrison, *supra* note 818, at 497-98.

[872] *Supra* Chapter III sec. C (assizes as medieval legislation).

[873] *Supra* notes 682-695.

[874] *Supra* note 693.

[875] *Supra* notes 690-705.

[876] *Supra* notes 694, 781; *cf.* Chapter V.C (Edward I's statutes); *supra* notes 317, 386, 448-454 (modifying law and Magna Carta's promises). Coke cited 42 Edward III, *supra* note 451, out of context when he commented in debates on the Petition of Right that parliamentary statutes contrary to the Magna Carta were void. *Supra* notes 696-698. Coke likely appreciated the concept of royal equity in the Council and Chancellor. *Supra* note 538. To the extent that Coke believed that the Magna Carta was unalterable, that position is not consistent with medieval history. *Supra* notes 448-456. Challenging Parliament was not the theme of the 1620s. Rather, it was challenging the king's power to commit without

Magna Carta and baronial reform established participatory government in place of an arbitrary king. Similarly, state and federal legislation create and update their respective law of the land.[877] Due process of law meant the rule of law.

For the American judiciary, however, due process of law came to mean not the rule of law or process by the law adopted by the sovereign and representative state and federal legislative bodies. Rather, it took on a self-executing and variable characteristic. As a self-executing power in the courts, due process of law was interpreted as a stand-alone provision capable of voiding state and congressional law. Due process of law became whatever the judge thinks ought to be the law.

Once the due-process-of-law and law-of-the-land language was inverted against participatory government, no legislative action touching life, liberty, or property was beyond its reach. Thrusting the liberty pendulum to the other extreme and against the legislature, the courts became superlegislative councils and judges became "evil councilors" separate from the people's will. The power to "interpret" the propriety of validly enacted law—especially based on ambiguous, open-ended constitutional text not intended for the judiciary—is the power to create and repeal the law.[878]

---

cause. In this fight, several statutes as well as the Magna Carta were the primary defense. The Commons wanted to limit the king in favor of Parliament. *Supra* Chapter VIII.

877 The interface between English law and American law in the context of law of the land and due process is very well put in Attorney General Haywood's argument reported in *State v.* ---, 2 N.C. (1 Hayw.) 50 (1794), *supra* note 806; *see also supra* notes 781-783, 791-792, 797.

878 *Supra* note 696 (Parliament declaring the law; king and royal judges limited in discretion).

The problems with substantive due process illustrated above tap a bigger problem with judicial enforcement of the Bill of Rights. The English Bill of Rights was a venerated set of principles, but those principles had meaning against the king's prerogative and rule *per voluntatem.* Where the English Bill of Rights limited the king, Parliament stepped in with representative government.[879] The founding generation adapted similar language in state and federal constitutions but without appreciating the difference between monarch and self-government.[880]

New Hampshire's 1784 Bill of Rights contained a list of thirty-eight "rights" including the "Law of the Land" provision.[881] The list included Lockean language that was also found in the Declaration of Independence—for example, "natural law," "inalienable rights," and "pursuit of happiness." Article 10 provided what could be construed as a right to resist government.

While New Hampshire and other states proclaimed that these declarations in their bills of rights were restrictions on the legislature, it is difficult to understand how such open-ended principles would be self-executing in the courts against the legislature without more. A much clearer view is that the state bills of rights were intended to be recommendatory principles to guide

---

879 The grievances ending in the Declaration of Rights and English Bill of Rights aimed to restrict the arbitrary king in favor of Parliament and common consent: Declarations (1), (2) were against the king's suspending and dispensing power (SCHWOERER, *supra* note 680, at 59-64); (3) prohibited executive courts in conflict with the common law; (4) rejected nonparliamentary taxation (SCHWOERER, 64-69); (5) claimed the right to petition the king (SCHWOERER, 69-71); (6) required parliamentary consent to raise or keep standing armies (SCHWOERER, 71); and (13) called for frequent parliaments. DECLARATION OF RIGHTS *in* SCHWOERER, *supra* note 680, at 295-98; PLUCKNETT, CONST. HIST., *supra* note 59, at 449-54 (English Bill of Rights).

880 *Supra* notes 784-790, 824, 847, 855.

881 4 THORPE, *supra* note 739, at 2453-57.

the state legislatures and educate the citizens. In reference to the right to a jury trial in civil cases, John Marshall commented in 1788 that "[t]he bill of rights is merely recommendatory. Were it otherwise, the consequence would be that many laws which are found convenient would be unconstitutional."[882]

In response to the demand for a national Bill of Rights following the Constitutional Convention, Thomas McKean of Pennsylvania, opined:

> The truth is, sir, that bills of rights are instruments of modern invention, unknown among the ancients, and unpracticed but by the British nation and the governments descended from them. . . . In short, though [the Bill of Rights] can do no harm, I believe, yet it is an unnecessary instrument, for, in fact, the whole plan of government is nothing more than a bill of rights—a declaration of the people in what manner they choose to be governed. If, sir, the people should at any time desire to alter and abolish their government, I agree with my honorable colleague James Wilson that it is in their power to do so, and I am happy to observe that the Constitution before us provides a regular mode for that event.[883]

Ultimately, the founding generation enacted state and national bills of rights despite general statements finding bills of rights unnecessary in republican governments.

If and how bills of rights were to be enforced against state and national legislatures was a matter of uncertainty. James Mad-

---

[882] 10 DOC. HIST. OF RATIF. CONST., *supra* note 745, at 1438.

[883] PENNSYLVANIA AND THE FEDERAL CONSTITUTION, 1787-1788, at 252 (John Bach McMaster and Frederick D. Stone eds. 1888); *see also* 1 STORING, *supra* note 769, at 68.

ison, the leading intellectual behind the Constitution, was critical of judicial review generally and ambiguous on the enforcement of the Bill of Rights. In one of his passages introducing the proposed Bill of Rights in the 1st Congress, he alluded to both judicial enforcement and senatorial or popular enforcement.

> It has been said that it is unnecessary to load the Constitution with [the Bill of Rights], because it was not found effectual in the constitution of the particular States. It is true, there are a few particular States in which some of the most valuable articles have not, at one time or other, been violated; but it does not follow but they may have, to a certain degree, a salutary effect against the abuse of power. If they are incorporated into the constitution, independent tribunals of justice will consider themselves in a peculiar manner the guardians of those rights; they will be an impenetrable bulwark against every assumption of power in the legislative or executive; they will be naturally led to resist every encroachment upon rights expressly stipulated for in the constitution by the declaration of rights. Besides this security, there is a great probability that such a declaration in the federal system would be enforced because the State Legislatures will jealously and closely watch the operations of this Government, and be able to resist with more effect every assumption of power than any other power on earth can do; and the greatest opponents to a Federal Government admit the State Legislatures to be sure guardians of the people's liberty. I conclude, from this view of the subject, that it will be proper in itself, and highly politic, for the tranquillity of the public mind, and the stability of the Government, that we should offer something, in the form I have proposed, to be incor-

porated in the system of Government, as a declaration of the rights of the people.[884]

Before this, Madison wrote in another context:

---

[884] James Madison, 1 ANNALS OF CONGRESS, *supra* note 773, 1st Cong., 1st. Sess. 456-57 (June 8, 1789) (minor formatting added). In 1787, shortly before the Constitutional Convention, Congress enacted the Northwest Ordinance, which provided an initial law for the western territories, including declarations of rights similar to our Bill of Rights. These declarations would be unalterable "unless by common consent" suggesting that the declarations were subject to participatory governance. The Ordinance:

> It is hereby ordained and declared by the authority aforesaid, That the following articles shall be considered as articles of compact between the original States and the people and States in the said territory and forever remain unalterable, unless by common consent, to wit:
> Art. 1. No person, demeaning himself in a peaceable and orderly manner, shall ever be molested on account of his mode of worship or religious sentiments, in the said territory.
> Art. 2. The inhabitants of the said territory shall always be entitled to the benefits of the writ of *habeas corpus*, and of the trial by jury; of a proportionate representation of the people in the legislature; and of judicial proceedings according to the course of the common law. All persons shall be bailable, unless for capital offenses, where the proof shall be evident or the presumption great. All fines shall be moderate; and no cruel or unusual punishments shall be inflicted. No man shall be deprived of his liberty or property, but by the judgment of his peers or the law of the land; and, should the public exigencies make it necessary, for the common preservation, to take any person's property, or to demand his particular services, full compensation shall be made for the same. And, in the just preservation of rights and property, it is understood and declared, that no law ought ever to be made, or have force in the said territory, that shall, in any manner whatever, interfere with or affect private contracts or engagements, *bona fide*, and without fraud, previously formed. . . .

1 DOC. HIST. OF RATIF. CONST., *supra* note 745, at 168, 172-73.

> In the State Constitutions & indeed in the Fedl. one also, no provision is made for the case of a disagreement in expounding them; and as the Courts are generally the last in making their decision, it results to them, by refusing or not refusing to execute a law, to stamp it with its final character. This makes the Judiciary Dept paramount in fact to the Legislature, which was never intended, and can never be proper.[885]

The United States Bill of Rights did not have an active presence in the first half of the nineteenth century. One explanation is that the founding generation considered the declarations to be principles rather than self-executing provisions for judicial enforcement against Congress.

This uncertainty in the enforcement of bills of rights is illustrated in an early nineteenth-century treatise. Chancellor Kent, a well-regarded American jurist in the early part of the nineteenth century, questioned the need for and the enforcement of bills of rights in self-governing republics.

> But the necessity, in our representative republics, of these declaratory codes has been frequently questioned, inasmuch as the government, in all its parts, is the creation of the people, and every department of it is filled by their agents, duly chosen or appointed according to their will, and made responsible for maladministration. It may be observed, on the one hand, that no gross violation of those absolute private rights, which are clearly understood and settled by the common reason of mankind, is to be apprehended in the ordinary course of public affairs; and as to extraordinary instances of faction and turbulence, and the corruption and violence which they necessarily engender, no

[885] James Madison to Thomas Jefferson, October 15, 1788 (observations on Jefferson's draft constitution), *available at* http://press-pubs.uchicago.edu/founders/documents/v1ch17s25.html.

> parchment checks can be relied on as affording, under such circumstances, any effectual protection to public liberty. When the spirit of liberty has fled, and truth and justice are disregarded, private rights can be easily sacrificed under the forms of law. On the other hand, there is weight due to the consideration that a bill of rights is of real efficacy in controlling the excesses of party spirit. It serves to guide and enlighten public opinion, and to render it more quick to detect, and more resolute to resist, attempts to disturb private right. It requires more than ordinary hardiness and audacity of character to trample down principles which our ancestors cultivated with reverence; which we imbibed in our early education; which recommend themselves to the judgment of the world by their truth and simplicity; and which are constantly placed before the eyes of the people, accompanied with the imposing force and solemnity of a constitutional sanction. Bills of rights are part of the muniments of freemen, showing their title to protection, and they became of increased value when placed under the protection of an independent judiciary, instituted as the appropriate guardian of private right. Care, however, is to be taken in the digest of these declaratory provisions, to confine the manual to a few plain and unexceptionable principles. We weaken greatly the force of them if we encumber the constitution, and perhaps embarrass the future operations and more enlarged experience of the legislature, with a catalogue of ethical and political aphorisms, which, in some instances, may reasonably be questioned, and in others justly condemned.[886]

Kent recognized that the Bill of Rights was a concept in relation to the king and that the legislatures in all or nearly all cases were the

---

[886] 2 KENT'S COMMENTARIES, *supra* note 799, at 50–51 (minor formatting added).

proper safeguard against arbitrary government. The Bill of Rights would be a paper parchment ineffective against true tyranny but may have value as a guiding principle to legislatures.[887] Kent commented that a constitution full of "ethical and political aphorisms" found in declarations constipates written constitutions and legislative processes. He continued:

> Several of the early state constitutions had no formal bill of rights inserted in them; and experience teaches us that the most solid basis of public safety, and the most certain assurance of the uninterrupted enjoyment of our personal rights and liberties, consists, not so much in bills of rights, as in the skillful organization of the government and its aptitude, by means of its structure and genius, and the spirit of the people which pervades it, to produce wise laws, and a pure, firm, and intelligent administration of justice.[888]

For Kent, protection from tyranny was found in the "skillful . . . structure and genius" of government rather than bills of rights. He went on to describe examples where states had declarations but did not or should not follow them to the letter—for example, an absolute right to trial by jury.[889]

A passage from Kent's Commentaries states in reference to the Bill of Rights:

> The absolute rights of individuals may be resolved into the right of personal security, the right of personal liberty, and the right to acquire

---

887 *See also* 1 STORING, *supra* note 769, at 69-70 (noting that one benefit of bills of rights was to educate the people).

888 2 KENT'S COMMENTARIES, *supra* note 799, at 53 (minor formatting added).

889 *Id.* at 51-57.

> and enjoy property. These rights have been justly considered, and frequently declared, by the people of this country, to be natural, inherent, and unalienable.[890]

For judicial activists, this passage would be discussed in a judicial opinion striking down federal or state legislation. But Kent understood the context of the Bill of Rights, even in America, was not different from the concept of liberty to Englishmen. Kent continued.

> The effectual security and enjoyment of [the absolute rights of individuals] depend upon the existence of civil liberty; and that consists in being protected and governed by laws made, or assented to, by the representatives of the people, and conducive to the general welfare. Right itself in civil society is that which any man is entitled to have, or to do, or to require from others, within the limits prescribed by law.[891]

Instead of recognizing that the United States Constitution and self-government were the end-game of bills of rights against arbitrary kings, American courts eventually treated the Bill of Rights as a type of constitution in itself, but worse than that, the phrase "due process of law" as its own multifaceted, judicial constitution self-executing against the legislative branch. The people have no place in these judicial constitutions. Principles like "tyranny of the majority," which is not in any state or federal constitution, provide a pretext to write off the legislature. With all of this power in the courts, the people would benefit from a second bill of rights to protect themselves from unelected judicial discretion and prerogative. Failure to explain the application of or to address problems with applying open-ended bills of rights

---

[890] *Id.* at 43.

[891] *Id.* (footnotes omitted).

against self-governing governments was the founding generation's major shortcoming.

D. The Fourteenth Amendment and Substantive Due Process

In the American system of government, the primary repository for the police power was the states. The states' police power covered life, liberty, and property—the community's general welfare and common utility.[892] Antifederalists demanded a Bill of Rights to protect state and local government from congressional imperialism. From a federal and theoretical perspective, the problems with judicial enforcement of the Bill of Rights did not affect the states as the Bill of Rights applied to federal powers.

But the American Civil War and the Reconstruction amendments changed the federalism relationship between Congress and the states.[893] Following the War, newly freed slaves and loyalists were being denied citizenship rights and enforcement of the law of the land by their own state and local government.[894] Accordingly, the Fourteenth Amendment extended due process

[892] *Cf. supra* notes 676-681, 695 (Parliament represents the nation's welfare).

[893] The Thirteenth Amendment outlawed slavery. The Fourteenth Amendment, among other things, authorized congressional legislation establishing citizenship and citizenship rights for newly freed slaves. The Fifteenth Amendment prohibited racial discrimination in voting among citizens. All male citizens were allowed to vote without distinction of race or former status as slaves.

[894] THEODORE BRANTNER WILSON, THE BLACK CODES OF THE SOUTH (1965); Thomas H. Burrell, *Justice Stephen Field's Expansion of the Fourteenth Amendment: From the Safeguards of Federalism to a State of Judicial Hegemony*, 43 GONZAGA L. REV. 77, 83-85 (2007).

and added equal protection language as provisions congressionally enforceable against the states.[895] The Fourteenth Amendment:

> Section one. All persons born or naturalized in the United States, and subject to the jurisdiction thereof, are citizens of the United States and of the state wherein they reside. No state shall make or enforce any law which shall abridge the privileges or immunities of citizens of the United States; nor shall any state deprive any person of life, liberty, or property, without due process of law; nor deny to any person within its jurisdiction the equal protection of the laws.
>
> Section five. The Congress shall have power to enforce, by appropriate legislation, the provisions of this article.[896]

The due process language of the Fifth and Fourteenth Amendments did not mean more to its framers than the language did to the barons, Lords, and Commons of the thirteenth and fourteenth centuries.[897] The due process language in both the Fifth and Fourteenth Amendments was proposed and adopted with little to no substantive debate. They were not intended to be substantive reaches into the law. The founders wanted to partici-

---

[895] For discussion, see Burrell, *Justice Stephen Field*, *supra* note 894, at Parts II–III.

[896] U.S. CONST. amend. XIV §§ 1, 5 (1868).

[897] Williams argued that by the Fourteenth Amendment's ratification, states, courts, and others considered "due process of law" and "law of the land" substantively. Therefore, the Fourteenth Amendment's ratification of "due process of law" justified substantive due process as that doctrine evolved. Williams, *supra* note 740, at 477–83. There's no doubt that Bingham advocated for a broad coverage of civil rights legislation. However, Bingham did not sway from the point that Congress would be enforcing the law, *the substantive law* that Bingham supported. *Infra* notes 920–921. Therefore, the Fourteenth Amendment must reinforce the rule of law and not substantive due process as defined above.

pate in and protect the law of the land and the rule of law. Colonists of the American Revolution despised taxation and governance over their lives and property without their common consent and representation.[898] Lack of participatory government was the essential cause of the American Revolution and an essential component of state and federal constitutions.[899] In the Reconstruction Congress, newly freed slaves were formally made citizens, and Congress protected citizenship rights and equal enforcement of the rule of law.[900] The Fourteenth Amendment empowered Congress to reverse the slave and black codes present in several states. Thus, despite the span of several hundred years, the aim of protecting participatory government constituted the same core component of the language—indeed the very essence of liberty.

As expected, the postbellum debates over civil rights and the Reconstruction amendments were controversial. After ratification, that controversy quickly spilled into the courts in the form of an internal division among the Supreme Court's members. The majority mostly limited the Fourteenth Amendment's reach. In *Munn v. Illinois*, for example, the majority upheld an Illinois statute regulating the maximum rate charged for grain storage against a Fourteenth-Amendment challenge.[901] Chief Justice Waite stated that "[e]very statute is presumed to be constitutional. The courts ought not to declare one to be unconstitutional, unless it is clearly so. If there is doubt, the expressed will of the legisla-

---

[898] *Supra* note 737.

[899] *Supra* Chapter IX sec. A.

[900] U.S. CONST. amend. XIV; *see also* Civil Rights Act of 1866 ch. 31, § 1, 14 Stat. 27 (1866).

[901] *Munn*, 94 U.S. 113, 123, 134 (1877).

ture should be sustained."[902] Waite discussed the social compact and the need for individuals to sacrifice some rights and privileges.

> When one becomes a member of society, he necessarily parts with some rights or privileges which, as an individual not affected by his relations to others, he might retain. "A body politic," as aptly defined in the preamble of the Constitution of Massachusetts, "is a social compact by which the whole people covenants with each citizen, and each citizen with the whole people, that all shall be governed by certain laws for the common good."[903]

Waite emphasized that it is the province of the legislature to cure the defects in the common law and bring regulations up to date.

> But a mere common-law regulation of trade or business may be changed by statute. A person has no property, no vested interest, in any rule of the common law. That is only one of the forms of municipal law, and is no more sacred than any other. Rights of property which have been created by the common law cannot be taken away without due process; but the law itself, as a rule of conduct, may be changed at the will, or even at the whim, of the legislature, unless prevented by constitutional limitations. Indeed, the great office of statutes is to remedy defects in the common law as they are developed, and to adapt it to the changes of time and circumstances.[904]

---

[902] *Id.* at 123. *Supra* notes 812, 848-849; *infra* notes 912, 915 (repugnance standard, beyond a reasonable doubt discussed or developed).

[903] *Munn*, 94 U.S. at 124 (citations omitted).

[904] *Id.* at 134; *supra* notes 676, 694, 783, 806.

Waite for the majority: "We know that [legislative power] may be abused; but that is no argument against its existence. For protection against abuses by legislatures the people must resort to the polls, not to the courts."[905]

The dissent and nonmajority opinions in *Munn* and subsequent decisions envisioned a much broader Amendment including a substantive due process theme that exploited the gap in the Webster-Taney umbrella theory of due process.[906] Nonmajority opinions adopted and expanded upon the notion that due process and law of the land extend to constitutional conflicts as well as to principles of fairness, justice, and English common law. For them, law deemed unreasonable was a violation of the Fourteenth Amendment. Eventually, the nonmajority ideology captured the majority as the Supreme Court harnessed substantive due process to police the states' general police power and thereby extract a common-welfare-common-utility standard from popular government and infuse that power into the judiciary's now arbitrary judicial prerogative.[907]

The horns of the dilemma can be seen in Justice Matthew's opinion in *Hurtado v. California*.[908] The California legislature provided for prosecution by magistrate and information without grand jury indictment. Similar to the above-discussed state court opinions, the question was whether the Fourteenth Amendment's "due process of law" incorporated some judicial procedure or

---

905 *Munn*, 94 U.S. at 134.

906 Burrell, *Justice Stephen Field*, *supra* note 894, at 128–57 (criticizing Justice Stephen Field's Due Process Clause opinions as placing the judiciary over the legislature and the former usurping the latter's role); *supra* notes 816–821, 869 (Webster-Taney umbrella interpretation).

907 Burrell, *Justice Stephen Field*, *supra* note 894, at 128–57.

908 110 U.S. 516 (1884).

"constitutional common law" such that the California law was a violation of the Fourteenth Amendment's Due Process Clause.

Justice Matthews came to the party sober. The beginning of his opinion did much to correct Coke's heresy and placed English provisions in context with the American form of government. Matthews commented that due process of law included settled usages as well as any other legislatively enacted process of law not forbidden by the Constitution.[909] Matthews and the *Hurtado* majority did not find that "due process of law" required indictment for criminal trial. Matthews continued:

> [Due process of law] refers to that law of the land which derives its authority from the legislative powers conferred upon congress by the constitution of the United States, exercised within the limits therein prescribed, and interpreted according to the principles of the common law. In the fourteenth amendment, by parity of reason, it refers to that law of the land in each state which derives its authority from the inherent and reserved powers of the state, exerted within the limits of those fundamental principles of liberty and justice which lie at the base of all our civil and political institutions, and the greatest security for which resides in the right of the people to make their own laws, and alter them at their pleasure.[910]

Matthews had a better grip on due process than his predecessors. But his definition would have left the legislature unrestrained by "due process of law," an outcome he did not support.

---

[909] By the time of *Hurtado*, the average law library was likely much improved over the law library of the latter eighteenth century in which Coke's writings predominated. William Stubbs's CONSTITUTIONAL HISTORY OF ENGLAND (1874-1878) was available by *Hurtado*.

[910] *Hurtado*, 110 U.S. at 535-36.

Matthews, citing Webster and the umbrella theory of due process, succumbed to the temptation of Fourteenth Amendment liquor.

> But it is not to be supposed that these legislative powers are absolute and despotic, and that the amendment prescribing due process of law is too vague and indefinite to operate as a practical restraint. It is not every act, legislative in form, that is law. Law is something more than mere will exerted as an act of power. It must be not a special rule for a particular person or a particular case, but, in the language of Mr. Webster, in his familiar definition, 'the general law, a law which hears before it condemns, which proceeds upon inquiry, and renders judgment only after trial,' so 'that every citizen shall hold his life, liberty, property, and immunities under the protection of the general rules which govern society,' and thus excluding, as not due process of law, acts of attainder, bills of pains and penalties, acts of confiscation, acts reversing judgments, and acts directly transferring one man's estate to another, legislative judgments and decrees, and other similar special, partial, and arbitrary exertions of power under the forms of legislation. Arbitrary power, enforcing its edicts to the injury of the persons and property of its subjects, is not law, whether manifested as the decree of a personal monarch or of an impersonal multitude. And the limitations imposed by our constitutional law upon the action of the governments, both state and national, are essential to the preservation of public and private rights, notwithstanding the representative character of our political institutions. The enforcement of these limitations by judicial process is the device of self-governing communities to protect the rights of individuals and minorities, as well against the power of numbers, as against the violence of public agents transcending the limits of lawful authority, even when acting in

> the name and wielding the force of the government.[911]

Matthews's speech did not support strict construction of the Constitution and did not limit judicial review to the letter of the written constitution.[912] Matthews, citing and expanding upon Webster, impregnated the Fourteenth Amendment's "due process of law" language with variable meanings such that "special, partial, and arbitrary" legislation—as determined by the courts—would be unconstitutional.[913] Matthews supported his substantive due process interpretation with variations of the "tyranny of the majority" theme. As noted above, the Framers dealt with interested majorities by building checks and balances into the Constitution. And the most important check and balance is frequent elections.

The late nineteenth-century battle over state regulation of oleomargarine provides a good illustration of the initial conflict over the Fourteenth Amendment's meaning. The majority in *Powell v. Pennsylvania* upheld the conviction of an individual for engaging in unlawful manufacture and sale of oleomargarine.[914] Justice Harlan, reasoning similar to T.A. Johnson's dissent in *Wynehamer*, commented in response to the Fourteenth Amendment argument:

---

[911] *Id.* at 535.

[912] *Supra* notes 812, 848-849, 902 (repugnance beyond a reasonable doubt).

[913] The *Hurtado* majority held that California's substitute for presentment and indictment did not offend the Fourteenth Amendment's "due process of law." Justice Harlan's dissent made much of Coke's arguments that "law of the land" meant "due process of law," which he felt required presentment and indictment. *Hurtado*, 110 U.S. at 538-57; *see also supra* notes 686-690.

[914] 127 U.S. 678 (1888).

> "Every possible presumption . . . is in favor of the validity of a statute, and this continues until the contrary is shown beyond a rational doubt. One branch of the government cannot encroach on the domain of another without danger. The safety of our institutions depends in no small degree on a strict observance of this salutary rule. . . ." It is not a part of [the judicial] function[] to conduct investigations of facts entering into questions of public policy merely, and to sustain or frustrate the legislative will, embodied in statutes, as they may happen to approve or disapprove its determinations of such questions.[915]

Justice Stephen J. Field, dissenting, would have ruled the regulation unconstitutional in violation of his open-ended interpretation of the Fourteenth Amendment. Justice Field:

> [P]revious to the adoption of the Fourteenth Amendment . . . the validity of such legislation [regulating the production and sale of oleomargarine] was to be determined by the constitution of the State. . . . If the legislation of the State thus sustained was oppressive and unjust, the remedy could be found only in subsequent legislation, brought about through the influence of wiser views and a more enlightened policy on the part of the people. . . . By the first section of the Fourteenth Amendment, which had its origin in the new conditions and necessities growing out of the late civil war, further restraints were placed upon the power of the States . . . which subjected their action to review by this court. . . .
>
> It is the clause declaring that no State shall "deprive any person of life, liberty, or property without due process of law" which applies to the present case. This provision . . . was designed to

[915] *Powell*, 127 U.S. at 684-85 (internal citation omitted); *supra* notes 812, 848-849, 902 (repugnance beyond a reasonable doubt).

prevent the arbitrary deprivation of life and liberty, and the arbitrary spoliation of property. As I said on a former occasion, it means that neither can be taken, or the enjoyment thereof impaired, except in the course of the regular administration of the law in the established tribunals. It has always been supposed to secure to every person the essential conditions for the pursuit of happiness, and is therefore not to be construed in a narrow or restricted sense.

By "liberty," as thus used, is meant something more than freedom from physical restraint or imprisonment. It means freedom not merely to go wherever one may choose, but to do such acts as he may judge best for his interest not inconsistent with the equal rights of others; that is, to follow such pursuits as may be best adapted to his faculties, and which will give to him the highest enjoyment. . . . "[T]he term 'liberty', as protected by the Constitution, is not cramped into a mere freedom from physical restraint of the person of the citizen, as by incarceration, but is deemed to embrace the right of man to be free in the enjoyment of the faculties with which he has been endowed by his Creator, subject only to such restraints as are necessary for the common welfare. . . ."

With the gift of life there necessarily goes to every one the right to do all such acts, and follow all such pursuits, not inconsistent with the equal rights of others, as may support life and add to the happiness of its possessor. The right to pursue one's happiness is placed by the Declaration of Independence among the inalienable rights of man, with which all men are endowed, not by the grace of emperors or kings, or by force of legislative or constitutional enactments, but by their Creator; and to secure them, not to grant them, governments are instituted among men. The right to procure healthy and nutritious food, by which life may be preserved and

> enjoyed, and to manufacture it, is among these inalienable rights, which, in my judgment, no State can give and no State can take away except in punishment for crime.[916]

By Field's standards, the Fourteenth Amendment was not limited to its text or its intended purpose to congressionally rectify slavery and racial injustice.[917] For Field and Field-like jurisprudence, the Fourteenth Amendment was a blank check for the judiciary to review and remedy perceived injustice violating any open-ended principles such as "pursuit of happiness." Open-ended dissenting viewpoints such as Field's more or less became the meaning and understanding of the Fourteenth Amendment.[918] With this broad interpretation of the Amendment, all state regulation was subject to the Court's reasonableness review.[919]

E. <u>Modern Supreme Court Law</u>

Two judicial assumptions of power made the late nineteenth-century situation worse. First, the Supreme Court interpreted the Fourteenth Amendment's due process language to incorporate the United States Bill of Rights for judicial enforcement against the states.[920] The Fourteenth Amendment's text and legis-

---

[916] *Powell*, 127 U.S. at 690-92 (internal citations omitted).

[917] In the first decade after the Amendment's ratification, there were several congressional enforcement acts and civil rights acts. Once the courts took over, those legislative efforts dissipated.

[918] Burrell, *Justice Stephen Field*, *supra* note 894, at Part IV.C.

[919] For a discussion and defense of judicial reasonableness review, see Haines, *Law of Nature in State and Federal Judicial Decisions*, *supra* note 835; *see also* Frederick Mark Gedicks, *An Originalist Defense of Substantive Due Process: Magna Carta, Higher-Law Constitutionalism, and the Fifth Amendment*, 58 EMORY L. J. 585 (2009).

[920] *See generally* Charles Fairman, *Does the Fourteenth Amendment Incorporate the Bill of Rights?: The Original Understanding*, 2 STAN. L. REV. 5 (1949).

lative history had envisioned congressional enforcement.[921] But the Court read "Congress . . . shall enforce" out of the text. The doctrine of incorporation and stand-alone judicial enforcement exponentially extended judicial discretion in governance of life, liberty, and property. Thereafter, the ambiguity of the self-executing Bill of Rights, joining substantive due process, strangled participatory government at the state and local levels in addition to the national. The Bill of Rights was designed to be a fence to curb a feared national imperialism in favor of state and local government. Incorporating the Bill of Rights to judicially protect state and local government from themselves transformed that national fence into a fortress protecting judicial oligarchism at the expense of representative state and local government.

Second, substantive due process, after the Fourteenth Amendment's ratification, slowly merged with the Equal Protection Clause and vice versa.[922] The Equal Protection Clause's foundation began with the Civil Rights Act of 1866 attempting to prohibit states from having unequal administration of the law.[923] Prior to this congressional prohibition, state laws and black codes had different punishments based on the criminal's race. Some states and localities had selectively enforced or selectively failed

---

[921] Elsewhere, I have discussed incorporation. In short, while Bingham desired that Congress be empowered to enforce and protect the Bill of Rights' principles against the states, Bingham was considered a radical, and an amending majority often disagreed with his desires for political and social rights. Second, Bingham himself maintained that any enforcement of the Bill of Rights' principles was to take place through congressional acts, that is, to be debated and amended by Congress. The Fourteenth Amendment expanded congressional powers, not stand-alone judicial powers. Burrell, *Story of Privileges and Immunities*, *supra* note 85, at 109-21.

[922] For discussion, see Adarand Constructors, Inc. v. Pena, 515 U.S. 200, 213-31 (1995).

[923] Burrell, *Justice Stephen Field*, *supra* note 894, at 97-99.

to enforce the law on the basis of race. Congress attempted to remedy the injustice. But the Civil Rights Act of 1866 was controversial and deemed unconstitutional because the Thirteenth Amendment only prohibited slavery and did not provide congressional authority for civil rights legislation. In response, Congress secured the right to legislate for and enforce equal protection and due process of law with the Fourteenth Amendment.

For the 39th Congress, equal protection of the law meant equal administration of the law. But substance judicially infected this provision as well. For judicial activists, "equal protection of the law" became "protection of equal laws,"[924] as its meaning was consumed by the judicial mudslide created by the Webster-Taney umbrella theory of due process and law of the land. While the judiciary's interpretation of the Equal Protection Clause requires the extra step of converting governmental action into one affecting a class or group and then finding unequal treatments of classes, the end result of the substantive Equal Protection Clause is the same as the substantive Due Process Clause.[925]

For a good example of the Court's interchanging due process and equal protection, see the school desegregation case *Bolling v. Sharpe*:

> [T]he concepts of equal protection and due process, both stemming from our American ideal of

---

[924] *Id.* at 151-56 (noting that the Court played on the language to substitute its view of "protection of equal laws" for the drafters' "Equal Protection of the Law").

[925] We also find efforts to use the Privileges and/or Immunities Clauses of Article Four and the Fourteenth Amendment. Litigants ground their desired outcome in alleged violations of Due Process of Law, Equal Protection of Law, or Privileges and Immunities. *See, e.g.*, Mont. Outfitters Action Grp. v. Fish & Game Comm'n of Mont., 417 F. Supp. 1005, 1007 (D. Mont. 1976) (all three Clauses argued). *See generally* Burrell, *Journey*, *supra* note 60, at Part III.

> fairness, are not mutually exclusive. The "equal protection of the laws" is a more explicit safeguard of prohibited unfairness than "due process of law" and, therefore, we do not imply that the two are always interchangeable phrases. But, as this Court has recognized, discrimination may be so unjustifiable as to be violative of due process.[926]

The drafters of the Fifth and Fourteenth Amendments never intended to put judiciary over the legislature on grounds of general fairness by the terms "due process of law" and "equal protection of the law." These principles of reasonableness and fairness were proper for legislature and the ballot box; judicially, they destabilized constitutionalism as the courts substituted their discretion for legislatures' discretion.

Much of the initial Fourteenth-Amendment judicial activism can be traced to Justice Field and Field-like jurisprudence in the latter part of the nineteenth century. As we saw above in *Powell*, Field's *modus operandi* was to exaggerate a discussion of "liberty" to such a degree that any governmental action naturally constituted a prohibited deprivation.[927] Field's methodology became textbook constitutional law in the twentieth century's heightened-scrutiny analysis.

The first step in the Court's twentieth-century adjudication of individual rights was to establish that the right was fundamental *in the eyes of a majority of the Court.*[928] The Court had

---

[926] Bolling v. Sharpe, 347 U.S. 497, 499 (1954).

[927] *Supra* notes 914–919.

[928] The Supreme Court has invented several tests and standards of review to determine the constitutionality of legislation. The three tests are: rational basis, intermediate review, and strict-scrutiny. The Court has created an additional standard, "undue burden," which falls somewhere in

a full range of ideological and political viewpoints to exercise in so doing. The first step provided the judge with the opportunity to air personal socioeconomic, cultural, and political views proving that "deeply held" *opinions* covering privacy, decency, dignity, equality or some other important matter were "fundamental rights."

Once such a "fundamental" status was proven, the Court applied a strict- or heightened-scrutiny standard of review to the offending legislation or governmental acts affecting the fundamental right. Only the state's narrowly tailored and compelling justification permitted the offending legislation to stand. In other words, the state had to convince the judge that the law was narrowly tailored as well as demonstrate to the court's satisfaction that it had a compelling justification for its legislation. Modern judicial review became a contest between the state's opinion and the judge's opinion.

As a matter of practice, the court often found a violation of a right along the first step's reasoning. The ideology traversed in the first step begged a violation in the second step, as the judge's strenuous effort to demonstrate that a "fundamental liberty" was at hand practically demanded his or her conclusion that a deprivation without a compelling justification had occurred.

---

the intermediate category. A governmental action, for example, affecting a fundamental right will be reviewed under heightened or strict scrutiny. The government must demonstrate to the Supreme Court that its action serves a compelling interest and is narrowly tailored to the Court's satisfaction. A government action affecting an economic concern, for example, will be reviewed under a rational basis; the government must articulate only a rational basis to pass the Court's review. The standard utilized depends on the judges' perception of the right at issue. There is a great degree of judicial discretion in choosing and applying a particular test. These standards of review break down into the judges' perception of the reasonableness of the legislation or action.

With open-ended tests and little to no external restraint, substantive interpretations of due process of law and equal protection spread throughout the twentieth century and undermined any legitimacy to the notion of constitutionalism. The Court deemed various rights and activities fundamental and governmental restraint thereof unreasonable or without compelling justification. Each case provided a foundation for the next. Substantive due process, equal protection, and other doctrines merged into a generic constitutional gloss divorced from any intent, meaning, or text. The Supreme Court merely articulated a persuasive foundation for its policy. With the order of five Justices, conflicting state and federal laws were void.

The Constitution was never intended to empower the federal government against the states in the police powers of life, liberty, and property. The Bill of Rights was designed to restrict federal government in favor of state and local autonomy. The Fourteenth Amendment, though changing original federalism designs in favor of more congressional powers, was limited in degree and scope and spoke to congressional enforcement of race relations stemming from slavery.

Unchecked Supreme Court adjudication of the Bill of Rights and the Fourteenth Amendment radically changed these principles. The Supreme Court has invaded every conceivable legislative setting, and its precedents resemble a legislative code.[929] The Court has cannibalized the most fundamental concept of lib-

---

[929] The chapters for the Due Process Clauses of the Fifth and Fourteenth Amendment in Congressional Research Service's annotated Constitution span more than 225 pages covering approximately twenty categories and more than fifty subcategories. THE CONSTITUTION OF THE UNITED STATES OF AMERICA: ANALYSIS AND INTERPRETATION (Johnny H. Killian, George A. Costello, Kenneth R. Thomas 2002 ed.). Due-process-of-law case law covers everything from taxation and liberty of contract to abortion, health, morals, and safety. *Id.*

erty—often in the name of liberty—which is participatory self-government and the notion of commonwealthism. In place of the people and representative government, the Court determines its own ideals of fairness, equality, dignity, happiness, privacy, and liberty in its due-process-equal-protection courtwealth.

A few of the famous or infamous Supreme Court decisions based on substantive due process or substantive equal protection include school desegregation, contraception, interracial marriage, abortion, and most recently, same-sex marriage.

In 1954, several states had segregated public facilities including their public school system. The issue of school integration was debated but failed to secure passage in postbellum civil rights debates.[930] The doctrine of "separate but equal" was lambasted by several facets of the American republic; however, it lived with the Fourteenth Amendment for three-quarters of a century. The Fourteenth Amendment's text itself was never intended to outlaw segregated schools. In *Brown v. Board of Education*, Chief Justice Earl Warren, 1953-1969, held:

> We conclude that, in the field of public education, the doctrine of "separate but equal" has no place. Separate educational facilities are inherently unequal. Therefore, we hold that the plaintiffs and others similarly situated for whom the actions have been brought are, by reason of the segregation complained of, deprived of the equal protection of the laws guaranteed by the Fourteenth Amendment. This disposition makes unnecessary any discussion whether such segregation also violates the Due

---

930 *See* Michael W. McConnell, *Originalism and the Desegregation Decisions*, 81 VA. L. REV. 947, 984-90 (1995); Burrell, *Justice Stephen Field*, *supra* note 894, at 119-20.

> Process Clause of the Fourteenth Amendment.[931]

For Warren, the Equal Protection Clause and the Due Process Clause were his own black box, and he decreed that that black box prohibited school desegregation.

As noted above, Justice Field was the architect of modern judicial hegemony. Justice Earl Warren filled in the blanks and handled construction. Warren did not care a lick for concepts of constitutionalism. The Constitution's text was mere pretext for his political ideology. The Warren Court, in no exaggeration, rewrote the Constitution with unwritten judicial code. America became a judicial state.

In 1965, several states prohibited the use of contraception. In *Griswold v. Connecticut*, Justice Douglas held for the majority that such laws violate the "right to privacy."[932] The "right to privacy" is not found in the Constitution or Bill of Rights, but the justices derived it from "zones" and "penumbras" of "fundamental guarantees" including the Due Process Clause.[933] *Griswold* and the power to invent constitutional text provided a convenient precedent for subsequent Supreme Court cases.

The interracial marriage issue was also cited and discussed in the postbellum civil rights debates.[934] In response to concerns

---

[931] Brown v. Bd. of Educ., 347 U.S. 483, 495 (1954).

[932] Griswold v. Connecticut, 381 U.S. 479 (1965).

[933] *Id.* at 484; *supra* note 835 (Court commenting on the "right to privacy" as a natural-law concept similar to vested property interests).

[934] Alfred Avins, *Anti-Miscegenation Laws and the Fourteenth Amendment: The Original Intent*, 52 VA. L. REV. 1224 (1966); Thomas H. Burrell, *Judicial Regimes and Same-Sex Marriage: Enforcing Judicially Determined*

over civil rights legislation interfering with state interracial marriage laws, drafters altered the language to reduce the likelihood of entanglement.[935] The drafters of civil rights legislation and the Fourteenth Amendment had no intention of proscribing state laws banning interracial marriage. Nearly one hundred years later, the Supreme Court in *Loving v. Virginia* intervened and concluded that state bans on interracial marriage violated the substantive Equal Protection and Due Process Clauses.[936] Chief Justice Earl Warren:

> Marriage is one of the "basic civil rights of man," fundamental to our very existence and survival. To deny this fundamental freedom on so unsupportable a basis as the racial classifications embodied in these statutes, classifications so directly subversive of the principle of equality at the heart of the Fourteenth Amendment, is surely to deprive all the State's citizens of liberty without due process of law.[937]

Before 1973, a majority of states banned abortion. Justice Rehnquist observed that bans occurred both before and after the Fourteenth Amendment's ratification. The Fourteenth Amendment did not intend to reach into state matters such as abortion. In *Roe v. Wade*, plaintiffs attacked the Texas abortion statute as a violation of the personal "liberty" found in the Due Process Clause and the "Bill of Rights or its penumbras."[938] The majority held—over a century after the Fourteenth Amendment's ratification—

Personal Autonomy at the Expense of Majoritarian Democracy, 35 OHIO N.U. L. REV. 619 (2009) (hereinafter Burrell, *Judicial Regimes*).

[935] Burrell, *Judicial Regimes*, *supra* note 934.

[936] 388 U.S. 1 (1967) (finding that laws prohibiting interracial marriage violate the Due Process Clause and Equal Protection Clause).

[937] *Id.* at 12 (internal citations omitted).

[938] 410 U.S. 113, 129 (1973).

that "due process of law" and *Griswold*'s "right to privacy" prohibited banning abortion in several situations.[939] The majority's holding:

> 1. A state criminal abortion statute of the current Texas type, that excepts from criminality only a lifesaving procedure on behalf of the mother, without regard to pregnancy stage and without recognition of the other interests involved, is violative of the Due Process Clause of the Fourteenth Amendment.
>
> (a) For the stage prior to approximately the end of the first trimester, the abortion decision and its effectuation must be left to the medical judgment of the pregnant woman's attending physician.
>
> (b) For the stage subsequent to approximately the end of the first trimester, the State, in promoting its interest in the health of the mother, may, if it chooses, regulate the abortion procedure in ways that are reasonably related to maternal health.
>
> (c) For the stage subsequent to viability, the State in promoting its interest in the potentiality of human life may, if it chooses, regulate, and even proscribe, abortion except where it is necessary, in appropriate medical judgment, for the preservation of the life or health of the mother.
>
> 2. The State may define the term "physician," as it has been employed in the preceding paragraphs of this Part XI of this opinion, to mean only a physician currently licensed by the State,

[939] Justice Rehnquist dissented.

> and may proscribe any abortion by a person who is not a physician as so defined.[940]

The *Roe v. Wade* Court, following Warren Court precedents, was clearly exercising a legislative function. The holding is even written in the form of a statute.

In the years preceding 2015, more than forty states defined marriage as a union between man and woman. In 2015, the Supreme Court in *Obergefell v. Hodges* concluded that such laws were a violation of the Equal Protection Clause and/or Due Process Clause.[941] For the *Obergefell* majority, the Due Process Clause, Equal Protection Clause, or an amalgam of both required that states recognize same-sex marriage on an equal basis with traditional marriage between a man and a woman. The majority did not give much or any attention to the text or history of either clause. By this date, the Court's individual-rights adjudication was so divorced from the Constitution's text and intent that the Court could issue its opinions following a color-coded scheme rather than citing text and continuing the pretext of constitutionalism. For the majority, the traditional definition of marriage was bad and therefore unconstitutional.

The *Obergefell* opinion had several dissenting opinions. Chief Justice Roberts emphasized in dissent that:

> [T]his Court is not a legislature. Whether same-sex marriage is a good idea should be of no concern to us. Under the Constitution, judges have power to say what the law is, not what it should be. . . .
>
> Five lawyers have closed the debate and enacted their own vision of marriage as a matter of con-

---

940 *Roe*, 410 U.S. at 164-65.

941 Obergefell v. Hodges, 576 U.S. ----, 135 S.Ct. 2584 (2015).

> stitutional law. Stealing this issue from the people will for many cast a cloud over same-sex marriage, making a dramatic social change that much more difficult to accept.[942]

The late Justice Scalia, in dissent, commented:

> When the Fourteenth Amendment was ratified in 1868, every State limited marriage to one man and one woman, and no one doubted the constitutionality of doing so. That resolves these cases. When it comes to determining the meaning of a vague constitutional provision—such as "due process of law" or "equal protection of the laws"—it is unquestionable that the People who ratified that provision did not understand it to prohibit a practice that remained both universal and uncontroversial in the years after ratification. We have no basis for striking down a practice that is not expressly prohibited by the Fourteenth Amendment's text, and that bears the endorsement of a long tradition of open, widespread, and unchallenged use dating back to the Amendment's ratification. Since there is no doubt whatever that the People never decided to prohibit the limitation of marriage to opposite-sex couples, the public debate over same-sex marriage must be allowed to continue.
>
> But the Court ends this debate, in an opinion lacking even a thin veneer of law. Buried beneath the mummeries and straining-to-be-memorable passages of the opinion is a candid and startling assertion: No matter *what* it was the People ratified, the Fourteenth Amendment protects those rights that the Judiciary, in its "reasoned judgment," thinks the Fourteenth Amendment ought to protect. That is so because "[t]he generations that wrote and ratified the Bill of Rights and the Fourteenth Amend-

942 *Id.* at 2.

> ment did not presume to know the extent of freedom in all of its dimensions. . . ." One would think that sentence would continue: ". . . and therefore they provided for a means by which the People could amend the Constitution," or perhaps ". . . and therefore they left the creation of additional liberties, such as the freedom to marry someone of the same sex, to the People, through the never-ending process of legislation." But no. What logically follows, in the majority's judge-empowering estimation, is: "and so they entrusted to future generations a charter protecting the right of all persons to enjoy liberty as we learn its meaning." The "we," needless to say, is the nine of us. "History and tradition guide and discipline [our] inquiry but do not set its outer boundaries." Thus, rather than focusing on *the People's* understanding of "liberty"—at the time of ratification or even today—the majority focuses on four "principles and traditions" that, *in the majority's view*, prohibit States from defining marriage as an institution consisting of one man and one woman.
>
> This is a naked judicial claim to legislative—indeed, *super*-legislative—power; a claim fundamentally at odds with our system of government. Except as limited by a constitutional prohibition agreed to by the People, the States are free to adopt whatever laws they like, even those that offend the esteemed Justices' "reasoned judgment." A system of government that makes the People subordinate to a committee of nine unelected lawyers does not deserve to be called a democracy.[943]

These cases provide only a glimpse of the modern Supreme Court's judicial hegemony. The point to keep in mind with these controversial cases is not the policy of the underlying issue but rather that the judicial aristocracy is interjecting itself into

[943] *Id.* at 4-5 (footnotes omitted) (minor formatting added).

societal debates and deciding the issue with no legitimate basis other than invented foundations built upon invented foundation and ambiguous text not intended to authorize judicial invention in the first place.

The Supreme Court socially reengineered society and constricted representative government in health, safety, and morals and thus in life, liberty, and property. In the twentieth century, the Court invented criminal procedure through its interpretation of the incorporated Fourth, Fifth, and Sixth Amendments. For the last fifty years, the judicial elite have targeted the death penalty. For them, judicial interpretation of the "evolving standards of decency" and the Eighth Amendment's prohibition against "cruel and unusual punishment" bars the government from executing convicted criminals.[944]

The American judiciary has pureed the Constitution into its own private code based on various tests and inserted language and meanings. Supreme Court decision-making is an up or down vote based on the justices' reasonableness review of the propriety of the law—whether it is good or bad—couched in terms of "liberty," "fundamental," and the like. Article V, the forgotten process by which the Constitution is legitimately amended, is a dead letter in these discussions. The judicial state has taken the people and Article V out of the Constitution. Supreme Court hegemony has relegated participatory government to a short window of indirectly weighing in on judicial nominations. The modern Supreme Court and its doctrine of judicial review is the exact type of thing that the founding generation feared the most—a centralized imperialism robbing the people and the states of the republican form of government.

---

[944] Furman v. Georgia, 408 U.S. 238, 242 (1972).

XI

Conclusion

EVOLVING FROM FEUDAL CONSILIUM, the Magna Carta and the rise of the High Court of Parliament developed parliamentary sovereignty alongside the reduction of the king. The seventeenth century completed the transformation as the Lords and Commons reduced the remaining prerogatives and established Parliament's sovereignty. No longer could the king suspend and dispense with the law under the theory of absolute or divine right of kings.

American colonies also celebrated the Glorious Revolution alongside their English brethren. Colonists claimed the privileges and immunities of Englishmen but were not on par with Englishmen. Many of the English Constitution's victories did not extend across the ocean. Colonies suffered, for example, taxation without representation.

The American Revolution challenged what many felt was England's arbitrary imperialism. The colonies wanted local control and protection against oppression by Parliament or the king. Following independence, the states adopted their own government and constitutions. Several states lauded republican principles and bills of rights. States handled local matters but ceded some sovereignty to the Confederation for national matters such as trade, boundaries, and collective defense.

But the federalism relationship between the states and the Confederation suffered from its inception. The Confederation was too weak and did not have sufficient powers to collect revenue or regulate interstate and foreign commerce. The leading members attempted amendments, but those amendments failed.

The Constitutional Convention of 1787 proposed a new form of government—a sovereign and supreme national government. After some deliberation, the Framers decided that there would be two houses of Congress: one built on the people and the other on the states. The Constitution and national laws would be supreme over conflicting state legislation. Instead of military enforcement or legislative vetoes of conflicting state law, Congress creates national law, which the judiciary has the power to interpret. The judiciary also has the power to void state law contrary to the Constitution and national laws.

The Constitution provided many checks and balances. But these checks and balances did not allay concerns over a national imperialism in Congress. Hence, after the Constitution's ratification, the founding generation also added the Bill of Rights to the Constitution. The Bill of Rights' Fifth Amendment contains due process language similar to the Magna Carta's Chapter 39 and was adopted without substantive debate. After the Civil War, the Fourteenth Amendment adopted similar due process language without significant debate on the meaning of "due process of law."

For purposes of the Magna Carta and the original concept of due process of law, "arbitrary" or "tyranny" were terms that described the king's deprivation without the rule of law.[945] The king was a tyrant because he ignored the will of the barons, Lords, Commons, and the law of the land.[946] A maxim of the Lockean commonwealth is that common consent purges tyranny.[947]

English heritage and western constitutionalism fought the monarchy to obtain a role in government. The rule of law had meaning against tyrannical and arbitrary actors acting without it. Colonial laws and the "privileges and immunities of Englishmen" cherished participatory government. The American Revolution was fought and independence gained based on participatory government and republican principles—We the People.

While the founding generation and Reconstruction Congress adopted due process language from the English Constitution without any suggestion for a different meaning than that used for the previous six centuries, the judiciary applied the text in a radically different way.

Proponents of judicial review emphasize that American constitutionalism placed written constitutions over the legislatures—enforced either judicially or by popular mechanisms. But early on, the courts mixed "due process of law" and "law of the land" with the common law and constitutional supremacy. Constitutional common law invoked by American courts was based on a mischaracterization of Coke without appreciating Coke's broader points or the context of Coke's commentary—which was arbitrary *royal* action. American courts created a judicial state.

---

945 *Supra* Chapters IV–VI.

946 *Supra* Chapter VI sec. G (Richard II and deposition).

947 *Supra* notes 700, 733–734, 825, 879.

In our modern judicial state, the Supreme Court arbitrarily determines whether validly enacted legislation is unconstitutional under ambiguous constitutional text and even more ambiguous tests constructed from the ambiguous constitutional text. In so doing, the Supreme Court might be appropriately compared to the tyrant king suspending and dispensing with the law, deciding questions of reason, necessity, and common utility *per voluntatem.*[948] The natural result of eviscerating the principle of common consent and participatory government—by the very language meant to safeguard its existence—was a new sovereignty shift in the political center of gravity. Modern constitutional political theory is "from God to Court to Community"—*vox curiae, vox Dei*! Outcome-determinative adjudication has devolved the rule of law into a standard of fundamental reasonableness—an unwritten custom capable of infinite expansion not by legislatures or the Constitution's Article V but by a handful of judges and judicial prerogative.

---

[948] *Supra* notes 32-36 (necessity, common profit, and utility); *supra* note 409 ("Common profit" in the *Confirmatio Cartarum* of 1297 and baronial grievances); *supra* notes 434, 461 (common profit and the idea that the Ordainers have a role in "right and reason" and common welfare of the realm); *supra* note 639; *supra* Chapter VIII (Glorious Revolution fought over and English Bill of Rights sought to limit or prevent the king's power to suspend and dispense with the law).

A

B

C

D

E

F

G

K

L

S

T

U

V

W

Z

Made in the USA
Monee, IL
20 September 2026

63772731R00166